The Oslo Accords

D1545800

The Oslo Accords
A Critical Assessment

Edited by
Petter Bauck
Mohammed Omer

Forewords by
Desmond Tutu
Össur Skarphéðinsson

The American University in Cairo Press
Cairo   New York

First published as an e-book in 2013. This revised and updated edition published in 2016.

Chapter 3 by Hilde Henriksen Waage is drawn from *Peacemaking Is a Risky Business: Norway's
Role in the Peace Process in the Middle East, 1993–96*, http://www.prio.no/Publications/Publica-
tion/?x=3075 (Oslo: Peace Research Institute Oslo, 2004). Reproduced by permission.

Chapter 4 by Amira Hass first appeared in *Haaretz* on 1 December 2015, and is reproduced by
permission. Copyright © Haaretz Daily Newspaper, Ltd. All rights reserved.

Chapter 11 by Are Hovdenak was first published in 2009 as "Hamas in Transition: The Failure of
Sanctions," *Democratization* 16 (1): 59–80. Special issue: *The European Union Democratization
Agenda in the Mediterranean: A Critical Inside-Out Approach*. Reproduced by permission of
Taylor & Francis Ltd.

Elements of Chapter 16 by Mads Gilbert appeared previously in *Eyes in Gaza* by Mads Gilbert
and Erik Fosse (London: Quartet Books, 2010), and *The Link* 45(5) (December 2012), published
by Americans for Middle East Understanding. Reproduced by permission.

Exclusive distribution outside Egypt and North America by I.B.Tauris & Co Ltd.,
6 Salem Road, London, W4 2BU

Dar el Kutub No. 22925/15
ISBN 978 977 416 770 6

Dar el Kutub Cataloging-in-Publication Data

Bauck, Petter
        The Oslo Accords: A Critical Assessment / edited by Petter Bauck and Mohammed
    Omer.—Cairo: The American University in Cairo Press, 2016.
        p.   cm.
        ISBN 978 977 416 770 6
        1. Arab–Israeli Conflict—1993—Peace
        2. International Law
        3. Peace Treaties
        956.94

1 2 3 4 5   20 19 18 17 16

Printed in the United States of America

Contents

Contributors

Haakon Aars is a medical doctor and specialist in psychiatry and clinical sexology. He also holds an MA in public health. He worked as a general practitioner for many years before he entered the field of psychiatry. He was also a producer of health information programs for Norwegian television and radio and a columnist for Norwegian papers and periodicals. He is the author of *Men's Sexuality* (2011) and the co-author of three medical textbooks. Aars was Health Delegate for the International Federation of the Red Cross/Red Crescent Societies in Palestine from 1998 to 2001. He now works at the Institute for Clinical Sexology and Therapy in Oslo.

Ahmed Abu Rtema is a journalist and author based in Gaza. Hundreds of his articles focusing on political and intellectual issues have been published by Arabic media outlets. In 2009 Abu Rtema was a correspondent for the London-based Al-Hewar satellite channel and his documentaries have been broadcast on Al Jazeera Documentary. He is known among Palestinians for his initiative for the peaceful return of Palestinian refugees in 2011.

Sufian Abu Zaida has a PhD in Middle East Politics from Exeter University, UK. From February 2005 until the establishment of the Hamas government, he served as minister of prisoners and ex-prisoners' affairs. In addition, from December 2005, he served as minister of civil affairs. He has served as a member of the Palestinian delegation responsible for negotiations for the release of Palestinian prisoners held in Israeli jails. Abu Zaida served as director of MA programs at al-Quds University in Gaza in 2006–2007. From 2008, he was head of the Culture of Peace Committee as part of the Palestinian negotiation team. He teaches at al-Quds and Birzeit universities. Since 2010, he has been head of the Gaza for Political and Strategic Studies think tank.

Petter Bauck holds an MA in Violence, Conflict, and Development from the School of Oriental and African Studies (SOAS), University of London. He served as deputy head of the Norwegian Representative Office to the Palestinian Authority from 2000 to 2003. After completing his studies in London, he worked as a senior adviser on conflict-related issues in the Norwegian Agency for Development Cooperation (Norad). Since July 2016 he has worked at the Norwegian

Embassy in Kiev, Ukraine, as a counselor for development. He has published several books and articles on Eritrea and Afghanistan.

Noam Chomsky is retired Institute Professor in Department of Linguistics and Philosophy at the Massachusetts Institute of Technology (MIT), where he has taught since 1955. He has published and lectured widely on linguistics, cognitive science, philosophy, international affairs, and social-political issues.

Richard Falk is the Milbank Professor of International Law Emeritus at Princeton University, where he was a member of the faculty for forty years. He is the author or editor of more than fifty books on world affairs, with a special emphasis on issues of international law and world order. He is currently senior vice president of the Nuclear Age Peace Foundation and has served as Special Rapporteur for Occupied Palestine on behalf of the UN Human Rights Council. He is also the director of a project on climate change, human rights, and democracy based at the Orfalea Center of the University of California, Santa Barbara. He is the author of *Power Shift: On the New Global Order* (2016).

Yasmine Gado was the rights and contracts manager for the American University in Cairo Press. Prior to that Gado practiced corporate law in the New York office of Latham & Watkins and the Washington, DC, office of Fried Frank. She also served as in-house counsel for the Export–Import Bank of the United States. She received her law degree with honors from George Washington University Law School and her undergraduate degree from Washington University.

Mads Gilbert is a Norwegian medical doctor and professor who has specialized in anesthesiology and emergency medicine. He works as the Clinical Leader at the Clinic of Emergency Medicine at the University Hospital of North Norway in Tromsø, Norway. As a medical solidarity worker, he has worked with Palestinians since 1982. Gilbert also has a broad range of international experiences in solidarity medicine in Burma, Cambodia, Angola, and Afghanistan. He has co-authored textbooks on pre-hospital lifesaving in remote communities in the global South, including *Save Lives, Save Limbs,* 2000. With his colleague, Dr. Erik Fosse, he was one of only two western medical doctors at al-Shifa Hospital in Gaza City during the first part of Operation Cast Lead in January 2009. Their experiences were described in their book *Eyes in Gaza* (2nd ed., 2013). His time at the hospital during Operation Protective Edge in summer 2014 formed the basis for another book, *Night in Gaza* (2015). He was made a commander of the Order of St. Olav by Norwegian King Harald in May 2013 for his overall contribution to emergency medicine and his international humanitarian work.

Amira Hass is an Israeli journalist for the daily newspaper *Haaretz,* Israel's oldest newspaper. She has lived in the occupied Palestinian territories since 1993, and is closely following the evolving system of Israeli restrictions on the movement of Palestinians, known as the closure regime. She is the author of *Drinking the Sea at Gaza: Days and Nights in a Land under Siege* (2000), and has also published two other books, compilations of her articles for *Haaretz* and her columns in the Italian weekly *Internazionale*.

Are Hovdenak is a Middle East researcher who has published articles and reports on various aspects of the Palestinian–Israeli conflict, including the negotiations on Palestinian refugees in the Oslo peace process; coping strategies of Palestinian refugees in exile; the emergence of Hamas as a political player on the Palestinian scene; and the relationship between Hamas and more radical, Salafist-jihadist elements in the Gaza Strip. He has also been a humanitarian worker in Lebanon and a journalist in North Africa and the broader Middle East. Hovdenak is a political scientist, with an MA/cand.polit. degree from the University of Oslo and Arabic studies at the University of Jordan, Amman. He has conducted his research at the Peace Research Institute Oslo (PRIO) and Fafo Institute for Applied International Studies and is today Senior Adviser at Landinfo, the Norwegian Country of Origin Information Center.

Gideon Levy is a *Haaretz* columnist and a member of the newspaper's editorial board. Levy joined *Haaretz* in 1982 and spent four years as its deputy editor. He is the author of the weekly "Twilight Zone" feature, which has covered the Israeli occupation in the West Bank and Gaza over the last twenty-five years, as well as the writer of political editorials for the newspaper. Levy was the recipient of the Euro-Med Journalist Prize for 2008; the Leipzig Freedom Prize in 2001; the Israeli Journalists' Union Prize in 1997; and the Association of Human Rights in Israel Award for 1996. His book, *The Punishment of Gaza*, was published in 2010.

Laura Dawn Lewis has spent twenty-five years in the media, print, online and broadcast industries in a variety of positions. Today Lewis is an entrepreneur, author, publisher and advocate for inter-faith understanding. She began researching and writing on the Middle East, propaganda, politics, and faith issues following the attacks of September 11, 2001 and has spent time living in Brazil, Saudi Arabia, and the United Kingdom. In addition to over one thousand articles under various names, in 2010 she co-authored the *Timeline & Inconsistencies Report Relating to the Gaza-bound Freedom Flotilla Attack*. She currently resides in Los Angeles, California.

Mohammed Omer is an award-winning Palestinian journalist from the Gaza Strip and winner of the Martha Gellhorn Prize for Journalism, among others. He has reported for numerous media outlets, including the *New York Times*,

Middle East Eye, *Al Jazeera*, the *Washington Report on Middle East Affairs*, *The Nation*, *Vice*, Inter Press Service, Free Speech Radio News, the Norwegian *Morgenbladet* and *Dagsavisen*, the Swedish daily *Dagens Nyheter*, the Swedish magazine *Arbetaren*, the Basque daily *Berria*, the German daily *Junge Welt*, and the Finish magazine *Ny Tid*. He has served as a development and communication advisor to several governments including Norway, the Netherlands, and Luxembourg. He holds a PhD from Erasmus University Rotterdam, and has studied at Columbia University, New York. His experiences during the Israeli offensive Operation Protective Edge in summer 2014 were recounted in his book *Shell-Shocked: On the Ground under Israel's Gaza Assault* (2015).

Ilan Pappé was born in Haifa. He graduated from Hebrew University in Jerusalem in 1978 and received his PhD from the University of Oxford in 1984. Pappé taught at the University of Haifa until 2006, when he moved to the University of Exeter in the UK. While in Israel, he founded and headed the Institute for Peace Research in Givat Haviva and was the chair of the Emil Touma Institute for Palestinian Studies in Haifa. At the University of Exeter, he is the director of the European Center for Palestine Studies and a fellow at the Institute for Arab and Islamic Studies. He is the author of fifteen books, among them *The Ethnic Cleansing of Palestine* (2006), *A History of Modern Palestine* (2003, 2006), and *The Modern Middle East* (2010), and co-author with Noam Chomsky and Frank Barat of *Gaza in Crisis: Reflections on Israel's War Against the Palestinians* (2010).

Lotta Schüllerqvist is a Swedish journalist and author living in Stockholm. She used to be based in Jerusalem as a correspondent for *Dagens Nyheter*, the most widely circulated daily in Sweden. Now she works as a freelancer in the Middle East, mostly in Gaza. She has published one book about Gaza (*Marnas hemlighet*, 2010) and contributed to an anthology about Jerusalem (*Jerusalem: en bok som hjälper dig att gå vilse*, 2011). Schüllerqvist was until recently the president of the Swedish section of Reporters Without Borders, and now serves as board member.

Matt Sienkiewicz is assistant professor of communication and international studies at Boston College. His research focuses on the west's investment in Middle Eastern broadcasting initiatives, as well as portrayals of race and religion on the American screen. His publications include articles in the *International Journal of Cultural Studies*, *Popular Communication*, the *Journal of Film and Video*, the *Velvet Light Trap*, and the *Middle East Journal of Culture and Communication*. He is the co-editor of *Saturday Night Live and American Television* (2013). In addition to his work as a scholar, Sienkiewicz is an Emmy-nominated documentary filmmaker and screenwriter. His most recent film, *Live from Bethlehem*, was released by the Media Education Foundation in September 2009.

Össur Skarphéðinsson was the minister of foreign affairs and external trade for Iceland from 2009 to 2013. He started his adult life as a fisherman on the Icelandic trawlers. He received a BSc in biology from the University of Iceland and a PhD in fish physiology from the University of East Anglia, UK. Skarphéðinsson has been a member of the Icelandic parliament since 1991, and was the first leader of the Socialdemocratic Alliance, from its foundation in 2000 to 2005. He has so far served in four governments. Skarphéðinsson has also had a journalistic career, having been the editor of three daily newspapers in Iceland.

Helga Tawil-Souri is associate professor of media, culture, and communication at New York University. The bulk of her scholarship analyzes culture and technology in everyday life in Palestine-Israel, focusing on the post-'peace process' time period and theorizing how media technologies and infrastructures function as bordering mechanisms and how territorial/physical boundaries function as cultural spaces. Tawil-Souri's publications have analyzed different aspects of contemporary cultural politics, including the Internet, telecommunications, television, film, and video games, as well as physical markers such as identification cards and checkpoints. She also researches and writes about the larger landscape of Arab media, and in particular about new technologies and their relationship to political and economic transformations.

Liv Tørres is currently the director of the Nobel Peace Center in Oslo. At the time of finalizing this manuscript, she was secretary general of the Norwegian People's Aid, a position she held since 2011. She was also the head of the international department at the Norwegian People's Aid (2006–2007). She has broad work experience, including academia, civil service, and politics, and has worked with organizations in Norway, South Africa, and at the international level. She has worked at the University of Oslo (Department of Political Science), the research institute Fafo, and the Norwegian Research Council. She has also been a political adviser to the minister of labor in Norway (2011).

Desmond Mpilo Tutu is a South African Nobel Peace Prize winner (1984) and social rights activist and retired Anglican bishop who rose to worldwide fame during the 1980s as an opponent of apartheid. He was the first black South African Archbishop of Cape Town and primate of the Anglican Church of Southern Africa. Tutu has been active in the defense of human rights and uses his high profile to campaign for the oppressed. He received the Albert Schweitzer Prize for Humanitarianism in 1986, the Pacem in Terris Award in 1987, the Sydney Peace Prize in 1999, the Gandhi Peace Prize in 2007, and the Presidential Medal of Freedom in 2009.

Harry van Bommel has been a Dutch member of parliament since 1998 and Spokesperson on European and Foreign Affairs for the Socialist Party. He was one of the founders of the NGO Stop the Occupation and has published various articles on the Israeli–Palestinian conflict. Van Bommel holds an MA in political science and a BA in education. Before entering parliament, he was a city councillor in Amsterdam and a teacher at a school for vocational training in Amsterdam.

Hilde Henriksen Waage is professor of history at the University of Oslo. She has worked extensively on Norway's involvement in the Middle East. Her current research project, "The Missing Peace," focuses on the lack of an ongoing peace process and why all mediation attempts between Israel and the Palestinians have so far proved unsuccessful.

John V. Whitbeck is an American-born, Paris-based international lawyer who has served as an occasional legal and strategic adviser to the Palestinian leadership for over twenty years; in Madrid in October 1991, in Cairo in April–May 1994, and in Camp David in July 2000, when the 'peace process' effectively ended. Since 1988, his articles on behalf of Palestinian rights and Middle East peace have been published more than 650 times in more than eighty different Arab, Israeli, and international newspapers, magazines, journals, and books. Between 1988 and 2000, both his 'Two States, One Holy Land' framework for peace and his 'condominium solution' for sharing Jerusalem in a context of peace and reconciliation were published more than forty times, in six different languages.

Ahmed Yousef is from Rafah in Palestine. He holds an MA in industrial engineering (USA, 1984), an MA in journalism (USA, 1987), and a PhD in political science (USA, 2004). He is currently head of the board of trustees of the House of Wisdom. He is former senior political adviser to the prime minister (Ismail Haniyeh, 2006–2009) and former deputy of the foreign affairs ministry (2009–2011). He has been executive director for the United Association for Studies and Research in the United States (1989–2004) and chief editor of the *Middle East Affairs Journal* (1990–2004). He is head of the Palestinian Reconciliation Committee and a member of the Palestinian Association for Writers. He has published more than twenty-six books in Arabic and English on topics related to the Arab–Israeli conflict, Islamist movements, and the relationship between Islam and the west. He has written many articles published in Palestinian and internationals media outlets addressing the issue of the reconciliation between Fatah and Hamas.

Foreword

Archbishop Emeritus Desmond Tutu

Those who follow the news know that history is made every day. But to appreciate the significance of history usually requires the distance of a little time, the benefit of hindsight.

While a twenty-two-year span is but a flash in the history of time, it is just about a wide-enough prism through which to view events in some perspective. This book therefore adds valuable context to our collective understanding of the making and unraveling of a peace process. To revisit these events is important not just for history's sake, but to inform the journey ahead.

Twenty-two years ago much of the world appeared to be on the verge of better things.

The collapse of the Berlin Wall symbolized the end of the Cold War and the possibility of reconciliation for Europeans driven apart since the 1940s by ideological dogma. The release of political prisoners in South Africa, including Nelson Mandela, and the peaceful negotiations that followed, bringing apartheid to an end, demonstrated that seemingly intractable racial chasms could be crossed. And the end of the terms of office of Prime Minister Margaret Thatcher and President Ronald Reagan promised a more people-centered approach to power relations on earth.

The leaders of Palestine and Israel signing the Oslo Accords on the White House lawn in September 1993 represented the proverbial cherry on this particular slice of history. Sadly, the cherry did not taste as sweet as it looked.

Making peace is in many respects much harder than waging war. It requires of combatants not only to lay down their arms but also to acknowledge the worth in, and to show good faith toward, one another. It cannot be half-hearted; magnanimity is to peace processes what oxygen is to people.

In South Africa, following the release of political prisoners who opposed apartheid and the unbanning of political organizations, as we lurched from one violent incident to the next on our journey to democracy, we were fortunate to have the caliber of leaders who understood the value of magnanimity. When at times it seemed inevitable that we would fall back into the abyss, they had the strength to pull us from the brink. But, most critically, these were leaders who could count on the support of the majority of the people. For, ultimately, it is the people who are the custodians of peace.

After South Africa's first democratic elections, our Government of National Unity (led by President Nelson Mandela) established a Truth and Reconciliation Commission. The TRC, as it was known, was a forum for the victims of apartheid-era violence to air their stories and for perpetrators of violence to receive amnesty in exchange for telling the truth.

It was a highly emotional, painful, and grueling process. For many, the most startling feature of the commission was the magnanimity of the survivors of apartheid-era atrocities, those who had lost loved ones, friends, and comrades. Their desire to forgive, and through forgiving, contribute to our national reconciliation process, outweighed the fear and hatred in their hearts. Our people were ready for peace.

When will the people of the Holy Land be ready for peace? What will it take for the majority of the people to assert their majority and demand of the warmongers that they cease provocations and lay down their arms?

In hindsight, the Oslo Accords may yet contain elements of the blueprint for lasting peace in the region. But the Oslo Accords collapsed because the signatories could not count on the support of their people.

The rest, as they say, is history — or a continuation of the history of encroachment, manipulation, dispossession, separation, discrimination, and mutual hostility and suspicion. At times, over these twenty years, it has seemed as if Israel has welcomed the provocation of Palestinian rockets as an excuse to respond with incommensurate hostility and force.

Ordinary people suffer most: They suffer the insecurity of living in a state of perpetual fear, and the indignity of conducting their lives under a set of rules and practices that amount to no less than a state of apartheid on the ground.

Those who dehumanize others little realize the extent to which they damage themselves, and so the cycle continues.

The people of Palestine and Israel are doing themselves a grave injustice — and the rest of the world is unwilling to see justice done.

God is weeping.

Foreword

Össur Skarphéðinsson

There was excitement in the air in 2010 as delegates to the United Nations General Assembly sat down to listen to US President Barack Obama's speech. Two years earlier, he had given the world new hope with his optimistic battle cry of "Yes, we can!" The speech was the performance of a virtuoso. On the Israeli–Palestinian issue, the president played all the diplomatic strings required to satisfy most of his audience, but nevertheless did not shy away from stressing the need to expand the moratorium on settlements being built by the Israelis. Dramatically, Obama tossed his audience a thinly veiled promise when he said to rapturous applause that next year we would possibly gather with the addition of a new member, an independent, sovereign State of Palestine.

It was pure music. The serious flaw of the Oslo Accords always had been the lack of a mechanism to block unilateral actions such as the illegal settlements, and only a firm commitment by the United States could breathe life into the stalled process. At the end of his speech, I was happy to believe that the president of hope would have the audacity to do whatever it took to kick-start the process.

A year later, Prime Minister Benjamin Netanyahu and the Israeli lobby had skillfully exploited the upcoming presidential election to water down dramatically the commitment of the US. In 2011, it was pretty clear that the Palestinians, under the able leadership of Prime Minister Salam Fayyad, were successfully completing the task of constructing a functioning state, as acknowledged not only by the Ad Hoc Liaison Committee and the World Bank but also by the International Monetary Fund. Many, including officials in Iceland, felt the Palestinians had a tacit understanding, at least with Europe, that in return they would be supported with a positive response to their forthcoming application to become a full member of the United Nations (UN). This was used as an argument to moderate the speed at which Iceland was approaching unilaterally declaring support for Palestinian statehood. Tragically, in the summer of 2011 it also became evident that the application would be blocked. The president of hope threatened not only to use his veto but also to cut aid to Palestine if President Mahmoud Abbas dared to take the proposal to the UN Security Council. The Palestinians' traditional supporters in the American camp could not avoid speculating on possible reactions to their continuing support for the Palestinian proposal. Once again, Palestine was left on the edge of betrayal by those who had the power and the glory.

In the policy manifesto of the Icelandic government that came to power in 2009, there was a very clear commitment to supporting the human rights of the Palestinian people and their right to self-determination. There was, however, no pledge to recognize their sovereignty. As foreign minister, it was my duty, as well as personal conviction, to speak out for Palestinians' rights at every opportunity. In 2011, I paid a visit to Gaza, the West Bank, and East Jerusalem to see things first hand. Gaza surprised me with its strange mixture of vigor, poverty, and desperation, while the over-optimism in Ramallah and the growing schism between Hamas and Fatah depressed me. The visit, combined with conversations with European colleagues, impressed on me the helplessness of the Palestinians. With the full support of the government, I decided that Iceland would take the final step to recognize the full sovereignty of Palestine, based on the borders established before the war of 1967.

Historically, such a decision was in line with our past, as Iceland has a proud history of strong support for the rights of small nations to self-determination. In 1947, it was the ambassador of Iceland who was a rapporteur for the resolution that led to the creation of Israel as a state. In 1991, Iceland became the first nation to recognize the renewed sovereignty of Estonia, Lithuania, and Latvia, when no one else dared, and later Slovenia, Croatia, and Montenegro. Our involvement in 1947 also means that we have a moral duty to Palestine beyond many others. In addition, our parliament, the Althing, had more than once reaffirmed its support for the two-state solution and the rights of the Palestinian people to have their own state.

Obviously, by stepping out of line with strong, historical allies such as the United States, a small country like Iceland took some risks. We had, however, given due notice. The government had a clearly stated pro-Palestinian foreign policy, and as foreign minister I had very strongly condemned the attacks on Gaza at the turn of 2008–2009 and publicly refused to meet an Israeli minister who wanted to 'correct' my views. Foreign Minister Avigdor Lieberman had engaged me in difficult correspondence where the Icelandic view had been forcefully stated. At the General Assembly, I had several times spoken out in strong terms against the Israeli violation of human rights in Palestine. We also had an earlier spat with the US due to Iceland blocking the admittance of Israel to JUS-CANZ (Japan, United States, Canada, Australia, and New Zealand), an ad hoc committee of like-minded nations under the human rights committee at the UN. To break this decision, US Secretary of State Hillary Clinton requested a phone call, but the call never materialized, as the very same day the WikiLeaks scandal broke. We also had vigorously campaigned for the adoption of Palestine into the UN Educational, Scientific and Cultural Organization (UNESCO). In short, Icelandic recognition of Palestine would not drop like a bomb on our allies.

The exact timing of our formal declaration was chosen for tactical reasons. Some European allies whom we consulted, not least in the North, asked if we could postpone it until 2012, and preferably until the fate of the Palestinian proposal at the UN became clear. Some even appeared to harbor hopes, despite the growing intensity of the American opposition, that the proposal somehow would be cleared through the Security Council. When the Council finally caved to pressure on the eve of the General Assembly, it seemed that Palestine could possibly emerge in an even weaker position than before, and consequently the hand of Hamas would be strengthened at the expense of Ramallah. That, we felt, was the correct time to stand on principle and honor. In my ensuing speech to the General Assembly, I declared Iceland's firm intention to recognize formally the sovereignty of Palestine.

Back home, the Althing concluded the matter in style. On November 29, 2011, the UN's International Day of Solidarity with Palestine, it accepted the resolution I put to it without a single opposing vote. A year later, Iceland again walked alone among western countries and co-sponsored the proposal on Palestine's status as an observer state to the UN. Despite some criticism at home and behind closed doors abroad, I felt the Icelandic view was vindicated when the proposal was overwhelmingly accepted, with all the Nordic countries voting for it and only nine countries voting against, sadly, including the United States.

We still are the only western nation that has recognized the sovereignty of Palestine since 1988. For a small nation, it sometimes is difficult to stand on a principle against powerful players. But it feels good.

Introduction

The Oslo Accords
—A Success or a Curse?

Petter Bauck and Mohammed Omer

More than two decades have passed since the Oslo Accords were signed in front of the White House in Washington by the Palestine Liberation Organization (PLO) and Israel. Ahead of the signing ceremony, they had agreed upon a formula of recognizing each other. The PLO recognized the State of Israel, while Israel recognized the PLO as the representative of the Palestinians. Oslo I was more like a procedural arrangement between Israel and the PLO concerning how they should each proceed in order to reach a final agreement. Among many Palestinians it was celebrated as a breakthrough toward independence, sovereignty, and a dignified life, as well as an end to the occupation. In Israel it was seen as an international diplomatic breakthrough, ending a feeling of isolation.

The Iranian Connection

Let us first introduce part of the background for the Norwegian engagement in promoting a dialogue between Israel and the Palestinians. Norway, especially the Norwegian Social Democratic Party, has historically had very close connections with its sister party in Israel. The creation of Israel and its policies, with a focus on the *kibbutz*, was by many seen as a socialist experiment. A number of leftist Norwegians went to Israel in the early days to participate in these developments.

With the Khomeini revolution in Iran in 1979, Israel lost its source of petroleum products. For the US, a staunch ally of Israel, the question became how to establish a new safe supply. The Norwegian government was contacted, as its government had recently begun extracting oil from wells in the North Sea. For Norway, though, a close ally of the US and a close friend of Israel, the request from the Americans raised a serious concern. At that time, Norway was heavily engaged with its soldiers in the UN's peace-keeping force in Lebanon, the United Nations Interim Forces in Lebanon (UNIFIL). The area patrolled by the Norwegians was mainly controlled by the PLO. What would the consequences be for Norway's soldiers if the PLO came to know that Norway was supplying Israel with oil? Better take the question directly with the PLO. The Norwegian charge d'affaires in Beirut, Hans Wilhelm Longva, was instructed to raise the issue with Yasser Arafat. He did, and to his surprise, Arafat responded, without hesitation, positively. No problem for him that Norway supplied Israel with oil, but he had one request to make: Some day in the future, when convenient, Norway would assist Arafat in establishing a secret back channel with the Israelis to negotiate a solution to the conflict and occupation.[1]

You can read more about Norway's role in the negotiations between Israel and the PLO in the essay "Champions of Peace?"

Oslo II—Toward a Solution?

In September 1995, more than twenty years ago, the Oslo II Accord was signed, also in Washington. Many believed that it was a further step toward a final peace deal between the two parties. The procedures agreed upon in Oslo I were developed into what was seen as a rather concrete step-by-step move toward an end to the occupation. An important element of Oslo II was the division of the occupied territories into A areas, the main populated Palestinian areas including major parts of Gaza, under "full" Palestinian security and civilian control; B areas with key Palestinian villages, under Palestinian civilian and Israeli security control; and C areas, scarcely populated, with important natural resources and water reservoirs, fully under Israeli control. The C areas in total comprised more than 60 percent of the territory defined by the Green Line, or the cease-fire agreement from 1949. The agreement also posed a time schedule implying a steady Israeli military withdrawal from B and C areas, and an orderly transfer of B to A areas and C to B areas. What was lacking, however, was a mechanism to control adherence to the agreed-upon time table, with no specified repercussions if the parties didn't follow up and no mention of the established guidelines in international law regarding the rights and duties of an occupying power.

Today we can conclude that the agreed-upon procedures and steps toward a withdrawal of the occupation have not been implemented. None of the agreements contained any guidelines regarding illegal Israeli settlements on occupied Palestinian land. The years since 1993 have been used continuously by Israeli governments to support the enlargement of existing settlements and the establishment of new ones. While settlers have been granted permits to build, Palestinians living in B and in particular C areas, and in East Jerusalem, have as a general rule had similar permits rejected, often with reference to laws introduced during the British Mandate.

From Hope to Hopelessness

Since 1993, hope among Palestinians has been replaced by hopelessness and despair. If we add the Israeli use of deadly force during the Second Intifada beginning in September 2000, plus three devastating wars on Gaza since 2008 which have aimed to eradicate or weaken Hamas and have killed thousands of civilians and destroyed peoples' dwellings and their means of living, agriculture, and industry, we see the emerging explosion among the young as well as the old, male as well as female. The result is an eradication of any future hope for the nearly two million people who are trapped on Gaza's 360 square kilometers of land and have lived through years of setbacks.

Oslo Is Dead, but the Oslo Parameters Are Alive

It is often said that Oslo is dead. But this statement needs some elaboration or correction. The Oslo Accords are dead, but the Oslo parameters are still alive and kicking. Any attempt to restart dialogue between the occupation and the occupied must revert to the Oslo parameters: a respect for signed agreements; a negotiated settlement between the occupier and the occupied; the non-use of violence; an acceptance of Israel's right to exist, which through the years has been expanded to "exist as a Jewish state," without an equal acceptance of Palestine's right as a sovereign state; the existence of Palestine as a non-armed entity; and a strong focus on Israel's security, again without equal focus on Palestinians' security. Any deviation from these "accepted parameters" results in Israeli political and economic pressure on the Palestinians, and the Palestinian Authority, through the withholding of tax and customs revenues collected by Israel on behalf of the Palestinian Authority, or on Hamas by reinforcing the siege of Gaza. International players headed by the Quartet[2] demand that Palestine adhere to these parameters, without imposing the same demands upon Israel.

In this book, the essay "The Illusion of Palestinian Sovereignty" illustrates how the Oslo Accords helped create an illusion that keeps the occupation alive.

National Reconciliation

Palestinian national reconciliation is something everyone agrees upon as important in order to reach a settlement of the conflict, an end to the occupation, and the establishment of an independent Palestinian state. That Hamas chose to participate in the national elections in 2006 along with other political parties was an important step in this direction. Negotiations between Fatah and Hamas for national reconciliation, including the reformation of the PLO governance bodies and organizational statutes, likewise allowed for a unified approach to further dialogue with the occupier and the international community, represented by the Quartet and the UN. These negotiations also paved the way for a unified approach toward including the diaspora in any acceptable solution, which is a vital element, and establishing national red lines for any settlement. The rejection of Hamas as the election winner in 2006 by key international players has contributed to the continued split, as has the continued Israeli siege of Gaza, supported by the present regime in Egypt under former army general Abd al-Fattah al-Sisi, and with silent acceptance from the Palestinian Authority under President Mahmoud Abbas.

From time to time the youth in particular have taken to the streets, both in the West Bank and in Gaza, to demand an end to the internal political split in the Palestinian polity and to call for a united front against the occupation. Again and again, such moves and attempts between Fatah and Hamas to reach a unified national platform have been met with fierce statements from the Israeli leadership, stating that President Abbas must choose between negotiations with Israel or cooperation with "terrorists."[3] With the emerged Palestinian elite seeing their interests best served by a Fatah-controlled Palestinian Authority, Israeli pressure strengthens the opposition to a national reconciliation.

Knowing that national elections are long overdue, both for the Palestinian Legislative Council (PLC) and the presidency, any talks on holding a vote are hampered by three concerns: the security situation, the possibility that Israel will prevent elections from taking place in East Jerusalem, and the uncertainty over whether Hamas will again show its strength and reach a high turnout in votes, given the weakened position of Fatah, in particular in the West Bank, while Gaza is crying out for new faces.

Palestinian Interests Include the Diaspora

The message from a wide spectrum of Palestinian voices is that the PLO represents Palestinian interests as long as a sovereign Palestinian state is not internationally recognized within acceptable borders. The PLO represents Palestinians' national aspirations, including the interests of refugees who were forced to flee from their homes in 1948–49 and 1967, and their rights to return or receive compensation, according to UN Resolution 194 stating that "the refugees wishing to return to their homes and live at peace with their neighbours should be permitted to do so at the earliest practicable date, and that compensation should be paid for the property of those choosing not to return and for loss of or damage to property which, under principles of international law or in equity, should be made good by the Governments or authorities responsible."[4]

The PLO represents Palestinian identity. The Palestinian Authority, established as a result of the Oslo Accords, should have represented a concrete step toward a sovereign state, but it is seen more and more as taking over the direct Israeli administration of the occupation. Nepotism and corruption have been allowed to undermine the legitimacy of important parts of its institutions, a development that was part of the run up to the Second Intifada that exploded in late September 2000.

Resistance Gives Legitimacy

Another message widely shared in the Palestinian public is that active resistance is one of the most important parameters strengthening the legitimacy of different political entities.[5] Negotiations have lost credibility as the sole way forward to end the occupation, a view that has only been intensified by Israel's demonstrated lack of adherence to agreements since 1993 in addition to an unwillingness by key international players to put pressure on the occupier to deliver on its past promises. As a consequence, any future dialogue between Israelis and Palestinians will probably not adhere to the Oslo parameters. This will pose a challenge for key international players engaged in promoting a "solution" to the continued occupation of Palestine. Will these advocates be able to reorient their analysis of the situation as well as their policies and relationship to the Palestinian polity in order to include these changes, thus allowing Palestinians to remain in the driver's seat when negotiations resume in the future? Or will they present themselves as uncritical supporters of an Israeli apartheid state, in line with Christian Zionists worldwide?

Departure from the Oslo Parameters?

In his speech to the UN General Assembly on September 30, 2015,[6] President Abbas implied that Palestine would no longer adhere to the Oslo Accords and subsequent agreements with Israel, stating, "We therefore declare that we cannot continue to be bound by these agreements and that Israel must assume all of its responsibilities as an occupying power, because the *status quo* cannot continue and the decisions of the Palestinian Central Council last March[7] are specific and binding." Palestinian patience had come to an end. Abbas said that Israel, as the occupier, had to take full responsibility according to international law for the occupied territory and its population. For Abbas this was clearly the only available option, given the state of affairs in occupied Palestine — the West Bank, East Jerusalem, and Gaza — and his dwindling legitimacy among Palestinians.

The steadfastness of President Abbas and his cronies in the Palestinian Authority regarding this changed approach to future negotiations with Israel has been questioned by many, and for good reason. The elite interests of important parts of the political and economic establishment in Palestine today are so entrenched in the Palestinian Authority project, with an economic safety net that is paid by international donors, that any move endangering international support will meet stiff resistance.

Two States or One State?

The conflict around Palestine is one of two national projects colliding. Jews received their homeland with the creation of Israel in May 1948, based on the UN General Assembly proposal of dividing the British Mandate of Palestine.[8] The resulting vote was made possible due to Zionist lobbying of European and American politicians and the Jewish deaths in the Nazi-led Holocaust during the Second World War. Ahead of the implementation of the decision, Jewish terrorist organizations like Stern and Haganah began clearing the land of its inhabitants, with seven-hundred thousand Palestinians fleeing either because of force or intimidation. Important forces among Jews wanted to make Israel a Jewish state, even if more than 20 percent of its population was non-Jewish, and a number of laws and practical arrangements were established to impose certain limitations on the possibilities of life for non-Jewish citizens of Israel.[9]

For Palestinians, the creation of Israel is seen as *al-Nakbah*, or the Catastrophe. Their national aspirations were trampled upon and put on the backburner for decades as they endured unbelievable sufferings. Many observers conclude today that the two-state solution is dead, as Israel has created such a reality on the ground that a division of territory now seems impossible.

It could still be argued that the two-state solution remains the only viable one. Anything else would undermine the two national projects, both Jewish and Palestinian. A one-state solution could only remain Jewish given that it at the same time established an apartheid system with Palestinian Bantustans, without full national rights. The political right in Israel has on several occasions in recent years made statements favoring such an arrangement. A one-state solution with equal rights for two peoples would not be Jewish as the majority would be Palestinian. Decades of suppression does not make such a solution very realistic, at least not in the short term.

Pragmatists argue that the two-state solution has long since been a dead option, with realities on the ground making it impossible. Even among Palestinians in the occupied territory, support for a two-state solution is declining. In a poll conducted by the Palestinian Center for Policy and Survey Research (PSR) in December 2015, only 45 percent supported this option.[10]

Israel is the result of the national aspirations of Jews that were developed over more than one-hundred years. But at the same time, Israel is the realization of the strong religious beliefs of important congregations, particularly those in the United States and Europe. The beliefs of Israel as the Holy Land and the Jews as the chosen people of God resonate well within these congregations, with certain circles focusing on Judgment Day. For Christian Zionists, the Holy Land should be cleaned of "non-believers" before Christ can return to pass judgment on humanity, and the Jews serve that purpose. For them, God's commandments regarding the end of the world, as outlined in the Old Testament, are far more important than human rights, Palestinians' national rights, international law, and UN resolutions. They believe that Israeli policies toward Palestinians are part of the necessary cleansing of the Holy Land, to prepare for the return of Christ. Through these circles, Israeli hawks have far more stable support for their policies, especially in the United States, which is discussed here in the essay "A War of Ideas."

A Dignified Compromise

Among the majority of Palestinians as well as Israelis, it is our impression that a compromise is seen as the only solution to the conflict. During an interview ten years ago, the Israeli officer heading the unit occupying Shuafat in East Jerusalem in 1967 said that he was not fond of the Palestinians but that he understood that a compromise along the Green Line would be the final result. "It is only a question how much blood is shed before that is reached," the officer said.[11] For Palestinians, the issue has always been a question of reaching a dignified compromise — and not a compromise forced upon them by the occupier. This is also the only way to obtain a sustainable compromise. It was possible that Yasser Arafat, due to his strong standing among all Palestinians, could have gathered wide support for an unfavorable compromise. Obviously no current Palestinian leader can dream of gathering similar support today.

Throughout the country's history, the Israeli attitude has been to strengthen its shares at the cost of Palestinians before a compromise is reached. No dignified compromise is reached this way. This compromise between the oppressor and the oppressed is a receipt for continued resistance and unrest, killing and bloodshed. Or, as some Israelis argue, the forced transfer of Palestinians from Gaza and the West Bank to somewhere else.

The Oslo Accords

Several essays included in this book were written with the ambition to highlight different aspects of the process preceding the signing of the Oslo Accords in September 1993 as well the consequences of the accords and the subsequent agreements. Other pieces focus on the context within which the accords were supposed to work. The development of public opinion and the media in the US is an important concern. While the Jewish opinion is moving toward a more critical position of Israel, especially among youths, Christian Zionists are uncritical supporters of Israeli policies. Similar situations will probably be found in other countries. The Oslo Accords are dead, but they remain alive through the parameters they have set for future dialogues.

Two essays, "The Oslo Accords: A Common Savior for Israel and the PLO in Exile?" and "Palestinian Identity in the Aftermath of Oslo," examine a particularly serious consequence of the accords: the undermining of Palestinian identity and the fragmentation of society. In this case, the authors indicate, it might be necessary to break with the Oslo parameters in order to restore a common Palestinian identity, reach national reconciliation, and, as a consequence, obtain a sustainable settlement in the future.

Back to 1947

No one can disagree that the parties, the occupier, and the occupied have to come to terms with one other if a sustainable solution is to be reached. At the same time, the international community should accept its responsibility for the present situation under which Palestinians are living. The UN decision in 1947 to divide the British Mandate of Palestine into a Jewish and an Arab state gave Jewish terrorist organizations the go ahead to clear as much land as possible before the State of Israel declared its existence in May 1948.

In the essay "Revisiting 1967," we are brought back to the first years of the existence of Israel and the time before the declaration of the state, as the author explores archives regarding the actual position of leading politicians in Israel at the time on the issue of the future ambitions of a Jewish state.

In the UN, the immediate assessment, represented by the UN-appointed negotiator Count Folke Bernadotte from Sweden, was that the erupting conflict would be solved within a few months. A specific UN organization, the United Nations Relief and Works Agency for Palestine Refugees in the Near East (UNRWA), was established a day ahead of the formation of the UN High Commissioner for Refugees (UNHCR) for the purpose of providing for the seven-hundred thousand Palestinian refugees who within a short time had spread to a number of the countries in the region. Developments didn't move as predicted. Today, more than sixty-seven years later, these refugees are still refugees and now number more than five million, and UNRWA remains responsible for the well-being of those residing in Syria, Lebanon, Jordan, and Palestine.[12]

At the same time, UNRWA represents the guarantee that UN Resolution 194 granting Palestinian refugees the right to return will be honored. Recent Israeli references to a number of refugee groups elsewhere in the world as not being able to return, thereby arguing that the Palestinians should also refrain from this demand, tells how important the refugee question remains to any solution. Among Palestinians, the fate of the refugees is engrained in their identity as a people.

The Oslo Accords were based on the established Green Line or Cease-fire Line signed in 1949. However, it could be argued that any future dialogue on a settlement should take the UN General Assembly recommendation from 1947[13] as a point of departure regarding how to divide the British Mandate of Palestine.

Why? This decision is the only one that is internationally recognized and in line with international law. According to the UN Charter, adopted in 1945, any change of borders through the use of military power is deemed illegal[14]

When Israel was approved as a member of the UN in 1949,[15] its membership was based on an assessment stating that Israel was a peace-loving country, ready to abide by the UN Charter and UN Resolutions 181[16] and 194, the latter of which was defined above.[17]

Israel Has Not Delivered

Israel's signing of the Oslo Accords over two decades ago was seen, among Palestinians especially, but also by important parts of the international community, as a first step toward ending an illegal occupation. The years since the signing have shown policies that are not at all conducive with the establishment of a sovereign Palestinian state. Settlements have expanded; the continued siege of Gaza has entered its second decade; severe limitations have been imposed on activities in C areas; and policies have been expressed concerning annexation, depopulation, and the annihilation of the Palestinian population. All of this indicates completely different intentions. Israel has not proven itself to be a trustworthy partner for peace with the intention to end occupation. In his most recent election campaign from 2015, the current Prime Minister Benjamin Netanyahu clearly stated that with him in charge, no Palestinian state would become a reality west of the Jordan River.[18] This contradicts US President Barack Obama's pledge in 2010 to Palestinian President Abbas: "I will make every effort to ensure Palestinian statehood."[19] During the latest war in Gaza in 2014, Israeli officials argued in favor of killing as many Palestinians as possible.[20] And this does not seem to be the only war, on the ground. There are indications that new wars could erupt at any moment. The dehumanization of Palestinians is widely accepted in Israeli political discourse.

With continued control of the C areas, Israel uses its military on a daily basis to forcibly transfer people, particularly Palestinian nomads. Attempts to build physical structures in existing villages are as a rule prevented. Possibilities to move from one village to another, to hospitals, or to agricultural land are severely hampered. At the same time, settlement activities expand under military protection. Sixty percent of the occupied West Bank is still outside what Palestinian authorities and inhabitants can utilize in a fruitful way for the future.

The combination of existing settlements and Israeli military control of the C areas results in a physical division of the West Bank into at least four separate clusters of Palestinian cities and villages. The settlements of Ariel, Ma'ale

Adumim, and Efrat, which impede Palestinians' freedom of movement, were the stumbling blocks in the negotiations in Taba, Egypt, in 2000, at the start of the Second Intifada, as they remain stumbling blocks today.

Returning to the UN recommendation adopted in 1947, both Israel and Palestine would be comprised of three geographical parts, connected by two land bridges. Major Palestinian cities like Akko and Nazareth were to be located within a future Palestinian state. The UN decision to govern Jerusalem and the holy sites under an international body could perhaps be replaced by the formula of "one city, the capital of two countries," with the freedom to move between the two parts of the city and visit the different holy sites.

Dangers Ahead

Kåre Willoch, the former Norwegian prime minister from the Conservative Party (Høyre), recently said, in reference to Palestine, that a history of suppression as a rule ends in an explosion if the suppression is not brought to an end. Palestinian ministers say the same. Steadfastness is a Palestinian characteristic. Their relation to the land on which they work and live has strengthened them to be able to cope with ongoing atrocities and a lack of hope for the future. Developments over the last twenty-two years have pushed more and more people to the brink, especially youths. In a world where they can better understand the realities elsewhere thanks to the Internet and social media, their frustration increases to a level that becomes difficult to control.

International trading in disrespect of Palestinian dignity and rights can continue as it has, with investments from state-owned pension funds, banks, and private investors in Israeli state bonds and company shares underpinning the occupation regime to a substantial level. However, we should be aware that that this will come at a heavy price: The brunt of the burden will no doubt be carried by the Palestinians. Meanwhile, Europe and the US will pay in terms of international reputation. Who will ever trust these countries in the future? International laws and conventions take their toll. What are they worth in a world where an occupation can just go on?

Two states living side by side is a far-fetched idea, commentators frequently say, given the realities of Israeli settlements, particularly in the occupied West Bank. But these settlements are the result of political will in Israel — and political will can disband them again. Some settlers, in particular the political orthodox, will protest violently. They are a minority. The Israeli army has again and again shown its ability to act against rioting populations: It can manage if Israel has the political will.

Most likely the Israeli leaders, regardless of political affiliation, have to be told that the alternative to ending the occupation will not be positive for Israel's politics and economy. Do the declared supporters of an independent Palestinian state have the courage to give that message and follow through with it? Palestine depends on courageous action from outside. Recognition of Palestine is a symbolic act today, one that implies hope. Two countries in Western Europe, Iceland and Sweden, have recognized the State of Palestine, joining together with most countries in Asia, Africa, South America, and Eastern Europe. Several parliaments in Western Europe have made non-binding recommendations to their governments to recognize Palestine. But this needs to be followed up with more concrete action in order for a sovereign and independent state to become a reality now — and not sometime in the future. Neither the Palestinians nor the international community can live with the occupation any longer.

A Success or a Curse?

The intention of this collection of essays is not to give a definite answer to the question over whether the Oslo Accords have been a success or a curse. "Oslo is dead" and "Oslo is the only option in town" are two contradictory statements often heard when discussing the issue of Palestine. The Oslo Accords in 1993 and the following years were seen as a breakthrough at the time regarding the most significant conflict in the Middle East. Indeed, Norway received a great deal of recognition for its role as a facilitator in the secret dialogue that took place between the Israelis and the Palestinians.

When the accords were first signed in 1993, a timeframe of five years was stipulated for when a final agreement between Israel and the PLO would be reached. But with no common understanding of what a "final agreement" might imply, and with no agreed-upon mechanisms for assuring that this determined time table would be followed by both parties, five years have now become more than twenty. Palestinians in Gaza and the West Bank experience severe atrocities due to wars and bombings, blockades, extrajudicial killings, and restrictions on movement and economic activity. Israelis are also facing insecurity and killings due to suicide bombings, rockets, and the "knife intifada" that began in late 2015, in which lone-wolf assailants began carrying out knife attacks against Israelis and members of the security forces.

Among Palestinians there is limited belief in negotiations as stipulated in the Oslo Accords. Resistance to end the occupation is a major factor that gives any political leader legitimacy. Two-thirds of the respondents in a December 2015 public poll said they were in favor of the knife attacks mentioned above, believing "that if the current confrontations develop[ed] into an armed intifada, it [would] help in achieving national interests in ways that negotiations could not."[21] There is severe frustration in huge segments of the population over the lack of progress in ending the occupation and granting Palestinians the same rights as anyone else in the world. Steadfastness is no longer a sufficient platform for enduring the hardships of occupation.

The Palestinian authorities, having accepted the role of custodians of the Israeli occupation, have lost the most credibility. Among Palestinians, an elite class has been fostered which is today clinging to the results of the Oslo Accords. Ordinary citizens, on the contrary, see the Oslo Accords as a curse, limiting their ability to resist the occupation and keeping an illegitimate leadership in place. Particularly among the youth, who are connected to the Internet and well aware of the world outside, the present situation offers no acceptable future. Resistance or escape are the only viable alternatives.

The Palestinian leadership has worked to engage the international community and international bodies like the UN and the International Criminal Court (ICC) in moving toward an end to the occupation and the declaration of a sovereign and independent Palestine. President Abbas's speech at the UN General Assembly in September 2015 indicated a breach with the Oslo parameters. But two-thirds of Palestinians don't believe that Abbas is serious in his statements about abandoning the Oslo Accords.[22] A reason for this is that previously announced threats to end security coordination with Israeli have not been implemented.

For years the Palestinian leadership has tried to internationalize its concerns, raising the case of war crimes with the ICC and the issue of ending the occupation with the UN, but with limited success so far. Regardless of whether the solution will involve one state or two, it is important to make the international community complicit and jointly responsible for a viable and acceptable outcome, in line with the UN decision in 1947 and taking into account the sufferings of Palestinians who are living in the West Bank and Gaza as well as outside in the wider diaspora.

For the younger generations of Palestinians, the more than 60 percent who were born after the signing of the Oslo Accords, the old symbols of resistance like *al-Nakbah*, Land Day, and the attitude of steadfastness, carry little—if any— meaning. For these youths, the unacceptable situations under which they are living, with limited movement, sudden arrests, and no prospects for the future, constitute the basis of resistance, in which there is only one way out: end the occupation. Many are willing to pay the price that this might cost them, even if it means their lives, since continuing to live under Israeli occupation is totally unacceptable.

For the younger generation, the Oslo Accords carry no positive message, only one of endless talks without any tangible changes on the ground, with the same old guards pursuing their own interests. With this in mind, it is time to question if the Oslo Accords have been a success or a curse for the Palestinians.

A Change in Attitude?

In January 2016, the foreign ministers of the 28 European Union member states issued a statement voicing their "strong opposition" to Israel's expansionist policy of settlements, which the ministers said were "illegal under international law, constitute an obstacle to peace and threaten to make a two state solution impossible."[23] The statement urged Israel "to end all settlement activity and to dismantle the outposts erected since March 2001, in line with prior obligations," arguing that "settlement activity in East Jerusalem seriously jeopardizes the possibility of Jerusalem serving as the future capital of both States."

The ministers stated that "the EU expresses its commitment to ensure that — in line with international law — all agreements between the State of Israel and the EU must unequivocally and explicitly indicate their inapplicability to the territories occupied by Israel in 1967. This does not constitute a boycott of Israel which the EU strongly opposes."

The EU foreign ministers' decision may prove to be an important change in international attitude regarding the ongoing occupation. Indeed, these ministers' statement serves as a balance between strong EU–Israel relations, on one side, and the principles of international law and their own commitment to a two-state solution, with a sovereign Palestine existing side by side with Israel. The EU operates on a tight rope, and its move might have unforeseen consequences for the situation, given the EU's international political and economic importance.

Additional assessments on the role of the EU can be found in the essay "The European Union and Israel since Oslo."

Notes

1. Longva revealed this information in an interview for the 2013 *Al Jazeera* documentary "The Price of Oslo," which was produced for the twenty-year anniversary of the Oslo Accords. He died shortly after the interview, in October 2013. http://www.aljazeera.com/programmes/aljazeeraworld/2013/09/2013910121456318891.html.

2. The Quartet consists of the United Nations, the United States of America, Russia, and the European Union. The Quartet was established in 2002 as a response to the deteriorating situation in the occupied territory after the outbreak of the Second Intifada in September 2000. Former British Prime Minister Tony Blair served as special representative for the Quartet from 2007 until he resigned in 2015.

3. Herb Keinon, "Netanyahu: Abbas Must Choose, Peace with Israel or Reconciliation with Hamas," *The Jerusalem Post*, April 23, 2014, http://www.jpost.com/Diplomacy-and-Politics/Netanyahu-Abbas-must-choose-peace-with-Israel-or-reconciliation-with-Hamas-350159.

4. See UN General Assembly Resolution 194, http://www.un.org/documents/ga/res/3/ares3.htm.

5. The Palestinian Center for Policy and Survey Research (PCPSR) has conducted a number of public polls that show increasing support for resistance, either civil disobedience or armed engagement, and weakening support for negotiations as the way forward. See http://www.pcpsr.org/en/node/625.

6. Mahmoud Abbas, "Full Text of Abbas's 2015 Address to the UN General Assembly," *The Times of Israel*, September 30, 2015, http://www.timesofisrael.com/full-text-of-abbas-2015-address-to-the-un-general-assembly/.

7. Abbas here is referring to a March 2015 statement issued by the Palestinian Central Council, which said that the council had decided "to end all forms of security coordination with Israel as it continues to violate signed Agreements." http://nad-plo.org/userfiles/file/statements/Statement_Central_Council.pdf.

8. UN General Assembly, Resolution 181 (II), "Future Government of Palestine," November 29, 1947, http://www.un.org/documents/ga/res/2/ares2.htm.

9. Khaled Diab describes this reality in his opinion piece "Israel's Six-State Reality," *Al Jazeera*, January 6, 2015, http://www.aljazeera.com/indepth/opinion/2016/01/israel-state-reality-160104113512447.html.

10. "Palestinian Public Opinion Poll (58)," Palestinian Center for Policy and Survey Research, December 14, 2015, http://www.pcpsr.org/en/node/625.

11. Interview made by Petter Bauck in connection while writing his Master's thesis at SOAS, London, "My House is My Castle," which deals with human security being under threat in relation to the demolition of houses in Gaza.

12. UNRWA website, http://www.unrwa.org/where-we-work.

13. UN General Assembly, Resolution 181 (II), "Future Government of Palestine," November 29, 1947, http://www.un.org/documents/ga/res/2/ares2.htm.

14. United Nation Charter, Article 2.4, http://www.un.org/en/sections/un-charter/chapter-i/index.html.

15. See UN General Assembly Resolution 273, http://www.un.org/documents/ga/res/2/ares2.htm.

16. The UN Partition Plan for the British Mandate of Palestine, UN General Assembly Resolution 181, http://www.un.org/documents/ga/res/2/ares2.htm.

17. See UN General Assembly Resolution 194, http://www.un.org/documents/ga/res/3/ares3.htm.
18. Barak Ravid, "Netanyahu: If I'm Elected, There Will Be No Palestinian State," *Haaretz*, March 16, 2015, http://www.haaretz.com/israel-news/elections/1.647212.
19. Natasha Mozgovaya, Avi Issacharoff, "Obama to Abbas: I Will Make Every Effort to Ensure Palestinian Statehood," *Haaretz*, July 9, 2010, http://www.haaretz.com/israel-news/obama-to-abbas-i-will-make-every-effort-to-ensure-palestinian-statehood-1.301054.
20. Gideon Levy, "Israel's Real Purpose in Gaza Attack? To Kill Arabs," *Information Clearing House*, July 13, 2014, http://www.informationclearinghouse.info/article39082.htm.
21. "Palestinian Public Opinion Poll (58)," Palestinian Center for Policy and Survey Research, December 14, 2015, http://www.pcpsr.org/en/node/625.
22. Ibid.
23. Press release, "Council Conclusions on the Middle East Peace Process," European Council of the European Union, January 18, 2016, http://www.consilium.europa.eu/en/press/press-releases/2016/01/18-fac-conclusions-mepp/.

1

The Oslo Accords:
Their Context,
Their Consequences

Noam Chomsky

In September 1993, United States President Bill Clinton presided over a handshake between Israeli Prime Minister Yitzhak Rabin and Palestine Liberation Organization (PLO) Chairman Yasser Arafat on the White House lawn — capping off a "day of awe," as the press described it with reverence. The occasion was the announcement of the Declaration of Principles (DOP) for political settlement of the Israel–Palestine conflict, which resulted from secret meetings in Oslo sponsored by the Norwegian government.

Independent negotiations had been underway between Israel and Palestinians since November 1991, initiated by the United States during the glow of success after the first Iraq war, which established that "what we say goes," in the triumphant words of President George H.W. Bush. The negotiations opened with a brief conference in Madrid and continued under the guiding hand of the United States (and, technically, the fading Soviet Union, to provide the illusion of international auspices). The Palestinian delegation, consisting of Palestinians within the Occupied Territories (henceforth the 'internal Palestinians'), was led by the dedicated and incorruptible left nationalist Haidar Abdel Shafi, probably the most respected figure in Palestine. The 'external Palestinians,' the PLO based in Tunis and headed by Yasser Arafat, were excluded, though they had an unofficial observer, Faisal Husseini. The huge number of Palestinian refugees were totally excluded, with no regard to their rights, even those accorded them by the UN General Assembly.

To appreciate the nature and significance of the Oslo Accords, and the consequences that flowed from them, it is important to understand the context in which the Madrid and Oslo negotiations took place. I begin by reviewing highlights of the immediate background that set the context for the negotiations, then turn to the DOP and the consequences of the Oslo process, which extend to the present, adding a few words on lessons that should be learned.

The PLO, Israel, and the United States had recently released formal positions on the basic issues that were the topic of the Madrid and Oslo negotiations. The PLO position was presented in a November 1988 declaration of the Palestinian National Council, carrying forward a long series of diplomatic initiatives that had been dismissed. It called for a Palestinian state to be established in the territories occupied by Israeli in 1967 and requested that the UN Security Council "formulate and guarantee arrangements for security and peace between all the states concerned in the region, including the Palestinian state" alongside Israel. The PLO declaration, which accepted the overwhelming international consensus on a diplomatic settlement, was virtually the same as the two-state solution brought to the Security Council in January 1976 by the Arab 'confrontation states,' Egypt, Syria, and Jordan, and vetoed by the US in 1980. For over thirty-five years the US blocked the international consensus, and still does, diplomatic pleasantries aside.

By 1988, Washington's rejectionist stance was becoming difficult to sustain. The outgoing Reagan administration had become an international laughingstock with its increasingly desperate efforts to pretend that alone in the world, it could not hear the accommodating proposals of the PLO and the Arab states. Grudgingly, Washington decided to "declare victory," claiming that at last the PLO had been compelled to utter Secretary of State George Shultz's "magic words" and express its willingness to pursue diplomacy. As Shultz makes clear in his memoirs, the goal was to ensure maximum humiliation of the PLO while conceding that peace offers could no longer be denied. He informed then President Ronald Reagan that Arafat in one place was saying "'Unc, unc, unc,' and in another he was saying, 'cle, cle, cle,' but nowhere will he yet bring himself to say 'Uncle,'" conceding total capitulation in the humble style expected of the lower orders. Low-level discussions with the PLO would be allowed, but on the understanding that they would be meaningless. Specifically, it was stipulated that the PLO must abandon its request for an international conference so that the US would maintain control over the process.

In May 1989, Israel's Likud–Labor coalition government formally responded to Palestinian acceptance of a two-state settlement, declaring that there can be no "additional Palestinian state" between Jordan and Israel (Jordan already being a Palestinian state by Israeli dictate, whatever Jordanians and Palestinians might think) and that "there will be no change in the status of Judea, Samaria, and Gaza [the West Bank and Gaza] other than in accordance with the basic guidelines of the [Israeli] Government." It stated that Israel would conduct no negotiations with the PLO, though it would permit "free elections" under Israeli military rule, with much of the Palestinian leadership in prison without charge or expelled.

The new Bush administration endorsed this plan without qualifications in December 1989 (the Baker Plan).

Those were the three formal positions on the eve of the Madrid negotiations, with Washington mediating as the "honest broker."

When Arafat went to Washington to take part in the "day of awe" in September 1993, the lead story in the *New York Times* celebrated the handshake as a "dramatic image" that "will transform Mr. Arafat into a statesman and peacemaker" who has finally renounced violence under Washington's tutelage. At the extreme critical end of the mainstream, *New York Times* columnist Anthony Lewis wrote that until that moment Palestinians had always "rejected compromise" but now at last they were willing to "make peace possible." Of course, it was the United States and Israel that had rejected diplomacy and the PLO that had been offering compromise for years, but Lewis' reversal of the facts was quite normal and unchallenged in the mainstream.

There were other crucial developments in the immediate pre-Madrid/pre-Oslo years. In December 1987, the Intifada erupted in Gaza and quickly spread throughout the Occupied Territories. This broad-based and remarkably restrained uprising was as much a surprise to the PLO in Tunis as it was to the occupying Israeli forces with their extensive system of military and paramilitary forces, surveillance, and collaborators. The Intifada was not limited to opposing the occupation; it was also a social revolution within Palestinian society, breaking patterns of subordination of women, authority by notables, and other forms of hierarchy and domination.

Although the timing of the Intifada was a surprise, the uprising itself was not, at least to those who paid any attention to Israel's US-backed operations within the territories. Something was bound to happen. There is only so much people can endure. For the preceding twenty years, Palestinians under military occupation had been subjected to harsh repression, brutality, and cruel humiliation while watching what remained of their country disappear before their eyes as Israel conducted its programs of settlement, huge infrastructure developments designed to integrate valuable parts of the territories within Israel, robbery of resources, and other measures to bar independent development, always with the United States' crucial military, economic, and diplomatic support and its ideological support in shaping how the issues were framed.

To take just one of the many cases that elicited no notice or concern in the west, shortly before the outbreak of the Intifada, a Palestinian girl, Intissar al-Atar, was shot and killed in a schoolyard in Gaza by a resident of a nearby Jewish settlement. He was one of the several thousand Israeli settlers who went to Gaza with substantial subsidies, protected by a huge army presence as they took over much of the land and scarce water of the Strip while living "lavishly in twenty-two settlements in the midst of 1.4 million destitute Palestinians," as the crime is described by Israeli scholar Avi Raz (2012).

The murderer of the schoolgirl, Shimon Yifrah, was arrested but quickly released on bail when a court determined that "the offense is not severe enough" to warrant detention. The judge commented that Yifrah only intended to shock the girl by firing his gun at her in a schoolyard, not to kill her, so "this is not a case of a criminal person who has to be punished, deterred, and taught a lesson by imprisoning him." Yifrah was given a seven-month suspended sentence, while settlers in the courtroom broke out in song and dance. And the usual silence reigned. After all, this was routine.

As Yifrah was freed, the Israeli press reported that an army patrol had fired into a schoolyard in a West Bank refugee camp, wounding five children, intending only "to shock them." There were no charges, and the event again attracted no attention. It was just another episode in the program of "illiteracy as punishment," the Israeli press reported, including the closing of schools, use of gas bombs, beating of students with rifle butts, and barring of medical aid for victims — an extension of a reign of more severe brutality, becoming even more savage during the Intifada, under the orders of Defense Minister Yitzhak Rabin. After two years of violent and sadistic repression, Rabin informed Peace Now Leaders that "the inhabitants of the territories are subject to harsh military and economic pressure. In the end, they will be broken" and accept Israel's terms. And they did, when Arafat restored control through the Oslo process.

The Madrid negotiations between Israel and 'internal Palestinians' continued inconclusively from 1991, primarily because Abdel Shafi insisted on an end to the expansion of Israeli settlements. The settlements are all illegal, as has repeatedly been determined by international authorities, including the UN Security Council (among other resolutions, Resolution 446, passed 12–0, with the US, the UK, and Norway abstaining). The illegality of the settlements has been affirmed by the International Court of Justice. It was recognized by Israel's highest legal authorities and government officials in late 1967 when the settlement projects were beginning. The criminal enterprise has included the vast expansion and annexation of Greater Jerusalem, in explicit violation of repeated UN Security Council orders.

Israel's position as the Madrid conference opened was summarized accurately by Israeli journalist Danny Rubinstein, one of the best informed analysts of the Occupied Territories. He wrote that at Madrid Israel and the US would agree to some form of Palestinian 'autonomy,' as required by the 1979 Camp David agreements, but that it would be "autonomy as in a POW camp, where the prisoners are 'autonomous' to cook their meals without interference and to organize cultural events." [1]

Palestinians would be granted little more than what they already had: control over local services. And the Israeli settlement programs would continue.

While the Madrid negotiations and the secret Oslo negotiations were underway, these programs expanded rapidly, first under Yitzhak Shamir and then Yitzhak Rabin, who became prime minister in 1992 and "boasted that more housing in the territories is being built during his tenure than at any time since 1967." Rabin explained the guiding principle succinctly: "What is important is what is within the boundaries, and it is less important where the boundaries are, as long as the State [of Israel] covers most of the territory of the Land of Israel [Eretz Israel, the former Palestine], whose capital is Jerusalem."

Israeli researchers reported that the aim of the Rabin government was to expand radically "the greater Jerusalem zone of influence," extending from Ramallah to Hebron to the border of Ma'ale Adumim near Jericho, and to "finish creating circles of contiguous Jewish settlements in the greater Jerusalem zone of influence, so as to further surround the Palestinian communities, limit their development, and prevent any possibility that East Jerusalem could become a Palestinian capital." Furthermore, "a vast network of roads has been under construction, forming the backbone of the settlement pattern."

The programs were expanded rapidly after the Oslo Accords, including new settlements and 'thickening' of old ones, special inducements to attract new settlers, and highway projects to cantonize the territory. Excluding annexed East Jerusalem, building starts increased by over 40 percent from 1993 to 1995, according to a Peace Now study. Government funding for settlements in the territories increased by 70 percent in 1994, the year following the accords. The journal of the governing Labor Party, *Davar*, reported that Rabin's administration maintained the priorities of the ultra-right Shamir government it replaced: while pretending to freeze settlements, Labor "helped them financially even more than the Shamir government had ever done," enlarging settlements "everywhere in the West Bank, even in the most provocative spots." The policies were carried forward in following years and are the basis for the current Netanyahu government's programs. They are designed to leave Israel in control of some 40–50 percent of the West Bank, the rest cantonized, imprisoned, as Israel takes over the Jordan Valley, and separated from Gaza, in explicit violation of the Oslo Accords, thus ensuring that any potential Palestinian entity will have no access to the outside world.

The Intifada was initiated and carried out by 'internal Palestinians.' The PLO in Tunis tried to exert some control over the events, but with little success. The programs of the early 1990s, while negotiations were in process, deepened the alienation of the 'internal Palestinians' from the PLO leadership abroad.

Under these circumstances, it was not surprising that Arafat sought a way to reestablish PLO authority. The opportunity was offered by the secret negotiations between Arafat and Israel under Norwegian auspices, undercutting the local leadership. As negotiations were concluded in August 1993, the growing estrangement was reviewed by Lamis Andoni, one of the few journalists who was keeping a close watch on what was happening among the Palestinians under occupation and in refugee camps in neighboring countries.

Andoni reported that the PLO was "facing the worst crisis since its inception [as] Palestinian groups—except for Fatah—and independents are distancing themselves from the PLO [and the] shrinking clique around Yasser Arafat." She reported further that "two top PLO executive committee members, Palestinian poet Mahmoud Darwish and Shafiq al-Hout, have resigned from the PLO executive committee," while Palestinian negotiators were offering their resignations and even groups that remained inside were distancing themselves from Arafat. The leader of Fatah in Lebanon called on Arafat to resign, while opposition to him personally and to PLO corruption and autocracy were mounting in the territories. Along with "the rapid disintegration of the mainstream group and Arafat's loss of support within his own movement, . . . the speedy disintegration of the PLO's institutions and the steady erosion of the Organisation's constituency could render any breakthrough at the peace talks meaningless."

"At no point in the PLO's history has opposition to the leadership, and to Arafat himself, been as strong," Andoni observed, "while for the first time there is a growing feeling that safeguarding Palestinian national rights no longer hinges on defending the PLO's role. Many believe that it is the leadership's policies that are destroying Palestinian institutions and jeopardising Palestinian national rights." For such reasons, she noted, Arafat was pursuing the Jericho-Gaza option offered by the Oslo Accords, which he hoped "will assert the PLO's authority, especially amid signs that the Israeli government could go the extra ten miles by talking directly to the PLO, thus salvaging for it the legitimacy it is losing internally."

Israeli authorities were surely aware of the developments within Palestine and presumably came to appreciate that it made good sense to deal with those who are "destroying Palestinian institutions and jeopardizing Palestinian national rights" before the population sought to realize its national goals and rights in some other way.

Reaction to the Oslo Accords among Palestinians within the Occupied Territories was mixed. Some had high hopes. Others saw little to celebrate. "The provisions of the agreement have alarmed even the most moderate Palestinians, who worry that the accord consolidates Israeli control in the territories," Andoni reported. Saeb Erekat, a senior Palestinian negotiator, commented, "Apparently this agreement aims at reorganizing the Israeli occupation and not at a gradual termination." Even Faisal Husseini, who was close to Arafat, said that the accord "is definitely not the beginning that our people were looking for." Abdel Shafi criticized the PLO leadership for accepting an agreement that permits Israel to continue its settlement program, land appropriation, "annexation and Judaization" of its expanded Jerusalem area, and its "economic hegemony" over Palestinians. He refused to attend the celebrations on the White House lawn.

Particularly grating to many was what they saw as "the shabby behavior of the PLO leadership, including a pattern of ignoring Palestinians who have suffered through twenty-seven years of Israeli occupation in favor of exiles coming from Tunis to take power," Youssef Ibrahim reported in the *New York Times*, adding that PLO representatives "were pelted with stones by Palestinian youths as they rode into [Jericho] in Israeli Army jeeps." Arafat's provisional list for his governing authority revealed "that he is determined to stack it with loyalists and members of the Palestinian diaspora," Julian Ozanne reported from Jerusalem in the London *Financial Times*, including only two 'internal Palestinians,' Faisal Husseini and Zakaria al-Agra, both Arafat loyalists. The rest came from Arafat's "loyal political factions" outside the territories.

A look at the actual contents of the Oslo Accords reveals that such reactions were, if anything, overly optimistic.

The DOP was quite explicit about satisfying Israel's demands, but it was silent on Palestinian national rights. It conformed to the conception articulated by Dennis Ross, Clinton's main Middle East advisor and negotiator at Camp David in 2000, later President Barack Obama's main advisor as well. As Ross explained, Israel has *needs* while Palestinians have only *wants*, obviously of lesser significance (see Finkelstein 2007).

Article I of the DOP states that the end result of the process is to be "a permanent settlement based on Security Council Resolutions 242 and 338." Those familiar with the diplomacy concerning the Israel–Palestine conflict should have no difficulty understanding what this meant. Resolutions 242 and 338 say nothing at all about Palestinian rights, apart from reference to a "just settlement of the refugee problem," left vague. Later resolutions refer to Palestinian national rights, but these were ignored in the DOP. If the culmination of the 'peace process' would be as clearly articulated in the DOP, then Palestinians could kiss goodbye their hopes for some limited degree of national rights in the former Palestine.

Other articles of the DOP spell all of this out more clearly. They stipulate that Palestinian authority extends over the "West Bank and Gaza Strip territory, except for issues that will be negotiated in the permanent status negotiations: Jerusalem, settlements, military locations, and Israelis" — that is, except for every issue of significance. Furthermore, "subsequent to the Israeli withdrawal, Israel will continue to be responsible for external security, and for internal security and public order of settlements and Israelis. Israeli military forces and civilians may continue to use roads freely within the Gaza Strip and the Jericho area" — the two areas from which Israel was pledged to withdraw, eventually. In short, there would be no meaningful changes. The DOP did not include a word about the settlement programs at the heart of the conflict, which even before their vast expansion under the Oslo process were undermining realistic prospects of achieving any meaningful Palestinian self-determination.

In brief, only by succumbing to what is sometimes called "intentional ignorance" could one believe that the Oslo process was a path to peace. Nevertheless, this became virtual dogma among western commentators and intellectuals.

The Oslo Accords were followed by additional Israel–Arafat/PLO agreements. The first and most important of these was Oslo II in 1995, shortly before Prime Minister Rabin was assassinated. The assassination was a tragic event no doubt, although the illusions concocted about "Rabin the peace-maker" cannot sustain analysis.

The Oslo II Agreement is what one would expect to be crafted by intelligent law students assigned the task of constructing a document that would allow US and Israeli authorities the option to do as they please while also leaving room for speculation about other forthcoming outcomes. When these remain unrealized, the blame can be laid on the 'extremists' who have undermined the promise of the agreement.

To illustrate, the Oslo II Agreement stipulates that Israeli settlers in the Occupied Territories (illegally, of course) will remain under Israel's jurisdiction and legislation. In the official wording, "the Israeli military government [in the territories] shall retain the necessary legislative, judicial, and executive powers and responsibilities, in accordance with international law," which the US and Israel have always interpreted as they choose, with tacit European acquiescence. The same latitude grants these authorities effective veto power over Palestinian legislation. The agreement states that any such "legislation which amends or abrogates existing [Israeli-imposed] laws or military orders ... shall have no effect and shall be void *ab initio* if it exceeds the jurisdiction of the [Palestinian] Council" (which had no authority in most of the territories and only authority elsewhere conditional on Israeli approval) or is "otherwise inconsistent with this or any other agreement" (in practice, as the US and Israel determine).

Furthermore, "the Palestinian side shall respect the legal rights of Israelis (including corporations owned by Israelis) related to lands located in areas under the territorial jurisdiction of the Council" — that is, in the limited areas in which the Palestinian authorities were to have jurisdiction subject to Israeli approval. Specifically, this refers to rights related to government and so-called 'absentee' land, a complex legal construction that effectively transfers to Israeli jurisdiction the land of Palestinians absent from territories taken by Israel. This constitutes most of the region, though the government of Israel, which determines its boundaries unilaterally, provided no official figures for the agreement. The Israeli press reported that "unsettled state lands" amounted to about half of the West Bank in the mid-1990s, and total state lands to about 70 percent.

Oslo II thus rescinded the decision of virtually the entire world, and all relevant legal authorities, that Israel has no claim to the territories occupied in 1967 and that the settlements are illegitimate. The Palestinian side recognized their legality, along with unspecified other legal rights of Israelis throughout the territories, including zones A and B (under conditional Palestinian control). Oslo II implanted more firmly the major accomplishment of Oslo I: all UN resolutions that have any bearing on Palestinian rights were abrogated, including those concerning the legality of settlements, the status of Jerusalem, and the right of return.

It wiped out with a stroke virtually the entire record of Middle East diplomacy, apart from the version implemented in the unilateral US-run "peace process." The basic facts are not just out of history within US commentary, but are now officially excised.

So matters have continued, to the present.

As noted, it is understandable that Arafat would leap at the opportunity to undercut the 'internal Palestinian' leadership and to reassert his waning power in the territories. But another important question is what the Norwegian negotiators thought they were accomplishing. The only serious scholarly study of the matter, to my knowledge, is the work of Hilde Henriksen Waage (2008), who was commissioned by the Norwegian Ministry of Foreign Affairs to research the topic and granted access to internal files, only to make the remarkable discovery that the documentary record for the crucial period is missing.

Waage observes that the Oslo Accords were certainly a turning point in the history of the Israel–Palestine conflict, which also established Oslo as the world's "capital of peace." The Oslo process was "expected to bring peace to the Middle East," Waage writes, but "for the Palestinians, it resulted in the parceling of the West Bank, the doubling of Israeli settlers, the construction of a crippling separation wall, a draconian closure regime, and an unprecedented separation between the Gaza Strip and the West Bank," as well as expectations that were completely unrealistic for reasons already reviewed, which were quite evident at the time and, indeed, discussed but only far from the mainstream (see Said 1993; Chomsky 1993).

Waage concludes plausibly that the "Oslo process could serve as the perfect case study for flaws" of the model "of third party mediation by a small state in highly asymmetrical conflicts," and that, as she starkly puts it, "the Oslo process was conducted on Israel's premises, with Norway acting as Israel's helpful errand boy." Waage notes,

> The Norwegians believed that through dialogue and a gradual building of trust, an irreversible peace dynamic would be created that could push the process forward to solution. The problem with this entire approach is that the issue is not one of trust, but of power. The facilitative process masks that reality. In the end, the results that can be achieved by a weak third-party facilitator are no more than the strong party will allow.... The question to be asked is whether such a model can ever be appropriate.

This is a good question, and one worth pondering, particularly as educated western opinion now adopts the ludicrous assumption that meaningful Israeli–Palestinian negotiations can be seriously conducted under the auspices of the United States — an 'honest broker,' — in reality a partner of Israel for thirty-five years in blocking a diplomatic settlement that has near universal support.

Notes

1. *Haaretz,* October 23, 1991. On sources here and below where not cited, see, Chomsky (1994).

References

Chomsky, N. 1994. *World Orders Old and New.* New York: Columbia University Press.
_____. 1993. "The Israel–Arafat Agreement." *Z Magazine* (October).
Finkelstein, N.G. 2007. *Dennis Ross and the Peace Process: Subordinating Palestinian Rights to Israeli "Needs."* Washington, D.C.: Institute of Palestine Studies.
Raz, A. 2012. *The Bride and the Dowry: Israel, Jordan, and the Palestinians in the Aftermath of the June 1967 War.* New Haven, CT: Yale University Press.
Said, E.W. 1993. "Arafat's Deal." *Nation* 257 (8): 269–70.
Waage, H.H. 2008. "Postscript to Oslo: The Mystery of Norway's Missing Files." *Journal of Palestine Studies* 38 (1): 54–65.

2

Revisiting 1967: The False Paradigm of Peace, Partition, and Parity

Ilan Pappé

The view that the realities in Israel and Palestine are an example of settler colonialism has wide implications for our understanding of the present debacle in the region's 'peace process.' The scholarly debate on the peace process more often than not lacks a historical dimension, and the analyses of failure and progress are based on power relations, the intentions of the local actors, and opportunities.

The chief aim of this chapter is to examine the peace process historically as a strategy of the settler colonialist state and as a native response to it. This chapter also argues that the peace process was conceived at a particular moment, in June 1967, as part of the settler colonialist state's attempt to reconcile Israel's wish to remain demographically a Jewish state and its desire to expand geographically without losing the pretense of being a democratic state in the post-1967 context. A third claim made here is that the Israeli political and military elite knowingly engaged in this dilemma, contemplating the possibility of a scenario of its own or of others' making that would place it in control of the West Bank and the Gaza Strip.

All three vantage points, I argue, suggest that the two-state solution and the process that is supposed to bring it about are an Israeli plan, the logic of which has been accepted, with modifications, by a powerful coalition of the United States, the European Union, Russia, the United Nations, most of the Arab states, the Fatah Palestinian leadership, the Zionist Left and Center in Israel, and some well-known figures in the Palestinian solidarity movement. It is the power of the coalition and not the logic of the solution or the process that has maintained the 'peace process' for so long, despite its apparent failure.

The University on the Hill

Givat Ram, 'the Hill of Ram,' is a wide hilly spread in the very western corner of present-day Jerusalem. It is host to various ministries, the Knesset, part of the Hebrew University, and the Bank of Israel. Israelis of a certain age, ethnic origin, and socioeconomic background have developed a highly nostalgic attitude toward the place. The hill makes a brief and pastoral appearance in Amos Oz's first and famous novel *My Michael*, published in 1968: "Where a small herd of sheep graze alongside the Prime Minister's Office" (Oz 1976: 186). There are no sheep in sight today and the grazing fields of yesteryear are long gone. They have been replaced by an elaborate system of highways, metal gates, hanging bridges, and quite a beautiful rose garden.

It is unlikely that sheep were anywhere to be seen near the prime minister's office when Oz's book was published, but sheep did graze this hill when the Palestinian rural neighborhood Sheikh al-Badr was standing on it. A few of its houses are still in existence, next to the Crown Plaza Hotel, frequented by Israeli members of the Knesset who do not live in Jerusalem. Sheikh al-Badr was gradually swallowed by the city, becoming an urban neighborhood until it was ethnically cleansed by Israeli forces in 1948. It was a famous spot in the city, as it overlooked one of Jerusalem's most renowned landmarks: the Valley of the Cross. Tradition has it that the tree from which Christ's cross was fashioned stood there, which is why Greek Orthodox monks built an impressive monastery in the area, still there today, caged in by roads and new Jewish neighborhoods.

West of the monastery lies one of the two main campuses of the Hebrew University in Jerusalem. It was built on Sheikh al-Badr's confiscated land and sold to the university by the Israeli custodian of absentee lands (allegedly decisions on the future of land are kept pending, but in reality land is sold to any Jewish individual or enterprise willing to pay a ridiculously low price for it). The university until 1948 was on Mt. Scopus, which subsequently became a 'no man's land' and therefore inaccessible.

North of the campus, a new site for Israeli government offices was chosen at about the same time as that for the university. Whereas the campus buildings are modest in appearance and surrounded by pleasant lawns and greenery, it seems that the serene charm of this hilltop did not inspire the architects who built the government offices. Paying little attention to the pastoral scenery or its biblical heritage, they opted for huge lumps of cement spread all over the hill, wounding the natural beauty of this crest of the Jerusalem Mountains.

In the summer of 1963, a group of unusual students arrived at the Hebrew University campus for a month-long course. Almost all of them had a legal background of one sort or another. Some were members of the military administration running the areas in which the 1948 Palestinians lived under strict rule that robbed them of most of their basic rights. Others were officers in the legal section of the Israeli army or officials in the Ministry of Interior, as well as one or two private lawyers.[1]

They were invited by the university's department of political science for a course that included lectures on the political situation in the West Bank and the Gaza Strip and lessons to be learned from Israel's military rule in the Sinai and Gaza in 1956 and inside Israel after 1948. A short introduction to 'Islam' was part of the curriculum, and it ended with a lecture on the 1948 ethnic cleansing of Jerusalem, the Yevusi Operation of April 1948, in which scores of Palestinian villages were emptied and wiped out (Pappé 2006). This was followed by "a celebratory meal and everyone was in an excellent mood," as reported by one of the participants (Inbar 2002: 3).

These individuals' presence on Givat Ram in 1963 was part of a new military strategy initiated by the Israeli chief of general staff on May 1, 1963, which was meant to prepare the army for running the West Bank as an occupied military area. It is highly significant that four years before the actual occupation, the Israeli military was readying the judicial and administrative infrastructure for ruling the lives of one million Palestinians.

The plan was code-named the Shaham Plan and it divided the West Bank into eight districts for the purpose of facilitating the imposition of organized military rule. Michael (Michel) Shaham was the general military governor of the Palestinian territories inside Israel. The official name of the program was the Organization of Military Rule in the Occupied Territories (Inbar 2002).

Three groups were behind the plan: members of the legal section of the army, academics at the Hebrew University, and officials of the Ministry of Interior. The ministry officials were mainly individuals who were already serving in one capacity or another in the military administration imposed on the 1948 Palestinians, still intact in 1963.

The plan included the appointment of a legal advisor to the future military governor of the Occupied Territories and four military courts. The appendixes to the plan consisted of translations into Arabic of Jordanian law as well the 1945 mandatory regulations. Although the latter were already in use inside Israel, the Israelis did not yet have them in Arabic. The reason may be that, according to Israeli law, these draconian measures, of which more is said later, applied to Jews and non-Jews alike. In the case of the West Bank, the measures were meant to apply only to Palestinians (indeed, when Jewish settlers began arriving, they were exempted from this legal regime). Zvi Inbar, who published for the first time the details of the plan in his memoirs, explains that every term had to be transferred from the reality of the mandatory period, when these regulations were issued by the British government in 1945, to the prospective occupation of the West Bank and the Gaza Strip in 1963. Thus, 'high commissioner' and 'His Majesty's government' were irrelevant terms that were replaced by 'military governor' and 'the Israel Defense Forces,' respectively.

The plan also indicated that international law and the Geneva Conventions were of concern in the case of a prospective occupation. Ominously for the Palestinians, the main concern was that the Geneva Conventions do not permit executions. The Israelis would eventually solve this problem by other means.

Jordanian law was studied in order to determine which of the laws should be abolished immediately so as not to interfere with Israeli strategy and objectives. "It is impossible for us to leave a law which would be against Israel and grant it the legitimacy of an Israeli law," recollects Inbar (2002: 147). Otherwise, the mode of rule during the Jordanian period fit well with Israeli conceptions of control. It was as comprehensive as the Israelis wished it to be, even providing for the censorship of books, especially children's books. The Jordanian list of censored literature included Anne Frank's diary. The Israeli list would include Thomas Khun's *Structure of Scientific Revolutions*, because it contains the word 'revolution.'

The Shaham Plan suggested names of people who should be appointed to high posts in the future occupation. Some would indeed be there in 1967, such as Haim Herzog and the plan's mastermind, Colonel Michael Shaham himself.

Under the terms of the plan, another group of potential recruits was invited to the Hebrew University a year later. The courses were later moved to Beit Hayahl, the "soldiers' dormitory" of Jerusalem, although their content and main purpose continued to be preparation for the eventuality of activating and managing military rule in the West Bank and the Gaza Strip (Inbar 2002: 148).

By May 1967, the plan became operative and the appointment of military governors and military judges to the West Bank and the Gaza Strip moved to a more detailed stage (including preparation for installing a regime in what the army called 'Syria'). Each governor received a box *(argaz)* containing instructions on how to govern an occupied Arab area; copies of the Geneva Conventions and other human rights treaties; the Arabic translation of the emergency regulations; a copy of *The Occupation of Enemy Territory: A Commentary on the Law and Practice of Belligerent Occupation* by Gerhard von Glahn (1957); and a set of international law reports on administrative rule published in 1929 by Elihu Lauterpacht, C.J. Greenwood, and A.G. Oppenheimer.

I mention these books in detail, as they were either prepared before the occupation of Germany or on the basis of lessons learned from that occupation. In hindsight, however, one can say that despite the elaborate preparations in practice an easier way was chosen: transferring the mode of rule according to the emergency regulations imposed on the Palestinians inside Israel from 1948 to 1966 into the reality of the West Bank and the Gaza Strip. The Israeli interpretation of these regulations — in 1948 as well as in 1967 — gave a military governor unlimited control over every aspect of life in his area. The governors became what the first head of the military regime in 1948, Colonel Elimelech Avner, described as 'absolute monarchs' in their own small domains.[2]

When they were first imposed in 1948 and later again in 1967, no one mentioned the fact that when the emergency regulations were introduced by the British they were condemned by all Zionist leaders as Nazi legislation. These leaders described them as regulations with "no parallel in any enlightened country" and noted that "even in Nazi Germany there were no such rules, and the actions of Maydanek and its like had been done out of violation of the written law."[3]

The two most notorious regulations were 109, allowing the governor to expel the population, and 110, giving him the right to summon any citizen to the police station whenever he saw fit. Another infamous regulation was 111, which sanctioned administrative arrest, or arrest for an unlimited period without explanation or trial. This would become more of a familiar feature of the 1967 occupation than of the oppression of the Palestinians in Israel. One practice that stemmed from an interpretation of several regulations was the right of governors to resort to preemptive measures, the most common of which was to declare whole villages 'closed military areas' whenever the Shin Beit or the Shabak (the General Security Services) had prior knowledge of plans for a meeting or demonstration.

This measure was first used in 1949 when Palestinians in Israel were demonstrating against land expropriation (see Pappé 2011).

The mandatory emergency regulations were the basis for the military courts that millions of Palestinians would go through, arrested without trial, tortured and abused, and only rarely left unscathed. Together with Von Glahn's and Lauterpacht's books, the regulations were the textual infrastructure on which the Israeli judiciary system in the Occupied Territories was founded. The judges were all officers in the army and were not required to have a legal background. Courts had one, two, or three judges. The three-judge courts had the right to order executions or life imprisonment. Among the theoretical outfits envisaged in 1963 was a special military court of appeal that would become operational in 1967 (Inbar 2002).

The instruction boxes were hurriedly distributed in May to a new unit duly called 'the Special Unit,' which was attached to the occupying forces. The graduates of the course on Givat Ram were among the members of the unit and they took over the military judicial administration of the West Bank and the Gaza Strip. Inbar, for instance, was attached to the forces that occupied the Gaza Strip, and within two days he and others had set up the military rule and judiciary system in the area. The four years of preparation facilitated the takeover and the establishment of a regime that would in all but name remain intact for the next forty years.

What these individuals planned and executed, and successive generations of Israeli bureaucrats maintained, was the largest-ever mega prison for a million and a half people, who became four million and still today in one way or another are incarcerated within the real or imaginary walls of this jail.

The Government on the Hill

The governmental complex erected on Givat Ram in the early 1950s and completed just before the 1967 war consisted of three buildings. These huge cubic edifices tower above the hill's summit and are now joined by the Knesset, the Supreme Court of Israel, and the Bank of Israel.

The prime minister's office was, and still is, on the third floor of the building closest to the Hebrew University's campus. On the same floor is the government's boardroom, which houses a huge rectangular wooden table that quite often makes a brief appearance when an item referring to the government of Israel is included in local or international television news bulletins. Since the 1960s, government officials have also used another boardroom on the second floor of the Knesset, where they sit around an oval table, also a familiar sight in the televised history of the Jewish state.

The thirteenth government of Israel convened almost daily around both tables in the immediate aftermath of the 1967 war and discussed intensively the fate of the West Bank and the Gaza Strip and the future of the people living in them. After almost three months of deliberations, the officials concluded their discussions with a series of decisions that in one way or another condemned the Palestinians in these two areas to life imprisonment. The Palestinians were incarcerated in their mega prison for crimes they did not commit and for offenses that were never admitted or defined. Today, a third generation of 'inmates' has begun life in that mega prison.

The particular government that took these callous and inhumane decisions represented the widest possible Zionist consensus, as every ideological stream and view was present at the oval and rectangular tables. Socialists from Mapam sat alongside the Revisionist Mencahem Begin and shared the glory and the power with the various factions that made up the Labor Zionist movement. They were joined by members of the most secular liberal and the most religious and ultra-religious political parties. Never before, nor after, this government's term in office would such a consensual partnership lead the State of Israel in its decisions.

Contrary to common wisdom about the history of the West Bank and the Gaza Strip, no one apart from the government of Israel played any crucial role, then or since, in deciding the fate of these territories or the people living in them. What these officials decided in June through August 1967 has remained the cornerstone of Israeli policy toward the Occupied Territories. None of the successive Israeli governments deviated from this policy, nor did they wish to deviate from it in any form or shape, even during the most dramatic events that followed, including the first and second Intifada as well as the Oslo peace process and Camp David summit of 2000.

One explanation for the resilience of this set of decisions is the extraordinary composition of the 1967 government. As already mentioned, this government represented the widest possible Zionist consensus. Another explanation is the euphoric mood that prevailed in the wake of the total devastation of six Arab armies by the Israel Defense Forces (IDF) and the successful blitzkrieg that ended with Israeli military occupation of vast tracts of Arab territory. A messianic aura surrounded the decision-makers in those days, energizing them to take bold and historic decisions, which their successors would find hard to refute or change.

These plausible explanations render the policies as the direct product of the particular and extraordinary circumstances of June 1967. I argue that they were mainly the inevitable outcome of Zionist ideology and history (however one chooses to define this ideology or whether one insists on its shades and innuendos). The particular circumstances made it easier to remind politicians of their ideological heritage and reconnect them once more, as they did in 1948, to the Zionist drive to Judaize as much of historical Palestine as possible. The principles of how to adapt the dramatic events of June 1967 to this ideological vision were laid out in those frequent meetings on Givat Ram. Because the decisions taken reflected the consensual Zionist interpretation of the past and present reality of Palestine as an exclusively Jewish state, none of the developments that occurred thereafter seemed to undermine their validity. The only way of challenging the decisions was and is by questioning the validity of Zionism itself.

Two fundamentals of Zionist ideology were inherited and adhered to religiously by the Israeli politicians of 1967: the struggle for the survival of the Jewish state depended on its ability to control most of historical Palestine and on its capacity to reduce considerably the number of Palestinians living in it. Realpolitik in Zionist terms meant reconciling to the possibility of not being able to achieve these two goals in full. There were times when leaders such as David Ben-Gurion attempted to quantify these two objectives (namely how much of Palestine was needed and how many Palestinians could be tolerated in a Jewish state),[4] but more often than not the assumption was that the best options were more land in the first instance and fewer Palestinians in the second. When Palestine was clearly defined as a geopolitical entity, as a British mandate after the First World War, having most of the country meant possession of the majority of mandatory Palestine (Israel today, with the Occupied Territories). Population-wise, the consensus dictated a wish to have a purely ethnic Jewish state. Again, at times, there were attempts to find out what a tolerable non-Jewish minority within a Jewish state would be, but the unspoken, and at times spoken, desire was to have only Jews in what was considered the ancient land of Israel.

The year 1948 provided the historical opportunity to maximize both goals. Several discrete processes fused together to allow the Zionist movement to ethnically cleanse Palestine in that year: the British decision to withdraw from Palestine after thirty years of rule; the impact of the Holocaust on western public opinion; the disarray in the Arab and Palestinian worlds; and the crystallization of a particularly determined Zionist leadership. As a result, half of the country's native population was expelled, half of its villages and towns were destroyed, and 80 percent of Mandatory Palestine became the Jewish State of Israel.[5]

The dispossession was witnessed at close hand by representatives of the international community: emissaries of the International Red Cross, correspondents of the western press, and United Nations personnel. However, the western world was not interested in listening to their incriminating reports and political elites chose to ignore them. The message from Europe and the United States was clear: whatever happens in Palestine is the inevitable final act of the Second World War. This 'correction' would enable Europe to atone for the crimes committed on its soil against the Jewish people, therefore a last massive dispossession of Palestinians was needed so that the western world could move on to postwar peace and reconciliation. The situation in Palestine, of course, had nothing to do with the movement of populations in Europe in the wake of the Second World War or with the genocide of Europe's Jews. It was the culmination not of the war in Europe but of Zionist colonization that had begun at the end of the nineteenth century. It was the final act in the making of a modern-day settler Jewish state at a time when the international community seemed to render colonization an unacceptable practice and a deplorable ideology of the past.

The message from the 'enlightened world' was unambiguous: the Israeli dispossession of the Palestinians, as well as the takeover of most of Palestine, was both legitimate and acceptable. Almost half of the Israeli officials attending the 1967 meetings were veterans of the 1948 ethnic cleansing of Palestine. Some were members of the small cabal that took the decision to expel almost a million Palestinians, destroy their villages and towns, and prevent them from returning to their homeland. Others were generals or officers in the machinery that perpetrated the crime. All were fully aware of the international community's indifference in 1948. This is why they were convinced that the international community would allow them once more to act unilaterally now that the Israeli army occupied the remaining 20 percent of Palestinian land. They had received a carte blanche for their acts in 1948, and there was no reason to expect any serious rebuke or obstacles for a similar policy of ethnic cleansing in 1967.

There was one huge difference between 1948 and 1967, however. In 1948, decisions regarding the fate of the Palestinians were taken before the Arab–Israeli war. In 1967, they were formulated after the war. Therefore, in 1967, there was more time to ponder the implications of a massive expulsion that could be carried out without any actual war. The government was determined, almost en bloc, to decide unilaterally about the territories' future, but it was more divided about the possibility or the wisdom of another massive ethnic cleansing after the official end of hostilities.[6] A postwar ethnic cleansing could awaken an otherwise dormant western conscience. Furthermore, it was doubtful whether the army had the will and mentality to carry out the policy. The 1967 government was also a larger forum than the one that devised the 1948 ethnic cleansing. The thirteenth government included quite a few conscientious ministers who would have objected to such a master plan on moral grounds.

So, ethnic cleansing on a grand scale was ruled out.[7] However, the prevailing sense in those boardroom meetings was that the international community had granted Israel immunity for land expansion. This was not an endorsement of expansionism per se but more an unwillingness to confront it.[8] The one crucial caveat was that there could not be a de jure annexation of the territories, only a de facto one.[9] One reason was that the West Bank and the Gaza Strip under international law were occupied territories, whereas the areas Israel occupied in 1948 were all recognized by the UN as part of the State of Israel. Another reason was that if the population could not be expelled, it could also not be fully integrated as equal citizens of the Jewish state, given its size and potential growth, which could endanger the decisive Jewish majority in Israel.

There was then, and there is now, a consensual Israeli desire to keep the West Bank and the Gaza Strip, as well as recognition of the undesirability of officially annexing these territories without being able to expel the Palestinians. Yet, keeping these territories seemed as vital as the need to maintain a decisive Jewish majority in whatever constituted the Jewish state.

The minutes of the 1967 governmental meetings are now available to historians. They expose the impossibility and incompatibility of the appetite for possessing the new land and the reluctance to either drive out or fully incorporate the people living on it. The documents also reveal self-congratulatory satisfaction with an early discovery of a way out of this ostensible logical deadlock and theoretical impasse. The officials were convinced that they had found the formula that would enable Israel to keep the territories it coveted without annexing the people it negated, while safeguarding international immunity and reputation.

In fact, the government did not discover anything new. Israel had already imposed military rule on Palestinians, lifting it after eighteen years, only to replace it with a regime of inspection, control, and coercion. With time, this regime eased somewhat and became more hidden and complex. In the meantime, the population of the West Bank and the Gaza Strip had grown, and while the limited citizenship granted to the Palestinian minority in Israel seemed to tally with the aim of maintaining a decisive Jewish majority in the state, the same would not have been the case had such citizenship been extended to the people of the West Bank and the Gaza Strip. The need, therefore, was to keep the territories without expelling the people in them but also without granting them citizenship. These three parameters or presumptions have not changed to this day. They remain the unholy trinity of the consensual Zionist catechism.[10]

When these three aims are translated into policies, they can only produce an inhumane and ruthless reality on the ground. There can be no benign or enlightened version of a policy meant to keep people without citizenship for a long period of time. Only one known human invention similarly deprives people of the basic human and civil rights of citizens: the modern-day prison. The prison, the penitentiary institution, and correctional facilities are contemporary outfits that impose such a reality either as part of a ruthless dictatorship or as a consequence of a long legal process in democracies.

The modern prison is a Panopticon, according to Jeremy Bentham, who was the first modern philosopher to justify the rationale of jailing within a new coercive penal system. The Panopticon, which was popular in the early nineteenth century, was designed to allow guards to see their prisoners but not vice versa. The building was cylindrical, with prisoners' cells lining the outer diameter and a large, circular observational tower in the middle. As guards could be looking into prisoners' cells at any time but carefully placed blinds prevented prisoners from seeing the guards, this left them to wonder whether they were being monitored at any given moment. It was Bentham's belief that the 'gaze' of the Panopticon would force prisoners to behave morally. As under the all-seeing eye of God, they would feel shame at their wicked ways (Bentham 1995).

If we substitute moral conduct with collaboration with occupation and change the circular structure to a variety of geometrical parameters of imprisonment, the 1967 Israeli decision was to imprison Palestinians in the West Bank and the Gaza Strip in a modern Panopticon.

A more elaborated application of the Panopticon facility as representing power over the powerless is offered by Michel Foucault. Indeed, one Israeli scholar has attempted quite successfully to deconstruct the present-day occupation in such terms (Dahan 2012). Foucault, like Bentham, stressed that the Panopticon as a system of control has no need for physical barriers. This applies to only one element in the matrix of power that cages the Palestinian population in its mega prison. Others are intentionally forcing the 'prisoners' to look at the guards and to sense in the most physical way possible the barriers, the wall, and barbed wire surrounding them.

Israel's official navigation between impossible nationalist and colonialist ambitions turned a million and a half people in 1967 into inmates. This is not a prison for a few inmates, wrongly or rightly incarcerated — it has been imposed on a society as a whole. Some of its architects searched for the most humane model for this prison, probably because they were aware that it was a collective punishment for a crime never committed (see Gazit 1985). Others did not even bother to search for a softer version or a more humane one. The two camps did exist, however, and therefore the government offered two versions of the mega prison to the people in the West Bank and the Gaza Strip. One was an open-air Panopticon and the other a maximum security one. Should the inmates not accept the former, they would get the latter.

The open-air prison allowed a measure of autonomous life under indirect and direct Israeli control. The maximum security one robbed Palestinians of all autonomy and subjected them to a harsh policy of punishment, restriction, and, in the worst-case scenario, execution. The reality on the ground was that the open-air prison was harsh enough and sufficiently inhumane to trigger resistance from the population and that the maximum security model was imposed as retaliation for this resistance. In general, the softer model was attempted twice, once between 1967 and 1987 and once between 1993 and 2000, and the retaliation occurred between 1987 and 1993 and again between 2000 and 2009.

The open-air prison became the false paradigm of peace as marketed by Israel and by its American and European allies — an ingenious idea for how to solve the conflict. The open-air prison was eventually propagated first as autonomy in the 1979 Camp David agreement between Israel and Egypt, which led nowhere, and later as an independent Palestinian state in the 1993 Oslo Accords. When the Oslo Accords were translated into reality by the sheer power of the occupier, the resemblance of this idea of a 'state' to an open-air prison became clear with the partitioning of the West Bank into Areas A, B, and C and the exclusion of the Jewish settlements in Gaza from any Palestinian authority.

The Oslo Accords II of 1995 gave autonomy only to small parts of the West Bank and the Gaza Strip, leaving control over the enclaves' security and sovereignty in the hands of the Israeli security apparatus. When security deteriorated for a short while in Israeli eyes, the maximum security model was reinstalled in 2002 and in many ways is still there today. The rebellious inmates of Gaza are being severely punished by a continuous siege and closure.

The selling of the open-air prison model as a diplomatic effort and a 'peace process' could not have been possible without the support of large sections of the Palestinian political elite, the Zionist Left, and even some well-known and highly respected international supporters of the Palestinian cause. But it is mainly a new formation, the Quartet — a kind of ad hoc international tribunal for Palestine consisting of the Europen Union (EU), Russia, the US, and the UN — that gave the prison a final push as a powerful paradigm for peace.

In Israel and in the west, a huge launderette of words and a very cooperative media and academia were essential for maintaining the moral and political validity of the open-air prison option as the best solution for the 'conflict' and as an ideal vision for normal and healthy life in the occupied West Bank and the Gaza Strip. The terms 'autonomy,' 'self-determination,' and finally, 'independence' were used, and mainly abused, to describe the best version of an open-air prison model the Israelis could offer the Palestinians in the West Bank and the Gaza Strip.

But this launderette did not cleanse the reality, and the hyperbolic discourse of peace and independence did not deafen the conscientious members of all the societies involved, in the Occupied Territories, in Israel, and in the outside world. In the age of the Internet, independent press, active civil society, and energetic nongovernmental organizations, it has been hard to play this charade of peace and reconciliation.

The Bureaucracy on the Hill

The open-air prison requires a huge staff. Thousands and thousands of soldiers, officers, officials, judges, physicians, architects, police, tax collectors, academic advisors, and politicians are the principal human face of this inhumanity.

At the top of the bureaucratic pyramid stands a committee of ministerial directors general.[11]

The committee was established on June 15, 1967, and for a few months devised the economic, legal, and administrative infrastructure for controlling and maintaining the Occupied Territories. This group of government officials enlisted the top academics at the time and veteran members of the previous system of control employed in the Palestinian areas inside Israel.

One should talk about these officials, academics, and bureaucrats as much as about the system they built in June 1967. There is already a second generation of them in place, and a third will soon arrive. Once one crosses that generational landmark, any discourse about temporality or even finality is useless. The system becomes a living organism that is very difficult to fight or dismantle. Hence the understandable desperation of the last chapter in the Palestinian resistance: suicide bombs.

The False Paradigm of Peace

The heroes, or rather the villains, of this story are the Israelis who worked out the fine details of the system to begin with, who upheld it over all these years, and who 'perfected' its operation on the ground, namely its power to abuse, humiliate, and destroy. They were and are servants of the bureaucracy of evil. They come quite innocent into the system, but only very few among them do not succumb to its raison d'être and modus operandi. As wardens of this largest prison on earth, they are constant abusers, dehumanizers, and destroyers of Palestinian rights and lives. The moment the last of them is discharged from this service, we will know that the mega prison has been abolished forever.

Seen from this perspective, the so-called 'peace process' begun in the 1970s and culminating in the 1993 Oslo Accords is a false paradigm that became a powerful discourse in a similar way that the discourse of Orientalism became a potent and hegemonic prism through which Middle Eastern realities were viewed in the past. As Edward Said (1978) put it in the opening pages of his seminal work, the discourse in this instance is a presentation, or rather mis-presentation, with institutions, political and economic power, academics and media, and a well-oiled public relations mechanism behind it.

The discourse of the two-state solution has been powerful enough to induce quite a few Palestinians to adopt it. Its basic assumptions, as seen from this historical perspective, are not only wrong but also frame reality in a way that enables Israel as a state to deepen its occupation and oppression of Palestinians while the world at large believes that a genuine effort is being made to solve the problem.

The 'peace process' has been based on the assumption that everything visible is divisible — land, resources, blame, and history. This business-like approach has offered at best 20 percent of Palestine to Palestinians (and even that was never on the table); punished them with a lesser offer when they refused the first offer; was adopted without consultation with Palestinians; and, all in all, is based on Israel's intention of having as much of Palestine as possible with as few Palestinians in it as possible and the western world's desire to be assured that a 'process' is occurring that absolves the international community of addressing Israel's impunity.

It is time to adopt a new discourse that shows Israel to be a settler colonial state and the Palestinians to be leading an anticolonial struggle. Decolonization is more relevant than a 'peace process' for the torn land of Palestine and Israel. Only a more accurate framing can help bring reconciliation for the benefit of Jews and Arabs alike.

Notes

1. The plan was the first and only one reported on by a participant in a scholarly article (Inbar 2002).
2. See an extended discussion of the employment of these regulations inside Israel in Pappé (2011).

3. Quoted in *Hapraklit*, February 1946, 58 (in Hebrew; translation by Ilan Pappé).
4. He did it in December 1947. See David Ben-Gurion's speech to the secretariat of Mapai on May 13, 1947, Central Zionist Archives.
5. See the evolution of this process in Pappé (2006: 39–86).
6. See, Israel State Archives, protocols of government meeting, Section 43.4, meetings throughout June 1967. See also Tom Segev's (2007) interpretation of these documents, which is not far from mine.
7. Some ideas of expulsion or forced transfer were discussed but eventually ruled out. The main desire was at least to move the refugees out of Gaza. See, ISA, government meetings, June 17–19, 1967.
8. Very early on, Prime Minister Levi Eshkol and Defense Minister Moshe Dayan said to the meetings protocol that when they talked publicly about Israel's willingness to withdraw from the territories it occupied in June 1967 they did not mean the West Bank and the Gaza Strip. See, ISA, government meeting, June 11, 1967.
9. Interior Minister Haim-Moshe Shapira explained with regard to Jerusalem and its environs, and with implication to any territory Israel would wish to hold, that he supervised a similar process when Israel illegally annexed in 1950 those areas of Palestine allocated to the Arab Palestinian state in the partition resolution of November 29, 1947. ISA, government meetings, June 17–18, 1967.
10. The discussion of this theme was summarized in the meetings by Defense Minister Moshe Dayan, who assumed that Israel could maintain the occupation for a long period of time. Some ministers were then already prepared to involve the Jordanians by offering them strong linkage to the territories, as did Minister Eliyahu Sasson and later on, Dayan. Some would seek the collaboration of Palestinian notables in having limited autonomy under Israel rule (an idea that never took off). See ISA, cabinet meeting, June 18, 1948.
11. ISA, cabinet meeting, June 15, 1967.

References

Bentham, J. 1995. "Panopticon." In *The Panopticon Writings*, edited by Mirzan Bozovic, 29–95. London: Verso.

Dahan, M. 2012. "The Gaza Strip as Panopticon and Panspectron: The Disciplining and Punishing of a Society." In *Procedures: Cultural Attitudes towards Technology and Communication*, edited by M. Strano, H. Harchovec, F. Sudsweets, and C. Ess, 25–37. Sydney: Murdoch University.

Gazit, S. 1985. *Ha-makel ve ha-gezer: Ha-mishal ha-Israeli be-Yehuda ve-Shomron*. Tel Aviv: Zemora and Bitan.

Inbar, Z. 2002. "The Military Attorney General and the Occupied Territories." *The Law and the Army* 16:147–49.

Oz, A. 1976. *Michael sheli*. Tel Aviv: Am Oved.

Pappé, I. 2011. *The Forgotten Palestinians: A History of the Palestinian Minority in Israel.* New Haven, CT: Yale University Press.

_____. 2006. *The Ethnic Cleansing of Palestine.* Oxford: Oneworld.

Said, E.W. 1978. *Orientalism.* New York: Pantheon Books.

Segev, T. 2007. *1967: Israel, the War, and the Year that Transformed the Middle East.* New York: Metropolitan Books.

Von Glahn, G. 1957. *The Occupation of Enemy Territory: A Commentary on the Law and Practice of Belligerent Occupation.* Minneapolis, MN: University of Minnesota Press.

3

Champions of Peace? Tools in Whose Hands? Norwegians and Peace Brokering in the Middle East

Hilde Henriksen Waage

On September 13, 1993, Norwegian Foreign Minister Johan Jørgen Holst was among the prominent international actors strolling in the sun on the White House lawn in Washington, D.C. The Oslo Accords were to be signed. Through a series of secret talks held in and around Oslo, representatives of the Israeli and Palestinian leaderships had managed to agree on a declaration of principles that paved the way for the establishment of the Palestinian Self-Government Authority and mutual recognition between Israel and the Palestine Liberation Organization (PLO).

Norway had made a decisive contribution to this, one of the most serious attempts at making peace in the strife-torn Middle East region since May 1948, when the State of Israel was established. Two archenemies — Israeli Prime Minister Yitzhak Rabin and PLO Chairman Yasser Arafat — were soon to speak and shake hands. United States President Bill Clinton was present as a witness, along with engrossed audiences throughout the world that followed the momentous events on their television sets.

Few adversaries have ever been enmeshed in a more vicious spiral of violence than the Israelis and their Palestinian neighbors. Countless previous efforts by individuals, organizations, and large and small states to open up direct contact between Israel and the PLO had all failed (Bercovitch 1997: 220–21). And then, little Norway managed to get the old enemies to agree both to a gradual Israeli withdrawal from some of the Occupied Territories and to local Palestinian self-determination. What had made Norway, of all countries, suitable for such an extraordinary task?

On the whole, Norway has been a country with limited influence on world politics. True, in the 1990s, the Norwegian policy of engagement involved a new and far more active and conscious mediating role than earlier. But Norway was also a supportive and loyal member of the North Atlantic Treaty Organization (NATO), with close ties to the United States. In addition, it was situated both geographically and politically on the outskirts of Europe. The 'Good Samaritan' Norway, with its big budget surplus, was one of the most generous countries in the world when it came to granting economic assistance to developing countries. And Norway had a postwar history of involvement in the conflict-torn Middle East (Waage 2000a; Tamnes 1997).

The fairy tales and the myths about the Norwegians, who, in a miraculous way, contributed to bringing peace to the Middle East in 1993 has been hard to repudiate. There has been a strong focus on the role of the Norwegian actors, followed by personality-centered explanations. The principal actor, Terje Rød-Larsen, today president of the International Peace Institute (IPI), was the clever, self-confident, and charming diplomatic man of action. He created the 'magic' during the Oslo process. His pleasant, elegant wife, Mona Juul, Norwegian ambassador to the United Kingdom, represented the specialist, working with Middle East questions in the Norwegian Ministry of Foreign Affairs. State Secretary Jan Egeland, today secretary general of the Norwegian Refugee Council, handsome, result-oriented, and idealistic by nature, had written a thesis in political science about how small states could create results in international politics that were unattainable for the superpowers. In 1993, he wanted to put his theory into practice. What happened next, according to the prevailing fairy tale, was that the so-called 'Oslo spirit' simply descended upon the Israeli 'peaceniks,' the PLO terrorists, and a few carefully chosen Norwegians.

In all that has been written, surprisingly little emphasis has been put on the very special relationship that existed between Norway and Israel long before the exciting days of the secret Norwegian back channel. Is this political past insignificant or decisive when it comes to understanding and explaining Norway's role in the Oslo back channel? Even more important, why did Israelis as well as Palestinians find Norway, of all countries, acceptable as a mediating partner? Not least, how can the outcome be explained? The Oslo peace process reflected the fundamentally asymmetrical power situation between the Israelis and the Palestinians, with Israel as the stronger party and the PLO as the weaker party. What room for maneuver did such a basic asymmetry of power provide for the Norwegians?

The Political Past

Norway had for decades been one of Israel's best friends. After the founding of the State of Israel in 1948, the Norwegians developed enormous admiration for the country, almost akin to a religious conversion. After the Arab–Israeli war in 1967, this extremely pro-Israeli attitude changed slightly. In the 1980s, although their relationship was somewhat weakened, Norway was still one of Israel's staunchest allies. Norway was isolated, both in Europe and in the United Nations on account of its position on the conflict. It was among the last and most cautious of the western countries to establish contact with the PLO, and it had one of the most restrictive policies toward the PLO in the world (Waage 1989, 1996, 2000a, 2000b, 2002; Jebsen 1997; Tamnes 1997; Stoltenberg 2001; Johansen 1980).

Surprisingly enough, it might seem, it was Norway's traditional position as Israel's best friend that made the remote Scandinavian country suitable and attractive as a possible mediating partner. Even more surprising, it was Arafat who took the initiative and brought Norway's name forward, already in 1979, because of its close relations with Israel. Norway also had close ties with the United States, which had to play a key role in any peace settlement in the Middle East (Tamnes 1997: 379–81; Johansen 1980: 62–66; Jebsen 1997: 21–24; Waage 2000a: 49–53).

The thought of Norway as a possible mediating partner and back channel option was raised on several occasions during the 1980s. At a meeting between Arafat and Norwegian Foreign Minister Thorvald Stoltenberg in January 1989, the two actually agreed on how to pursue a peaceful solution. This peace plan, which included a Norwegian role, was Arafat's idea and was, four years later, to serve as a blueprint for the Oslo back channel. Arafat wanted Stoltenberg to forward the plan to Israel, but Stoltenberg got nowhere. The Israelis turned down the idea. Thus, the Norwegians were forced to shelve their mediation plans at the very end of the 1980s (Tamnes 1997: 382–83; Stoltenberg 2001: 266–67; Butenschøn 1989: 8–11; Waage 2000a: 49–67).

However, at the beginning of the 1990s, the Norwegians were no longer loyal fans of Israel. The outcome nevertheless reflected previous attempts: it was based on Israel's premises and bowing to Israel's 'red lines' and security concerns. Yet, the explanations for the role of Norway in the Oslo peace process cannot be sought in Norway's biased political past. While Norway's close relationship to Israel explains how it all began, it does not explain the process and the outcome.

The Negotiations in the Oslo Back Channel

Thus, the Norwegians did not stumble by coincidence into the Middle East peace process at a time when it needed a push and an alternative track. In January 1993, the Norwegians started off with a small and to a large degree unplanned role.[1] The Norwegian goal was to serve as a modest facilitator and not to mediate. The aim was only to develop more informal political contacts to see if anything could be done to help or improve the stalemate in Washington. Any new ideas or results produced in Norway would be transferred back to the official negotiations in the United States.

However, in Norway—in contrast to the situation in the US capital—the Israelis and the Palestinians quickly managed to agree on the road to be taken. In Norway, Arafat had the position and opportunity to make whatever concessions he found suitable or necessary. As a result, the Israelis and the Palestinians soon managed to agree on a joint declaration of principles (DOP).

The declaration consisted of three major elements. First, Israel agreed to withdraw completely from Gaza, which was then to be placed for a limited period of time either under Egyptian trusteeship or under a UN or multinational mandate. Meanwhile, negotiations were to continue on an interim autonomy scheme for the West Bank. Second, a mini-Marshall Plan was to be worked out for the Gaza Strip and the West Bank. Third, economic cooperation between Israel and the Palestinian interim authorities was to be developed.

Difficult questions such as sovereignty, refugees, borders, settlements, and that of Jerusalem would be discussed in future negotiations. Only an interim agreement was on the agenda. Israel had given nothing on final status issues, and every single one of the interim arrangements could be halted and reversed. In fact, many of them were. Only such an approach would stand a chance, so both the Israeli and the PLO representatives agreed to it. The will, the mandate, and the flexibility shown in Norway made the setting, the progress, and the results very different from those in Washington (Makovsky 1996: 31–34; Peres 1995; Corbin 1994: 59–63; Elon 1993; Abbas 1995: 119–138; Beilin 1999: 69–73).

In this first phase, the Norwegians played an extremely modest role. Norway's strength was to keep a low profile and to facilitate only. The intention of the Norwegians was to bring the parties together and to use their good offices to promote trust. Without the willingness of the parties, there would be no Norwegian role or any Norwegian back channel (Corbin 1994; Beilin 1999: 68–69; Elon 1993: 80–81; Makovsky 1996: 22).

In May 1993, Israel upgraded the negotiations in Norway. This meant that real negotiations could begin. The process of clarifying, hardening, and withdrawing Israeli concessions from the first draft of the DOP now began, or, as Israeli Foreign Minister Shimon Peres chose to put it, Israel began to "revise [its] position on ... basic ideas" (1995: 333. Also, Peres 1995: 329–30; Beilin 1999: 80–88; Corbin 1994: 76–94; Makovsky 1996: 45–49; Savir 1998: 5–28).

Israel's goal in the negotiations was to maintain as much control as possible, to give away as little land as possible, and to protect Israel's security. Therefore, when the formal negotiations started, most of the concessions given in the previously drafted declaration were withdrawn. Jerusalem would not be included in any autonomy arrangement. The Palestinians also had to drop their demand that all outstanding questions should be referred to binding international arbitration. There would be no third party to replace the Israelis during the transitional period, nor would there be any trusteeship proposal for Gaza. Israel's alternative was full autonomy for the Gaza Strip. In the West Bank, Israel would grant partial autonomy, meaning that autonomy would only be applied in a few places and spheres, starting with Jericho. Autonomy would be limited to five specific areas of activity: education, health, tourism, welfare, and taxation. This would give Arafat the foothold he needed in the West Bank (Beilin 1999: 80–85; Peres 1995: 329–36; Savir 1998: 5–28; Corbin 1994: 76–94; Makovsky 1996: 45–52).

This second phase changed the role of Norway gradually, triggered by the Israeli upgrading, the arrival of new Israeli participants, the new Israeli demands, and the entrance of a new Norwegian foreign minister in April 1993. From May 1993, Norway became an active mediator. When Foreign Minister Johan Jørgen Holst took over, the exploratory rounds were over and the upgrading of the talks was eagerly pursued (Holst 1993: 32; Beilin 1999: 79; Savir 1998: 21–22; Corbin 1994: 95–113).

Foreign Minister Holst wanted to explore the commitment, involvement, and seriousness of both the Israelis and the Palestinians for himself. He was still in the dark about the role of Prime Minster Rabin, although he had a clear picture of the prevailing attitude of the rest of the Israeli team. However, the crucial person was Arafat and his undefined positions. Consequently, the man to investigate was Arafat, and the party to reassure was Israel. Holst traveled. He wrote letters. Along with two other important Norwegian players, Terje Rød Larsen and his diplomat wife Mona Juul, he held a number of meetings with key players from the Palestinian and Israeli sides (Corbin 1994: 95–96; Beilin 1999: 106–10; Savir 1998: 42–44; Peres 1995: 337–42; Makovsky 1996: 60–61).

An important sequence of meetings, held in July 1993 among the main Norwegian actors, Arafat and his advisors, and subsequently the whole Israeli peace team, illustrates how far the Norwegians were willing to go in order to conduct a process on Israel's premises (Waage 2004b: 112–14).

On July 13, 1993, Holst, Juul, and Rød Larsen met Arafat at his headquarters. Holst sent a letter to Peres, in which he gave a full assessment of the meeting (Waage 2004b). According to letters from Holst to Peres, Holst had told Arafat that the latter was "deviating from the substance of realistic proposals." The PLO could "never achieve a better deal than now" (Peres 1995: 342). Holst, however, did point out to Peres that if Jericho were not added to the package, Arafat would be confronted with an "impossible sales problem" (Peres 1995: 332).

Holst told Arafat that the Israeli government was prepared to take "a bold step." Yet, continuation of the Intifada or terrorist acts against Israel would immediately kill an agreement. The Palestinians had a unique opportunity to obtain self-rule. This could be "converted at a later stage to full independence, as well as economic development." "Holding up the process" as Arafat and the PLO were doing, according to a letter Holst sent to Peres, "endangering it for the sake of arguing over a formula, was likely to be a fateful mistake" (Beilin 1999: 109).

So much is well known. But, in the still classified archives of the Norwegian Ministry of Foreign Affairs, no documents have been found on the negotiations in the Oslo back channel from January to September 1993. In October 2005, a Norwegian journalist, Odd Karsten Tveit, published *War and Diplomacy: Oslo–Jerusalem 1978–96*. All the missing documents and many more are referred to in this book. Information from these documents sheds a clearer light on the most important phase of the Oslo process (Tveit 2005; Waage 2008).

What did the Norwegians report to the Israelis from these crucial meetings with Arafat? How much of Arafat's negotiating position did the Norwegians reveal? According to *War and Diplomacy*, we can read, "Holst [was] compos[ing] long and detailed minutes in English from the meeting with Arafat" (Tveit 2005: 414).[2]

In addition, Holst wrote, "Terje Rød-Larsen and Mona Juul, who belong to my secretariat, have both played a key role in administrating 'the Norwegian channel' and are my special envoys. They are going to inform your people [the Israelis] directly." He also noted that "Rød-Larsen and Juul arrived at Ben Gurion airport outside Tel Aviv on Saturday 17 July," bringing with them various documents containing information about Arafat and his negotiating position (Tveit 2005: 415). The Norwegians fully informed the Israelis on crucial information with regard to areas in which the Palestinians were prepared to make concessions (Waage 2008: 54–65).

Norway had become an active mediator. But, during this official phase of the negotiations in the summer of 1993, Norway agreed with Israel that it was Arafat and the PLO that were jeopardizing the whole peace-seeking enterprise. Israel's demands were "red lines," and they had to be understood and accepted. If not, there would be no deal. No evidence has been found to show or even suggest that the Norwegians argued in the same way with the Israelis as they did with the Palestinians.

The result achieved in 1993, the Oslo Accords, was not an ordinary peace agreement. In essence, it was more of a timetable, a point of departure with many vaguely formulated intentions. Arafat's willingness to accept the Oslo Accords, with all their shortcomings and compromises, was clearly a result of his fear of being permanently marginalized. However, given the enormous imbalance of power between the Palestinians and Israel, the PLO could hardly have expected a better deal (Lia 1998: 21).

Norway's Role and the Asymmetry of Power

With the signing of the Oslo Accords on September 13, 1993, Norway enjoyed its moment of glory as the broker of the agreement. The breakthrough brought Norway fame and glory, and the country was catapulted to the top division of international peacemakers.

However, Norway's role in the peace process cannot be analyzed meaningfully without reference to the evolution of the process itself. Basically, the Norwegian actors saw themselves as playing only a facilitating role in the process, at least initially. The talks were mainly held in isolated locations, where the participants were forced to spend most of their time with each other. The Norwegian actors emphasized the small group setting and, above all, the secrecy and intimacy of the facilitative approach. The emphasis was on breaking down stereotypes, smoothing over existential obstacles, removing misunderstandings, and overcoming a lack of willingness to talk (Jones 1999: 143–44; Pruitt 1997: 178–81).

One of the advantages of facilitation is that at the outset, only minor issues are put on the negotiating table. Once some sort of compromise has been reached on these, the parties move on to the more difficult problems. However, all difficult questions in the Oslo process were deferred to future negotiations, with no guarantees.

This is exactly what causes trouble. Many of the problems associated with the Oslo Accords might be seen to have occurred simply because a powerless facilitation process carried the entire burden of conflict resolution designed to solve one of the twentieth century's most intractable international conflicts (Jones 1999: 18–19).

Another serious problem with the facilitative approach is that it fails to deal adequately with problems related to power asymmetry between the two parties. The Norwegians did everything they could to ensure a symmetrical process. However, Norway had no opportunity to force solutions on unwilling parties. Such a third-party role could only be played by a strong mediator, basically a superpower like the United States.

Norway's role was dictated neither by sympathy for Israel nor a desire to help it. Yet, the outcome was the same: Norway invariably acted on Israel's premises and bowed to Israel's "red lines." The main reason for this position was that it was the only way to protect Norway's role in the process. The Norwegians knew full well that they had to be acceptable as a facilitator — and later as a mediator — first and foremost to the stronger party. The secret Norwegian role in the Middle East peace process would yield no results if the Palestinians refused to accept Israeli terms. Israel decided the conditions and the rules of the game. With no muscles, this was Norway's room for maneuver. Norway basically decided to persuade the PLO to give up positions Israel found unacceptable and to get the PLO to accept the positions put forward by Israel.

Norway had neither carrots nor sticks that it could use in relation to Israel. With regard to the Palestinians, though, Norway could employ both means. It could use sticks by arguing that the Palestinians would ruin all chances for peace if they failed to clinch a deal with Israel within the Oslo setting. It could also tempt the PLO with carrots such as getting a foothold in Palestine, recognition by Israel, or offers of international economic assistance.

But, if Norway was negotiating peace on Israel's premises, so was the PLO. The weak PLO had few options. It did not leave the negotiations, nor did the Norwegians. Both the PLO and Israel wanted the negotiations to produce an outcome.

The Norwegians wanted to achieve results through dialogue and a basically facilitative approach to conflict resolution. They believed in the principle of grad-ualism, that trust could be built up and that positive developments might eventu-ally lead toward a lasting peace in the Middle East. They believed that an irreversible peace dynamic would push the process forward. Their ambitions were to create peace between the Israelis and the Palestinians and a new international role for Norway. It paid off: Norwegians were asked to contribute to solving con-flicts all over the world.

As for Norway's primary goal — peace between the Israelis and the Palesti-nians — after three years of intensive efforts, an entire process was mapped out and a number of additional agreements were signed. No peace was reached, how-ever, and none was in sight. In cases of great asymmetry of power, the results that can be achieved by a powerless facilitator, in this case Norway, are no more than the stronger party will allow. Any other outcome could only be achieved by a superpower — an actor with both strong muscles and the willingness to use them to achieve a sustainable peace between Israel and the Palestinians.

Notes

1. The back channel negotiations in Norway are extensively elaborated on in Waage (2004a).
2. All translations are the author's.

References

Abbas, M. 1995. *Through Secret Channels*. London. Garnet.

Beilin, Y. 1999. *Touching Peace: From the Oslo Accord to a Final Agreement*. London: Weidenfeld and Nicolsen.

Bercovitch, J. 1997. "Conflict Management and the Oslo Experiece: Assessing the Success of Israeli-Palestinian Peacemaking." *International Negotiation* 2 (2): 217–35.

Butenschøn, N. 1989. "Fredsprosessen i Midtøsten og Norges rolle: Utenriksminister Thorvald Stoltenberg intervjuet av Nils A. Butenschøn." *Internasjonal Politikk* 1–2 (7–11): 8–11.

Corbin, J. 1994. *Den norske kanalen: De hemmelige Midtøstenforhandlingene.* Oslo: Tiden.

Elon, A. 1993. "The Peacemakers." *New Yorker* (December), (77–85), 81.

Holst, J.J. 1993. "Reflections on the Makings of a Tenuous Peace." *Middle East Insight* 9 (6): 30–34.

Jebsen, A.H. 1997. "Why Norway? Norway's Involvement in the Middle East Prior to the Secret Oslo Channel 1948–1993." PhD diss., London School of Economics and Political Science.

Johansen, J.O. 1980. "Tendenser i norsk Midt-Østen-politikk." In *Norsk Utenrikspolitisk Årbok 1979*, edited by Jon Kristen Skogan, 56–66. Otta: Norsk Utenrikspolitisk Institutt.

Jones, D. 1999. *Cosmopolitan Mediation? Conflict Resolution and the Oslo Accords.* Manchester: Manchester University Press.

Lia, B. 1998. *Implementing the Oslo Peace Accords: A Case Study of the Palestinian–Israeli Peace Process and International Assistance for the Enhancement of Security.* Oslo: FFI.

Makovsky, D. 1996. *Making Peace with the PLO: The Rabin Government's Road to the Oslo Accord.* Washington, D.C.: Westview.

Peres, S. 1995. *Battling for Peace.* London: Weidenfeld and Nicolson.

Savir, U. 1998. *The Process: 1,100 Days that Changed the Middle East.* New York: Random House.

Pruitt, D.G. 1997. "Ripeness Theory and the Oslo Talks." *International Negotiation* 2 (2): 237–50.

Stoltenberg, T. 2001. *Det handler om mennesker.* Oslo: Gyldendal.

Tamnes, R. 1997. *Oljealder 1965–1995.* Vol. 6 of *Norsk utenrikspolitikks historie.* Oslo: Universitetsforlaget.

Tveit, O.D. 2005. *Krig og diplomati: Oslo–Jerusalem 1978–96.* Oslo: Aschehoug.

Waage, H.H. 2008. "Postscript to Oslo: The Missing Files." *Journal of Palestine Studies* 38 (1): 54–65.

_____. 2004a. "Norway's Role in the Middle East Peace Talks: Between a Strong State and a Weak Belligerent." *Journal of Palestine Studies* 34(4): 6–24.

_____. 2004b. *Peacemaking Is a Risky Business: Norway's Role in the Peace Process in the Middle East, 1993–96,* http://file.prio.no/Publications/Report-1-2004/. Oslo: Peace Research Institute Oslo.

_____. 2002. "Explaining the Oslo Backchannel: Norway's Political Past in the Middle East." *Middle East Journal* 56 (4): 597–615.

_____. 2000a. *"Norwegians? Who Needs Norwegians?" Explaining the Oslo Back Channel: Norway's Political Past in the Middle East.* Oslo: Norwegian Ministry of Foreign Affairs.

_____. 2000b. "How Norway Became One of Israel's Best Friends." *Journal of Peace Research* 37 (2): 189–211.

_____. 1996. *Norge–Israels beste venn: Norsk Midtøsten-politikk 1949–56.* Oslo: Universitetsforlaget.

_____. 1989. *Da staten Israel ble til: Et stridsspørsmål i norsk politikk 1945–49.* Oslo: Gyldendal Norsk Forlag.

4

The Illusion of Palestinian Sovereignty

Amira Hass

Israeli military incursions into the West Bank's Area A and even Area B — the districts where only Palestinians live and the Palestinian Authority operates — have one positive aspect. Yes, even when they include the destruction of radio stations or raids on hospitals. Despite all the shock and the denunciations, these raids are a lesson in reality. For a few hours, they destroy the illusion of Palestinian sovereignty. It's a virtual sovereignty, fragmented and curtailed. Therefore, it's an illusion — but an illusion that works.

Broadcasters in Hebron think they can tell their listeners where soldiers are located, in order to get out and clash with them, as if they lived in an independent state. Palestinian Facebook users inhabit a virtual reality twice over: They see the real world in cyberspace and are convinced that it protects them from raids and arrests. Doctors treat people with bullet wounds and forget that the sovereign is the settlement defense forces, which don't recognize the sanctity of medical treatment and the immunity of medical institutions.

Palestinian Authority President Mahmoud Abbas receives ambassadors with great pomp, but when leaving Ramallah he is dependent on exit permits from the army. And professors from abroad are shocked when Israeli security services raid the campus of Al-Quds University in Abu Dis; their political geography classes evidently ended in 1993, when Zionism achieved one of its greatest military and diplomatic successes.

Short of expelling every Palestinian or "causing them to flee," this is the outcome most closely resembling transfer that was possible to achieve. The international political circumstances didn't allow the territory to be emptied (again) of its Palestinian inhabitants. So reservations were set up (Areas A and B). They were supposed to be temporary, but meanwhile they've become permanent.

It's not important for now whether this is exactly what Zionist leaders (the late Yitzhak Rabin and Amnon Lipkin-Shahak, Shimon Peres and Ehud Barak) intended when they concocted the Oslo Accords' interim agreements. The result is the same either way: Palestinian pseudo-sovereignty in territorial capsules, which is one of the main reasons why the current — and inevitable — uprising hasn't taken off.

The checkpoints that surround these enclaves block any mass demonstration that might, for instance, seek to march toward another water-sucking, land-swallowing settlement or a shepherds' village that's about to be demolished. But what's most effective of all, from the standpoint of Israeli interests, is that people have gotten used to the illusion. Within these population enclosures, life is lived in a way that closely resembles normalcy.

In Tel Rumeida, the silence is bloodcurdling. But beyond the concrete that isolates the neighborhood, one hears the enticing municipal clamor of Hebron. Cars honk, vendors in the market sell their wares, pedestrians chat. A multitude of seminars takes place in the hotels of cozy Jericho and Ramallah, while half an hour's drive to the north, Israel's Civil Administration is demolishing the houses of the tiny village of Hadidiyeh and the army is once again expelling thirteen families from their tents in Khirbet Khumsa. Studies at An-Najah National University in Nablus take place as normal, but a few kilometers southward, settlers burst into the villages of Madama and Burin and sow fear.

Just how strong the delusion of sovereignty is can be seen in the way East Jerusalem residents, and even Palestinian citizens of Israel, often travel to these West Bank enclaves and feel a sense of relief. In these enclosures, which are free of any army presence, they get a break from routine Israeli racism and vulgarity. This temporary feeling of rest and relief is only strengthened by the necessary return to Israel via an intimidating path of walls, barbed-wire fences, pointed rifles, threatening policemen and soldiers, and deluxe, verdant suburbs for Jews only.

The foreign ruler and his permanent aggression are divided into fractions and experienced differently in every Palestinian "territorial cell," as they are called in army jargon. The more numerous, smaller, and fragmented these territorial cells are, the harder it is for the Palestinians to develop a uniform response to Israeli aggression and violence.

That is how the phenomenon of the lone-wolf stabbers emerged — for lack of any other choice. This is a privatizing of the natural and general urge to rebel, a response to Israeli violence that breaks up into dozens of supposedly unconnected little incidents. This privatization of the struggle is the opposite of an intifada, which is a mass uprising. But because it has become such a widespread phenomenon, it constitutes an internal message: that the normalcy of the enclaves isn't normal.

This article was originally published in *Haaretz*, and can be read online here: http://www.haaretz.com/opinion/.premium-1.689502.

5

The Oslo Accords and Palestinian Civil Society

Liv Tørres

> Facing military occupation, many Palestinians wished to take up arms. Under such circumstances, only ideological and institutional discipline could contain the will to rebel within the realms of mass nonviolent protest. (Pearlman 2011: 123)

Civil society plays a pivotal role in struggles for liberation and democracy in many parts of the world. Social movements, nongovernmental organizations (NGOs), and organizations such as civics, women's groups, trade unions, and student groups generate ideas, enhance political skills, build social capital, and mobilize people for collective action. In the Occupied Palestinian Territories (OPT), both social capital and collective muscles would come in handy. Palestinian organizations have developed in the absence of the state, independence, sovereignty, and citizenship (Costantini et al. 2011). Still, organizational capacity and activism are an efficient tool and building block for unity and power here as elsewhere, which in turn will help Palestinians challenge their circumstances.

This is also our starting point in the Norwegian People's Aid (NPA), which has been active in the OPT since 1987. Our goal is to help build the organizational and collective muscles of Palestinians to challenge occupation, oppression, and internal division. It is against this background that we work in partnership with local Palestinian organizations. It is on this basis that we believe it is important to work with local forces rather than simply provide services. And it is from this perspective that we have watched the development of Palestinian civil society and the tensions, changes, and challenges that followed the Oslo Accords.

Civil Society Prior to the Accords

Palestinian civil society dates back to the 1920s and 1930s, when attempts were made to match the Jewish community in building institutions in preparation for the end of the British mandate (Kamrava 1999). Faith-based and religious organizations emerged, as well as labor movements, youth clubs, and women's groups focusing on the national issue. Yet, associational life as well as representation of Palestinians was divided, weak, dominated by notables, and continuously subject to 'divide and rule' tactics from successive regimes, first under the British mandate, then after the establishment of Israel and the Palestinian Nakba in 1948, as well as under Egyptian and Jordanian rule (Robinson 1997). With the 'national revolution' of the late 1960s, as Palestinians took control of the Palestine Liberation Organization (PLO) and Israel of the West Bank and the Gaza Strip, the stage was set for the development of new civil society formations. From then on, the development of Palestinian civil society was closely linked to the PLO.

After the 1967 war, numerous organizations emerged in the West Bank and Gaza with the aim of challenging Israeli occupation. They initially focused on providing services and relief, not on development (Costantini et al. 2011). The PLO's departure from Lebanon for Tunisia in the 1982 greatly increased its distance from the OPT and contributed to an increase in organizational mobilization at home (Kamrava 1999). Furthermore, the outbreak of the first Intifada in 1987 served as an important stimulus for Palestinian civil society. With Israel's heavy-handed response to the uprising and Jordan's 1988 renunciation of its claim to the West Bank, further incentives to mobilization arose (Kamrava 1999). A multitude of new NGOs emerged during the Intifada, including human rights groups, women's groups, community organizations, medical societies, and the like. They mobilized broad segments of the population and promoted largely nonviolent resistance to Israeli occupation. Popular committees became instrumental in sustaining and deepening the uprising (Pearlman 2011).

At the same time, political divisions shaped much of civil society, and many organizational forms were duplicated along factional lines. As political organizations were illegal, political and national issues were expressed through forces of civil society. Associational life became increasingly difficult to separate from the liberation struggle. Politically, Palestinian civil society could be divided into three groups in the pre-Oslo Accords period. Many organizations were affiliated with the secular left, with factions more popular and grounded than post-Oslo, and among which people were particularly active in setting up civic organizations. An Islamist, Hamas-linked civil society came to light during the Intifada. Set up by the Muslim Brotherhood in late 1987, Hamas emerged with an array of social and charitable work and organizations, in addition to militant resistance. A third group of NGOs, associated with Fatah, which is dominant within the PLO, developed gradually throughout the 1980s and acquired particular weight after the Oslo Accords.

While civil society was relatively united during the early Intifada, it gradually cracked thereafter. Fatah and the PLO also struggled with internal tensions. Those in exile sought to maintain a top-down revolutionary structure. Those from the OPT who had risen to leadership during the Intifada wanted to transform Fatah into a political party and the PLO into more of a democratic structure. During the early years of the uprising, Hamas pledged solidarity and unity with the PLO. On the streets, however, it organized differently and refused to acknowledge the sole representative status of the PLO (Usher 1999).

In spite of tensions, by the mid-1990s, the number of unions, professional associations, youth and women's groups, and the like had climbed sharply. By 1995, there were 700 NGOs in Gaza and some 1,500 in the West Bank (Sullivan 1995). An estimated twenty to thirty thousand individuals worked for NGOs (Sullivan 1996).Palestinian NGOs ran a formidable social provision infrastructure, handling as much as 30 percent of all educational services for Palestinians, 50 percent of hospital care, and 100 percent of disability care (Sullivan 1996). Forged around nationally contested issues such as agriculture, human rights, and labor, the NGOs comprised a counterhegemonic, nationalist bloc against the occupation, an "infrastructure of resistance" (Usher 1995).

Israel failed to crush the Intifada: "By April 1993, the occupied territories were hovering on the brink of an anti-colonial war, with military forms of resistance replacing the uprising's earlier modes of mass protest and civil disobedience" (Usher 1999: 9). The result was an iron curtain across the territories with massive Israeli interventions attempting to stop terrorists and take out activists. The stage and conditions were set for political negotiations.

The Oslo Accords and the Aftermath

The Oslo Accords were finalized and the Declaration of Principles (DOP) signed in 1993. Challenges soon emerged. The majority of Palestinians accepted the DOP, preferring it to bloodshed. Yet, as the return of PLO Chairman Yasser Arafat and the PLO was celebrated, distress and uncertainty about the future also prevailed. The subsequent establishment of a Palestinian Authority (PA) in the West Bank and the Gaza Strip established a new chapter in 'state'–society relations. In addition to functioning under Israeli occupation, the PA was to establish itself in a Palestinian society where a plethora of organizations had served, brought together, and represented people in the face of direct occupation.

One of the most notable aspects of the DOP was the shift from direct Israeli military rule in the OPT to an indirect form of domination. The accords gave the PA a clear mandate of demobilization, first and foremost of the militants but also of the society at large. The national question was no longer an issue to be solved through organizing in 'the street,' but one to be fixed at the negotiation table by the PLO elite. Herein lay the starting point for the main contradictions that have come to characterize Palestinian 'state'–society relations and civil society development after Oslo. With the establishment of the PA, civil society was to start relating to a new quasi-state and a new set of state-like institutions. Yet, the future was unclear, making it harder for civil society to identify its 'opponent,' the responsible institution, and expected progress on delivery. The occupation had not gone away. The question was where the attention of civil society should be directed: toward the occupier or toward the PA, PLO, Fatah, or the elite that had signed the accords?

There was also major political disagreement among Palestinians regarding the Oslo Accords, not only between the PLO and Hamas but among all political factions. This 'pro–con Oslo cleavage' not only divided previously established groups but also changed the power balance in favor of the elite that was 'pro Oslo' and had been part and parcel of settling the deal. The cleavage resulted in strong tensions and shifts in the power balance within civil society. Institutionally, the agreement distributed power among Palestinian groups. It established the PLO as an entity outside the PA and gave it almost absolute powers over the PA (Usher 1995). In practice, though, a PLO elite was moving into power while the PLO as an institution became more marginalized.

The PA set out quickly to impose tight political controls on nongovernmental organizations (NGOs). Many in the PLO and the PA saw the political independence of existing organizations as an obstacle. The PA required that NGOs and other organizations supply detailed information regarding their members (Kamrava 1999). NGOs soon found themselves closely monitored by the intelligence services. In 1993, sixty Palestinian organizations endorsed the principle of an independent civil society. In 1995, sixty-three NGOs formed a Palestinian Non-Governmental Organization Network (PNGO) to safeguard their "freedom to associate, organize, and operate." Yet, damage had already been done. Many hoped that the relatively dynamic progressive civil society that had evolved during the Intifada would manage to challenge the centralism and bureaucracy that grew in the PA. However, the pressure from the PA combined with continuous harassment by Israeli authorities forced civil society to redefine and relocate its role in the national struggle. The contraction of space available to civil society, along with bureaucratic expansionism in the public sector and recruitment of many civil society leaders into the PA, made it difficult to maintain the vibrancy and collective muscle of those left.

The PNGO fought for a legal base for an independent civil society, while at the same time trying to deal with the confusion over what role civil society should play with respect to the national question between the PA and the occupier. At the same time, many NGOs started orienting themselves toward service provision in response to the needs of the people, in order to build constituencies, for reasons of economic survival, or simply to assure their survival as regards the PA. Yet, as the PA began systematically to undo and socially demobilize the OPT's vibrant NGO networks (Parsons 2005), it also took over their tasks. Strain between the PA and civil society was exacerbated by historical tensions within and between the PLO and many NGOs. Organizations like relief committees, women's groups, and human rights groups were bastions of Palestinian independents and the PLO left, reflecting Fatah's historical neglect of developing organizations inside the OPT (Usher 1995). Organizations that were 'pro Oslo' experienced less pressure from the PA. Their funding was often maintained or increased. NGOs were hence coopted into the orbit of the PA elite to provide services and win adherence to the newly defined nationalist agenda.

Donors simultaneously created strong incentives to engage in peace-related activities. The 'pro–con Oslo cleavage' was reinforced with peace rhetoric and a strong expectation that civil society should be supportive of the new agenda if it wanted to maintain good links with the PA or other donors. The drying up of financial support from outside donors, who now mostly funneled funds through the PA, further curtailed civil society. The World Bank estimated in 1995 that external support for Palestinian NGOs was cut in half after Oslo (Parsons 2005). Many NGOs saw the PA's attempt to represent them with donors as a scheme to marginalize them. About 800 out of 1,400 organizations disappeared in the period following the establishment of the PA (Costantini et al. 2011). Many social services, clinics, and other projects were closed.

Simultaneously, a new generation of organizations was born. By 1996, around 40 percent of organizations were founded after the establishment of PA (De Voir and Tartir 2009). Arafat successfully resisted attempts by foreign donors to earmark contributions for specific projects, instead preferring the flow of unspecified 'operational funds.' Financial support to politically allied NGOs helped consolidate party apparatuses and ensure political control (Waage 2004), although it also contributed to further divisions in civil society. The PA invited organizations to incorporate themselves into its structures. While some agreed, this generated tension and increased competition for funds and activities (Costantini et al. 2011). Simultaneously, the number of Islamic organizations as well as international agencies and NGOs expanded, with the latter often having limited linkages to local communities (Costantini et al. 2011).

By the end of the 1990s, NGO politics had become increasingly careful. It no longer meant openly criticizing the authorities but rather cooperating with the PA or looking after projects to which the PA did not attend. In an attempt to control NGOs, the PA presented a draft law in 1997 to 'license' NGOs rather than simply 'registering' them. Due to successful mobilization by the PNGO, disagreements within the PA, and international pressure, civil society won this battle. One of the most liberal NGO laws in the region was hence enacted in 2000. When push came to shove, however, the law had limited value as the second Intifada broke out.

In September 2000, frustrations that years of negotiations between the Israeli government and the PLO had failed to deliver a Palestinian state boiled over. Many progressive local Fatah leaders were behind the second Intifada (Bishara 2001). They had stood up against corruption and elitism in the PLO and they had been advocating to give Oslo a chance. Now they thought the time had come for collective action. The early demonstrations were met with brutality by the Israeli army and the Intifada soon escalated into violence, high death tolls, and major destruction of infrastructure and property.

The level of violence was also an indication of civil society no longer having the muscles to manage coordination and restraint. The first Intifada had the ideological and institutional discipline to contain violence because the bulk of society was integrated into institutions and a united leadership. By the end of the 1990s, leadership, institutions, and collective purpose had begun to crumble (Pearlman 2011). Civil society provided important relief and services, reducing the costs of the uprising. Many organizations were also crucial in documenting violations of human rights. The collective unified purpose, however, was not there. What Usher called the "infrastructure of resistance" had ruptured.

Facing Failed Democracy and Donor Agendas

The contradictions imposed on Palestinian society post-Oslo were not eliminated with the second Intifada. Rather, they were deepened, and more layers were added. As part of their response to the second Intifada, the Israeli authorities imposed severe movement restrictions in the West Bank and the Gaza Strip, which resulted in further severe setbacks for the Palestinian economy and increased poverty. In addition, the blow to the PA's institutions was significant. After smashing much of the PA infrastructure, the joint Israeli and international demand became 'reform' of the PA. Arafat was no longer the partner they wanted. Local civil society actors had voiced their concerns for democracy and protested corruption and bad institutions since they were set up. Now, after having stood silently on the sidelines while civil society criticism was suppressed, these issues became the main agenda for Israel and the international community, with the political aim of getting the PA into line.

In the period leading up to the elections of 2005 and 2006, democratization became part of the call for reform, with support from both civil society organizations and donors. The end result was going to be difficult to handle, however, both for Palestinian civil society and for outside stakeholders. Consistently critical of the Oslo Accords and its institutions, willing to spoil the process by military means, and with a steady focus on building a genuine social base through a network of charities, mosques, unions, and sports clubs, Hamas ended up winning a majority in the Palestinian parliament. Total confusion, a fair amount of hypocrisy, and a 180-degree turn in the attitude of international powers followed. Now, the international community wanted to move the power of the Hamas prime minister back to the presidency that they previously sought to weaken.

The rush to move PA funding over to institutions controlled by the presidency was complemented by an attempt to run to civil society as an 'alternative channel' for funding. Could organizations take additional funds and cover more of the services provided by the PA? The principled answer from several Palestinian organizations was no. If the international community was serious about its reform and democracy talk, then the PA would have to be supported. In Norway, the response of larger NGOs working in Palestine was similar.

The subsequent split that led to a Hamas-governed Gaza and a Fatah-controlled West Bank has brought another disturbing trend: forced closing of numerous civil society organizations linked to the respective opponents. Freedom of organization, assembly, and speech has been increasingly curtailed.

In the meantime, the massive influx of international funding, donors, and international NGOs over the years has left its mark on Palestinian civil society. Palestinian organizations with genuine constituencies and agendas are being undermined by international donors or NGOs that are promoting their own interests. International organizations entering the OPT to do their own relief and service delivery, for example in Gaza in the aftermath of Operation Cast Lead in 2009, are also effectively undermining the capacity of local civil society. All in all, interventions driven from outside the OPT have in many cases done little to help the development of genuine Palestinian civil society.

Civil Society at the Twenty-Year Anniversary of the Oslo Accords

Slavoj Žižek (2012) begs us to ask what goes on in the Middle East "when nothing goes on," that is, when there are no reports of attacks or negotiations. With its slow expansion of settlements and the micromanagement of daily life, argues Žižek, Israel is engaged in a slow, invisible process, a kind of mole's underground digging, which will one day lead to the world awakening and realizing that the land is without Palestinians. Do civil society actors manage to challenge that slow, steady process of 'underground digging'?

The picture painted here may seem bleak. The post-Oslo period is a story of a total makeover when it comes to the characteristics of Palestinian civil society. It is a story of diminishing cohesion, of a more fragmented, professionalized, and service-oriented civil society. And it is a story of a less united, politically focused, and collectively oriented civil society. The combined effect of new institutions, political restrictions and divides, initial loss of funding, and pressure to depoliticize, as well as the shortage of alternative agendas in civil society together with the continued harassment, suppression, and military actions of the Israeli side, has turned civil society into far less of the 'infrastructure of resistance' it was before the Oslo Accords. Both the international community and the PA should have given more attention to the need to build popular Palestinian support for the peace process. Although in different ways, and possibly with different motives, both they and the Israelis were more concerned with demobilization. The international community's push for, or contribution to, a service-oriented clientilistic civil society also did little to build strength locally. Civil society's limited ability to develop alternative agendas, unity, and collective muscle contributed to its weakening.

As we mark the 'Oslo anniversary,' there are, however, some small promising signs. We have witnessed attempts to revive mobilization, as with the civil resistance to the wall in the West Bank. Starting 'from below' in the villages affected by the building of the wall since 2003, it has inspired thousands to demonstrate. The campaign has not yet managed to create a unified movement and has in many places been limited by the wall itself or been crushed by the Israelis. As such, one of the main obstacles for civil society since the Oslo Accords remains that if mobilization is not coopted or demobilized by the PA, it will be crushed by the occupation.

On the ground, however, people have not stopped organizing. In May 2011, refugees from Syria, Lebanon, Israel, and the OPT marched in protests commemorating the Nakba—the dispossession and exile caused by Israel's creation. In Jerusalem in January 2013, the protest tent village of Bab al-Shams was set up to resist Israel's plans for settlement expansion. It was torn down by Israeli forces, but activists have vowed to set it up again. There are other examples of collective action, such as the movement to boycott Israeli products and products from illegal settlements. Palestinian youth may have been slower than other Arab Spring sisters and brothers to mobilize for change, but since 2011 we have witnessed new forms of youth organization that are challenging the authorities as well as NGOs, political factions, and the authorities.

The immediate call of these movements is for unity, as a stepping stone to challenging the occupation. It is within such different and evolving forms of organizations, unions, self-organized groups, and campaigns that we should look for the fabric that will build the new 'infrastructure of resistance.' A new agenda would demand a focus on building strong united civil movements on the ground, rather than separate West Bank and Gaza organizations. As the experiences of South African anti-apartheid activists show, gains can be made by combining campaigns at home with the support of sympathizers abroad in building strong civil society activism and organizations.

Palestinians are left with only one choice: to summon the resolve to mobilize and revive the culture of collective activism. It is only through building and sustaining a unified collective campaign of resistance that the Palestinians stand a chance of challenging Israeli occupation.

References

Bishara, M. 2001. *Palestine/Israel: Peace or Apartheid.* London: Zed Books.

Costantini, G., J. Atamneh, K. Ayesh, and F. Al Husseini. 2011. *Mapping Study of Civil Society Organisations in the Occupied Palestinian Territory.* Brussels: European Union Commission and SOGES.

De Voir, J., and A. Tartir. 2009. *Tracking External Donor Funding to Palestinian Non-Governmental Organizations in the West Bank and Gaza 1999–2008.* Ramallah: MAS–NDC.

Kamrava, M. 1999. "What Stands between the Palestinians and Democracy?" *Middle East Quarterly* 6 (2): 3–12.

Parsons, N. 2005. *The Politics of the Palestinian Authority.* New York: Routledge.

Pearlman, W. 2011. *Violence, Nonviolence and the Palestinian National Movement.* Cambridge: Cambridge University Press.

Robinson, G.E. 1997. *Building a Palestinian State: The Incomplete Revolution.* Bloomington, IN: Indiana University Press.

Sullivan, D.J. 1996. "NGOs in Palestine: Agents of Development and Foundations of Civil Society." *Journal of Palestine Studies* 25 (3): 93–100.

_____. 1995. *Non-Governmental Organizations and Freedom of Association: Palestine and Egypt, a Comparative Analysis.* Jerusalem: Palestinian Academic Society for the Study of International Affairs.

Usher, G. 1999. *Dispatches from Palestine: The Rise and Fall of the Oslo Peace Process.* London: Pluto Press.

_____. 1995. *Palestine in Crisis: The Struggle for Peace and Political Independence after Oslo.* London: Pluto Press.

Waage, H.H. 2004. *Peacemaking Is a Risky Business: Norway's Role in the Peace Process in the Middle East, 1993–96.* Oslo: PRIO.

Žižek, S. 2012. "What Goes On When Nothing Goes On." In *The Case for Sanctions against Israel,* edited by Audrea Lim. London: Verso.

6

"We Have Opened Doors, Others Have Been Closed": Women under the Oslo Accords

Lotta Schüllerqvist

The majority of Palestinian women are seldom seen or heard in public. They have strong voices and strong minds, but the patriarchal culture requires them to keep their opinions and experiences within the family. A strong culture of silence hides most of the daily life and struggle of Palestinian women.

As in all societies, however, there are exceptions: strong and brave women who have made remarkable careers, both in politics and society. Three of them will tell their stories in this chapter.

The chapter will also discuss several Palestinian organizations that work actively to support women's rights and improve their situation. They deal with everything from charity to education and empowerment of women, as well as research, advocacy, and lobbying for women's rights.

A Long History of Struggle

The first women's organization in the country, the Palestinian Women's Union, was established as early as 1921. This organization led the demonstrations against the Balfour Declaration and organized the first Women's Conference in 1929.

The Palestinian women's movement has always been closely linked to the national struggle. After the 1948 war, women organized food aid and healthcare for the poor and needy among the refugees. After the 1967 war, they became involved in the resistance movement and started building women's grass-roots committees all over the occupied territories.

During the first Intifada (1987–92), women took an even more active role in society. Some worked as political agents, others were imprisoned, and many became the family providers when their husbands were sent to prison or deported or were killed or injured in the resistance struggle.

These new roles for women were seen as necessary under the prevailing circumstances. For Palestinian women, this step onto the public scene meant new experiences and a new awareness about society and politics. The male-dominated society, however, did not allow them to break out of the patriarchal culture, arguing that the struggle for women's social rights should be postponed until the national struggle was over and an independent state had been created.

Hanan Ashrawi, One of the Pioneers

"The first Intifada was a really transformative period in Palestinian society. The women were in the forefront of the struggle, defying the norms of behavior and the standard definitions of shame and honor," says Hanan Ashrawi, a well-known politician and women's activist (interview, Ramallah, January 8, 2013). "But after the signing of the Declaration of Principles (I never call it the Oslo Accords) everything changed. Now the fighting and risk-taking was over and the time had come for reaping the fruits of the struggle. So the male system went back into effect — the men wanted to take the rewards. They felt that this was a period for political decision-making, and it was the men who had to do the serious business of government."

Ashrawi describes how women were sidelined and excluded in the competition for positions of power. For a long time, men were left in charge of politics while women went back to the issues of social justice, good governance, and institution building. Ashrawi herself is one of the few women who have been able to compete for a position. She was elected to the Palestinian Legislative Council

(PLC) in 1996 and appointed minister of higher education and research in the first government. Since 2009, she has been a member of the Palestine Liberation Organization (PLO) executive committee — the first woman ever in this body.

She describes this achievement as the result of a women's mutiny: "The political factions had agreed on a list of only men for the executive committee, but the women in the PNC [Palestinian National Council] refused to accept this. Together with the youth, the trade unions and the reformers, they demanded elections, and they all supported me as their consensus candidate. And we won, after challenging the male power system."

According to Hanan Ashrawi, the situation for women in Palestinian society has started to improve. Seven women are now in the government, several women have been appointed mayors and governors, and there are at least twenty-two female judges. Still, a lot remains to be done to get women involved in all aspects of society, for example in the reconciliation talks between Fatah and Hamas, in political committees, and in strategic committees for negotiations. "When women are active in different fields they open up the closed system and create role models who can stretch the limits," Hanan Ashrawi.

Double Oppression: Occupation and Patriarchy

For the vast majority of women in Palestine, society has been going in a negative direction over the last decade. The pressure from the Israeli occupation has increased tremendously since the start of the second Intifada, and it severely affects everyday life. Walls and checkpoints restrict the movements of all. Gaza is under siege and cut off from the West Bank. The economy has been almost paralyzed, at least in the Gaza Strip, where thousands of jobs have been lost and poverty has grown deep and widespread.

The recurrent military actions of the Israeli army take a heavy toll on the population, in terms of deaths, injuries, and damage to property. The constant threat of new attacks creates an overwhelming feeling of insecurity and helplessness.

As usual, it is the women who have to carry the heaviest burden in this situation. They must do what they can to make ends meet, to feed and care for their children and husbands. If the husband has lost his job and his role as the provider, he might take out his frustration on his wife, but she has to put up with that, too.

Another burden that weighs heavily on women is society's growing conservatism and religiousness, which puts severe restrictions on women's lives. This is a trend that can be seen in many parts of the world, not least in the Arab countries. Palestine used to be a more open society than many of its neighboring countries, but this trend toward conservatism is accentuated by the occupation, which has destroyed most civil society functions. Lack of security and hope for the future makes people turn to tradition and religion in search of other sources of hope and strength.

Amal Syam, Women's Affairs Center

According to Amal Syam, the executive director of the Women's Affairs Center (WAC) in Gaza, the situation of women has deteriorated in many ways. "Early marriages have become more common, both here and in the West Bank," she notes. "The main reason is the bad economic situation — marrying off the daughters is a way to ease the economic burden of the family" (interview, Gaza City, January 14, 2013).

The legal age for marriage is seventeen for girls and eighteen for boys. In Gaza, where Egyptian law is applied (Egyptian Law of Family Rights of 1954), the minimum marriage age for girls used to be twelve. In 1995, the supreme sharia judge increased it in order to coordinate it with the Jordanian law applied in the West Bank (Jordanian Personal Status Law of 1976). One paragraph in the family law, however, allows for girls to be married at fifteen if a sheikh judges her to be physically mature enough for marriage.

"Early marriage is a really bad phenomenon because it prevents the girls from finishing their studies," says Syam. "Marriage means no more going to school, and the girl is left without a real education. That can be a true disaster if she becomes a widow, which is not uncommon in our society. Without education she will not be able to find a job to support herself and the children."

WAC works hard to encourage young women to continue their studies, as education is the most important thing, not only for the woman but also for her children. Even if it is not easy to find a job, education improves women's chances in the labor market.

Ever since the Palestinian Authority came to power in 1994 and established the legislative council in 1996, women's and human rights organizations have been pushing hard for a new family law for both Gaza and the West Bank and to improve the legal status of women. A committee was formed to write the new law, but without any result between 1996 and 2006. Since then, because of the split between Hamas and Fatah, the legislative council has not been able to work at all.

Mona Shawwa, Palestinian Center for Human Rights (PCHR)

Mona Shawwa, the head of the women's rights unit in the Palestinian Center for Human Rights (PCHR) in Gaza, points out that after severe Israeli attacks, such as Operation Cast Lead in the winter of 2008–2009, the number of early marriages increases. "Families who have lost their homes and are living in tents take any chance to marry their daughters because of the economic pressure . . . . We are still working hard to prevent the underage marriages," says Shawwa.[1]

She has discussed this with the supreme judge, trying to convince him to forbid girls from getting married at fifteen. His answer was, "If I forbid marriage from fifteen years of age, how can I solve the problem of a young girl who has been raped? Then I cannot allow her to marry the man who raped her."

Shawwa notes, "He said that there are many cases like this, and that marriage is the only possible solution to save the girl's honor. In my eyes this is totally crazy, but obviously this is still happening today in our society."

Increasing Family Violence

Another serious problem for Palestinian women is violence in the family, which is twice as common in Gaza as it is in the West Bank. Every second woman in Gaza and every third woman in the West Bank are exposed to some form of violence, according to the Palestinian Central Bureau of Statistics.

Physical and psychological violence against women has been increasing over the last decade. The reason for this, according to Palestinian medical anthropologist Jamileh Abu-Duhou, is that the home and the family are the only arena where men can freely exercise control and compensate for the psychological wounds inflicted by the loss of personal dignity under the occupation.

In *Giving Voices to the Voiceless*, Abu-Duhou (2011) paints a bleak picture of the daily life of the Palestinian woman. In the dominant patriarchal tradition she is seen as a second-class citizen whose main duty is to be obedient and submissive to her husband and male relatives. Every single step she takes, especially outside the home, requires permission from her husband, father, or brother.

This means that even if a woman is severely abused she is prevented from searching for help and support outside the family. If she is desperate or brave enough to go to the police, they usually tell her to go back home and solve the problem inside the family. Exposing family problems to the outside world is seen as a breach of the rules and a threat to family honor.

No Legal or Physical Protection

"The lack of legal protection for women is a serious problem — our criminal law is from 1936, the time of the British mandate. In the West Bank they have another old-fashioned law that also lacks real protection against violence in the family," says Syam.

She also mentions honor killings, which seem to be on the rise, although there are no clear statistics. In some cases the real motive for the killing of a woman is not honor but a conflict about inheritance or something else. The perpetrator pleads honor as his motive nonetheless, trying to obtain a more lenient verdict in court.

In honor killing cases the perpetrator can get away with just two or three years in prison. In 2009, President Mahmoud Abbas by decree raised the prison sentence for such killings to fifteen to twenty years, as for other murder cases. But, according to Shawwa, this decree is not implemented in all cases.

Women's organizations in Gaza tried for several years to create a shelter for women who need protection for their life and safety. Finally, they were allowed to open a shelter but not to let women stay overnight, just to receive them in the daytime and offer some help and support. Instead, Hamas opened a shelter of its own, with twenty beds where women can stay overnight. This is, at least, better than the prison where they used to put women who were under serious threat. But the staff working at the Hamas shelter lacks education and knowledge about how to care for women in violent families.

Economic Violence

Another common infringement on women's rights is economic, especially when it comes to inheritance. Most women do not obtain their legal share of inheritance, even though the rules for this are clearly stated in the Qur'an. The basic rule is that a woman shall inherit half as much as her brother. In most cases, she does not receive even that because it is seen as shameful for a woman to go to court and make claims against her brother.

Economic protection is also lacking for widows. The family of a deceased husband often claims his property, and in some cases it even takes over his house and throws the widow and her children into the street. Few women can afford to hire a lawyer to take their case to court.

Widows of *shahid* s (fallen resistance fighters) can face a very difficult situation, says Syam: "Some of the *shahid* families try to marry the widow to one of the brothers of the dead man, to get hold of his pension and property. As the children belong to their father's family they want to include their mother so she can take care of them. This can be a really terrible situation for the widow — she can be forced to marry a much older man, or to be taken as a second or third wife of one of her husband's brothers. Her life will be destroyed not only by the loss of her husband, but also economically and socially."

Many of the *shahid* widows are young — twenty-five to thirty-five years old — and have young children. If they continue living on their own, they can keep the custody of children up to fifteen years of age. If they want to marry again, however, they must leave their children to their deceased husband's family. Many widows remain single for the rest of their lives in order not to lose their children.

Divorce on the Rise

Even though the family unit is guarded by strong traditional rules, the number of divorces is increasing. Today, around 7 percent of all marriages end in divorce. "We see a new phenomenon here," says Syam. "Some 40 percent of the divorces happen before the wedding, in the time after the signing of the marriage contract. This period can be up to one year, and during this time the couple may find that they cannot live together for one reason or another. For example they discover that their families sympathize with different factions — one with Hamas and the other with Fatah. That can make their future family life impossible, at least in the present situation."

When the marriage contract is signed, the woman's name and status is changed in her papers. If the marriage does not go through, she is defined as a divorced woman. This can make it difficult for her to find another man because there is a clear social stigma attached to being a divorced woman.

If a woman is divorced after some years of marriage, she usually keeps her children — boys until the age of nine and girls until the age of eleven. After that, the father takes over custody and the mother can only meet her children for a few hours now and then. There is a question regarding where they can meet, however, as the mother cannot visit the house of her former husband, and vice versa. The only option used to be a police station, but lately women's organizations have created more neutral meeting places.

A Law of Empty Words

This is just a brief overview of the miserable social conditions for Palestinian women today. It stands in stark contrast to the wording of the Palestinian Basic Law of 2003. Article 9, under the headline "Public Rights and Liberties," asserts that "Palestinians shall be equal before the law and the judiciary, without distinctions based on race, sex, color, religion, political views or disability." Article 10 says that "basic human rights and liberties shall be protected and respected." According to Article 11, "Personal freedom is a natural right, shall be guaranteed and may not be violated."

Seen from a woman's perspective, these articles are only empty words that have changed nothing in real life during the ten years since the law's enactment. This leads me to think that a women's Intifada may be necessary.

Maisoun Qawasmi, Political Challenger

One woman who has succeeded in making some cracks in the wall of traditional male hegemony is Maisoun Qawasmi, a forty-three-year-old journalist and women's activist in Hebron. In the autumn of 2012 she took a step that echoed all over the world: she formed a women-only list for the upcoming municipality elections. Qawasmi notes, "I wanted to do something to improve the situation here in Hebron, where the women are suffering more than in other places."[2]

Hebron is under heavy pressure from the occupation. The city is divided into two parts, one under Israeli control and the other under Palestinian control. The Palestinian population lives under daily harassment from extremist settlers in the nearby settlement of Qiryat Arba.

In addition, Hebron is a highly conservative city with many restrictions on the daily life of women. A female initiative of this kind is thus a real challenge to traditional male dominance. But Qawasmi is a brave and strong woman and an excellent speaker. Maybe even more important, she belongs to one of the most respected families in Hebron and has the full and outspoken support of her husband. "It was not easy to convince the women to join my list," she notes. "Most of those I asked said that their father or brother were running for the election, so they couldn't compete with them. Or their families didn't allow them. But finally I succeeded to gather twelve names for the list under the label 'by participating, we can.'"

When the list was completed, she announced it on Facebook: "That was the most amazing moment in my life—after fifteen minutes questions started to come from journalists all over the world. Suddenly I was big, breaking news. I gave around a hundred interviews in the weeks before the elections."

The initiative also elicited lots of negative reactions among the people of Hebron. They tried to have the election committee cancel the list, and some of the candidates were put under pressure to back out. Qawasmi convinced them all to stay on.

During the campaign weeks she spent a lot of time in the streets, talking to all and sundry. She met a lot of resentment for this 'unbecoming' behavior, especially from women.

Working through Men

"I started thinking that to reach the women I had to work through the men," says Qawasmi.

> So after persistent asking I was allowed to come and speak in the *diwan* of one of the most powerful families, the Abu Sneinehs. To my surprise around five hundred men had gathered there, and I was speaking to them for one and a half hours. They all listened carefully, and afterward the *mukhtar* of the family came to shake my hand, and he said, "You are very strong, more than the men." . . . They had realized that my intention was not to tell the women to take off the hijab or something like that; I just wanted to tell them to take their rights in society. I said that if the donors come here and see the women in a weak position they might decide to stop funding water projects and such, and invest more in support for women instead. This was a message they could understand.

The candidates on Qawasmi's list did not get a seat in the municipal government, but she will try again in the next election: "We got 503 votes, which was more than I had expected. So I feel I have succeeded in ringing a bell, and sending the message that women must take their rights with their own hands. My inspiration comes from Samiha Khalil, who ran for president in 1996, challenging Abu Ammar [Yasser Arafat] himself. She was an amazing woman, who turned on the first light for me."

Kholoud Al Faqeeh, First Female Sharia Judge

Another remarkable woman is Kholoud Al Faqeeh. She is the first female sharia judge in Palestine, and one of very few in the Arab world. She is thirty-five years old and lives in the village of Beit Rima outside Ramallah with her husband and four children. After graduating from Al Quds University, she took a Master's degree in international family law.

In 2001, when she was training to be a lawyer, Al Faqeeh realized that there were no women in the sharia court system. She saw this as a big problem because these courts are concerned with family and personal law, dealing with marriage, divorce, inheritance, custody, and maintenance — issues that are very sensitive for women.

She says, "I made a study along two lines, the legal and the religious, to find the reason for this, and I found that there is no text that prevents a woman from being a sharia judge. So I went to the chief of justice and told him I wanted to be a sharia judge. He smiled and shook his head; it was a shock to him that a woman could ask such a question."[3]

Some years later there was a competition for a sharia judge position and Al Faqeeh wanted to take part in it, but she found that the deadline had passed: "In the following years up until 2008 I insisted that I wanted to be a sharia judge. Every time I had the opportunity I repeated this, to force the male judges to change their mind."

In the meantime she established a private practice and worked as a law counselor for Women's Center for Legal Aid and Counseling (WCLAC). She represented many abused women, both in civil and sharia courts, which gave her much experience in this field.

In 2008, another competition for a sharia judge position began, and Al Faqeeh passed both the written and the oral exam with top results. A few months later a new competition was held, and she passed it again, along with another female candidate who also became a sharia judge. President Abbas gave the two women their official documents as the first female sharia judges in Palestine. Sudan is the only other country with women in this role.

Making a Difference

Al Faqeeh has worked in the sharia court for five years now, and I ask her if she makes a difference in this function:

> There is no difference when it comes to applying the text of the law, there is no space for personal interpretations. But when a woman comes to the court and meets another woman it makes a big difference: the woman feels more at ease and can speak openly about all the details of her case. For example about abuse from

her husband, oral, physical, or sexual. She would never speak about that in front of a male judge, because our culture says it is shameful to talk about things that should be kept secret between man and wife. As a woman I can encourage her, like a counselor. So a woman in this role is the first step to achieve justice for women.

Al Faqeeh points to inheritance rights as one main problem for women:

It can be very difficult for a woman to get her rights, because of our male-dominated culture. The rules are very clear, and in the sharia court we produce the documents that state the share for the woman and the man respectively. And then they go to the civil court which decides how this document shall be implemented . . . . In many cases men refuse to share the inheritance with their sisters. This is really a bad pattern, because it is against the religion—the Qur'an is very clear on this point. But sadly enough many men are far too in love with themselves and only look for their own economic advantage. Money is power, and the women are the weak part in this society.

Influential Feminists

Al Faqeeh notes that she was a feminist long before she started to study:

When a woman comes to the court to ask for her inheritance share, I explain to her that God gave you this right, so your brother can't force you to relinquish it. If he wants to buy you out he must pay the full price. I try my best to encourage her . . . . There is a lot of work for the women's organizations to do to make the women aware of their rights. And the men of course, but that will take a long time. Our education ministry should also take up this issue in the school books, so the younger generation can learn how to build a new and better society.

In 2012, *Arabian Business* magazine named Al Faqeeh the tenth most important woman in the Arab world out of a hundred women. Some years earlier, Washington University, with support from Saudi Arabia, listed her as one of the five hundred most influential people in the Islamic world.

"So far we are just a few women who have opened some doors so other women can see that it is possible to follow us. And we will work hard to help them, by keeping the doors open," says Al Faqeeh.

Notes

1. Interview, Gaza City, January 13, 2013.
2. Interview, Hebron, January 7, 2013.
3. Interview, Beit Rima, January 8, 2013.

References

Abu-Dohou, J. 2011. *Giving Voices to the Voiceless: Gender-Based Violence in the Occupied Palestinian Territories*. Cairo: American University in Cairo Press.

7

After Oslo: A Legal Historical Perspective

Richard Falk

Points of Departure

When the Oslo Accords were signed on September 13, 1993, and confirmed for the world with the famous handshake on the White House lawn between Yasser Arafat and Yitzak Rabin with a smiling Bill Clinton looking on, many thought that finally the Israel–Palestine conflict was winding down or, at worst, entering its final phase. It seemed like there was a shared commitment between the parties, with strong backing from the United States, to strike a compromise more or less along the borders established by the 1948 armistice agreement that enlarged Israeli territory from the 57 percent of the British mandate allocated for a Jewish homeland by United Nations General Assembly Resolution 181 to the 78 percent of Palestine held by Israel at the start of the 1967 war. The other issues in dispute, although deferred until the so-called final status negotiations, including the arrangements governing Jerusalem, Palestinian refugees, Israeli settlements, permanent borders, water rights, and security guarantees, were all widely assumed at the time to be open to compromise and mutual acceptance. The accords proposed resolution of these issues within five years, which then seemed reasonable, as was the commitment to begin final status negotiations no later than 1996.

From the perspective of 2013, twenty years later, the prospect of peaceful resolution seems more elusive than ever, and indeed conditions have changed so
adversely as to make any assertion of an attainable and sustainable peace seem to
be at best an exercise in wishful thinking and at worst an expression of bad faith.
How can we explain, then, that the Oslo Accords, widely celebrated in 1993 as a
historic breakthrough, now appear to have been an insidious roadblock that
diverted the Palestinian struggle for self-determination while granting time to
Israel to expand its territorial claims and virtually extinguish any realistic prospect
of realizing Palestinian rights in the near future. What can we learn from this
experience? Were the Palestinians blindsided, or did the Palestinians themselves
contribute to this overall weakening of their position by engaging in violent forms
of resistance that gave Israel time, space, and world sympathy, which enabled the
pursuit of its expansionist ambitions? Or were the Palestinians insufficiently
united behind the Oslo Accords to provide the needed political support for the
necessary compromise implicit in the idea of legitimating Israel as a Jewish state?

There are other issues it seems appropriate to raise after twenty years. Did
Israel overreach in such a way as to undermine its long-term security as a result of
regional power shifts that made its situation more precarious than ever? It is
important to appreciate that technological progress in weaponry and doctrinal
shifts in tactics make all political actors, including those with apparent military
dominance, vulnerable to devastating attack. This is part of the lesson of the 9/11
attacks, carried out with minimal capabilities and almost no material resources.
What Israel has done is to create a seemingly irreversible situation in the Occupied Territories of the West Bank and East Jerusalem that has the collateral effect
of depriving Tel Aviv of a peace option.

The Palestine Liberation Organization (PLO) in 1988, five years before Oslo,
committed the Palestinians to such an option by accepting the existence of Israel
within the 1948 armistice borders, with the territorial remnant providing the basis
for a Palestinian state that was significantly smaller than what the UN had proposed in its partition plan. This plan had been disastrously rejected by Palestinians when put forward because it then seemed grossly unfair to the majority
Arab Palestinian resident population, and flagrantly violated the ethos and politics of the Palestinian people's right of self-determination.

In a sense, the overarching question twenty years after the Oslo Accords is
whether this dismal conclusion that the peace option is now foreclosed for both
sides is persuasive or not. If so, what now?

Recovering the 1993 Outlook

It seemed to many of us that the secret discussions in Oslo that produced the framework for negotiations would steer the parties in the direction of a sustainable peace, but even at the outset there were skeptics and many good reasons for skepticism. To begin with, there was no reference made in the framework to Palestinian sovereign statehood as a stipulated goal of the process. There was not even a reference to the Palestinians' right of self-determination.

An even more serious omen of trouble ahead was the absence of a clear-cut political consensus on either side in support of the approach and assumptions embodied in the Oslo Accords. In retrospect, the accords were more pleasing to Washington than to either of the parties, as they seemed to dispose of the conflict in a manner that allowed the United States to realize its grand strategy of oil energy geopolitics in the region. In the Israeli Knesset, despite the Labor government being in power, the vote on the Oslo Accords was too close for comfort, with sixty-one in favor, fifty opposed, and nine abstentions. The depth of Israeli right-wing opposition was disclosed by the assassination of Yitzhak Rabin in 1995 by Yigal Amir, a religious Jew associated with hardcore settler outlooks and emboldened by biblical claims. This eliminated the most respected Israeli leader identified with the Oslo approach to Israel's future well-being.

It is significant that Benjamin Netanyahu and his Likud Party were openly opposed to the Oslo Accords from the outset, particularly its implications of Israeli withdrawal and the ensuing establishment of a Palestinian state. Netanyahu attacked Rabin for his accommodationist views, accusing him of "being removed from Jewish traditions . . . and Jewish values" at anti-Oslo rallies. Such attitudes exhibited so provocatively within Israel were not expressed internationally, as the pretense was maintained that all political tendencies in Israel were seeking a negotiated peace.

In addition, the Israeli electorate was drifting toward the right, which signaled political trouble ahead for the Oslo timetable and the overall negotiation process, as well as a reluctance to travel very far down the Oslo road. Israeli ambivalence toward the Oslo Accords reflected the tension between those who sought a peace based on a two-state consensus and those who believed that Israel's destiny and security depended on the prevention of Palestinian statehood, and coupled this with the belief that all of Jerusalem and as much as possible of the West Bank should be incorporated into an expanded Israel that was biblically ordained.

On the Palestinian side there was also strong opposition to the partition implications of the Oslo process. The process seemed to promote the two-state approach to achieving a peaceful solution to the conflict, which meant both legitimizing Israel and splitting Palestine in two. It also appeared to look toward a state based on the 1967 borders, as adjusted, rather than the partition proposed by the UN. Further, the dominant PLO position since 1988 seemed to overterritorialize the dispute, as expressed by the formula 'land for peace,' thereby diluting the claims of those several million Palestinians living in refugee camps or being unwilling participants in an involuntary diaspora.

The more militant Palestinian factions refused to endorse such a prospect, including Hamas, Islamic Jihad, and the Popular Front for the Liberation of Palestine. Many prominent Palestinian intellectuals, including Edward Said, felt that the partition approach based on ethnic states was doomed to failure from the perspective of a just peace, and that in any event an acceptance of the ethos of modernity required that all sovereign states be secular rather than politically enshrining an ethnic or religious identity (see Said 2000; Abunimah 2006; Makdisi 2008). The argument against partition was that it would produce unequal polities given the power and diplomatic disparities between the parties, that it would subject the large Palestinian minority in Israel to permanent second-class citizenship, and that it would never produce a sustainable peace because it was totally unacceptable to those Palestinians who had fled or been forced from their homes and villages in the course of 1947–48 war.

Yasser Arafat was clearly the most dominant leader among the Palestinians, yet even he lacked the full support of the Palestinian people with respect to a peacemaking approach that was premised on the creation of two ethnic states. At best, Arafat's embrace of the Oslo Accords enjoyed fragile political support, as many on the Palestinian side worried that refugee rights would be sacrificed given Arafat's eagerness to achieve statehood or that the Israelis would not in the end agree to a reasonable compromise on the final status issues, given their refusal to abate the settlement process and their formal moves to annex and enlarge Jerusalem in defiance of the UN and international consensus. These worries were reinforced by the power imbalance embedded in the diplomatic process to be followed. Israel was much stronger in negotiating capabilities and circumstances than the Palestinians, and this disparity was greatly reinforced by the United States playing the mediating third-party role despite being an undisguised and unconditional ally of Israel. Indeed, it was an unmistakable sign of Palestinian weakness to have accepted this kind of framework and not to have insisted at least on neutral auspices for further negotiations. Could one even imagine Israel accepting the auspices of the Arab League as the supposed honest broker in the negotiations? Actually, the American relationship was far closer than this reversal of third-party identity, as the United States was a major donor and supplier of weaponry to Israel, as well as its strategic partner in the region, especially since the Israeli victory in the 1967 war.[1]

The historical timing of Oslo also seemed to maximize Israeli bargaining power, as the PLO (and Arafat) had badly miscalculated in backing Saddam Hussein's Iraq in the recently concluded Gulf War, thereby losing major diplomatic and financial support among Gulf countries. Once again the Palestinians found themselves backed against the wall. It seemed like the ideal time for Israel, with American backing, to make an advantageous deal that would allow it to retain many of the gains of its 1967 victory and yet win public approval by backing a diplomatic approach that promised to resolve the conflict through a mutually acceptable negotiated peace agreement.

In the years that followed, those with views hostile to the Oslo Accords gradually darkened the clouds that had always hung over this peace process. From the Israeli point of view, an upsurge of terrorist incidents, including suicide bombings, made it appear as though the Palestinian side was still committed to violent resistance and that Arafat was either insincere in his endorsement of the Oslo approach or could not control the behavior of those in the Palestinian camp who refused to accept the legitimacy of the Israeli state. It was also being reported in the west that Arafat sounded more militant when addressing Arab audiences than when talking at the UN or in international venues, and that he was alleged to be doing less than was possible to control the violent activities of the more radical groups in the Palestinian camp. Such interpretations were relied upon to discredit Arafat and to embolden Israel even to attack his compound and declare him an unfit 'partner' for peace talks.

At least as disillusioning for the Palestinian side was continuing Israeli settlement activity, abetted by an expensive network of settler-only roads, which seemed decisively inconsistent with implementing the five-year timetable for Israeli withdrawal from the Palestinian territory occupied in 1967, as was also the case with respect to various moves in Israeli law involving the further consolidation of control over the whole of Jerusalem. Such mixed signals given the postulates of the Oslo Accords were strongly reinforced by the rising strength of the settler-dominated Likud Party, which resulted in Benjamin Netanyahu's first period as prime minister between 1996 and 1999. Netanyahu had been an opponent of the Oslo Accords from their inception, as well as a proponent of the settlement phenomenon and biblical claims, and this cast further doubt on Israel's commitment to any conception of peace that involved the establishment of a Palestinian state, let alone resolution of the other nonterritorial Palestinian grievances. As with Arafat, suspicions were aroused when Netanyahu within Israel spoke of the West Bank as "Judea and Samaria," a coded complicity with the Greater Israel forces in the country that formed an important part of his political base, while in international settings continuing to profess faith in direct negotiations and refrained from any public repudiation of the Oslo Accords.

This undermining of Oslo was hidden from world public opinion, as neither side wanted to seem to be 'rejectionist' in relation to the two-state solution, a posture that would have angered the United States. It may have been the case that Arafat, up to the end of his life, continued to believe in the attainability of the core Palestinian goal of statehood. It could be argued that such a diminished conception of Palestinian self-determination was the realistic outer limit of what could be achieved given the power disparities, and that such an outcome was far preferable than enduring the torments of occupation and refugee camps for the indefinite future.

In addition, it remains to this day far easier for the international community to continue to uphold the 'peace process' as it was set forth in the Oslo Accords than to acknowledge its breakdown. The United States in particular has continued to act as if this was the only means to resolve the conflict and as if such a course of action is far more politically acceptable than either exerting sufficient pressure on Israel to halt and substantially reverse the settlement process or acknowledging to the world that conditions no longer favored Palestinian self-determination in the form that had been prefigured in UN Security Council Resolution 242 and in subsequent diplomatic commentary. Even if stalled, the Oslo process enabled the west to avoid a direct challenge to Israel without frontally alienating the Arab and Muslim worlds.

The high point of this approach came when Labor was once more briefly in control of the Israeli government, with Ehud Barack as prime minister. The 'last hurrah' of Oslo was the Camp David initiative of Bill Clinton at the very last stage of his presidency in 2000. Barack put forward proposals that were described as "generous" in the west but did not clearly commit Israel to a full withdrawal nor specify what land would be swapped for the territory ceded to Israel so as to enable its incorporation of the so-called settlement blocs. They also did not satisfactorily resolve issues pertaining to refugees, East Jerusalem, or water rights. Some effort was made at the follow-up Taba negotiations to address several of these Palestinian concerns, but such proposals were not put in writing and as reported seemed unlikely to be accepted by the Israeli electorate, which needed to endorse the agreements in a referendum. These negotiations led to one more diplomatic failure, with Arafat and the PLO cruelly blamed by the United States despite having been lured to participate against their political will based on their correct perception that too wide a gap between the minimum demands of the two sides existed to allow negotiations to succeed. The populist Palestinian rejection of the Camp David/Taba outcome resulted in the second Intifada, which seemed as much directed at the leadership of the PLO for allegedly going along with arrangements that so weakened Palestinian claims as it was against Israel and its policies of occupation and expansion.

Oslo beyond Oslo: The Roadmap and the Quartet

What followed was the presidency of George W. Bush in the United States, with Ariel Sharon as prime minister of Israel, and a seeming further strengthening of the relationship between the two countries, especially after the 9/11 attacks. Sharon claimed that Arafat was Israel's Osama bin Laden and that Israeli security tactics against the Palestinians and the Palestinian leader represented counterinsurgency warfare of the same character and as justified as that used by the United States against al-Qaeda. Bush did for the first time clearly indicate that the US conception of a solution to the conflict depended on the establishment of a contiguous Palestinian sovereign state with secure borders and convenient links between Gaza and the West Bank. This result was to be achieved in an incremental process that was named 'the Roadmap' and placed under the auspices of a new framework called 'the Quartet,' consisting of the United States, Russia, the European Union, and the United Nations, which turned out to be a change in form more than in substance. The United States continued to command the diplomatic process associated with all attempts to resume direct negotiations between Israel and the Palestinian Authority (PA).

Again, there were problems with acceptance of such an approach on both sides. Israel set forth fourteen conditions as qualifying its willingness to go along, including its refusal to freeze settlement expansion. There was also no reference made to the protection of Palestinian rights under international law, which seemed to express an intention to resolve the nonterritorial dimensions of the conflict (especially, refugees, the status of Jerusalem, and water resources) by diplomatic bargaining rather than by reference to rights. This implicitly deferred to the power disparities between the parties, which was bad news for the Palestinians (Falk 2005).

In this sense, the Roadmap reproduced two of the worst features of the Oslo Accords as text and as evolving process. It enabled Israel in the course of the occupation to engage in activities unlawful under international humanitarian law, to benefit from the delay in resolving the conflict, and to convert what was clearly unlawful into a new de facto reality that must be taken into account without authorizing challenges prior to the final status negotiations. It also demonstrated an unwillingness to allow the Palestinian side to overcome its disadvantages with respect to diplomatic support and power by acknowledging the relevance of international law and Palestinian rights as relevant to the resolution of final status issues. In effect, the Oslo Accords, as superseded in negotiating contexts by the Roadmap, have worked out to be a formula for the nonrealization of the vision of a sustainable peace between the two sides as projected in general terms by the canonical Resolution 242. The disconnect between text and de facto circumstances is disguised to this day by continuing to espouse the 242 + Oslo + Roadmap approach without any formal reference to Israel's actions, which have undermined such an outcome as a practical political possibility.

Although the format was adapted to a new phase in the process, the Roadmap approach essentially maintained continuity with Oslo, sustaining the disparity between the two sides, which allowed Israel to assemble more and more facts on the ground while the clock of the occupation continued to tick. Time was not neutral. Delay was beneficial for Israeli expansionism and continuously diminished Palestinian hopes and prospects. These facts included the construction of a separation wall mainly on Palestinian territory, appropriating Palestinian land, the demolition of Palestinian homes and olive groves, and the cutting off of many Palestinians from their villages and farmlands in a manner found unlawful in a July 2004 advisory opinion of the International Court of Justice. They also included the elaborate network of settler-only roads that contributed to the growing apartheid structure of the occupation and made it ever clearer that Israel had no intention of ever completely withdrawing from the West Bank in accord with the plain meaning of Resolution 242.

The United States continued to shield Israel from censure and sanctions despite its unlawful activities, which rendered the prospect of a truly sovereign Palestinian state less and less plausible with each passing year, and to dominate the diplomatic interactions of the parties. And, of course, the Palestinians were not entirely passive, with Hamas firing rockets at southern Israeli towns, which, while doing little damage, created fear and anxiety on the Israeli side of the border with Gaza and maintained the sort of tension and climate of violence that was incompatible with a politics of reconciliation. There is much controversy over the interactive timeline of violence, determining which side was the provoker and which the retaliator. Further, from Gaza it was not always clear whether the rockets were being launched with Hamas' approval or by militias that eluded or defied Hamas' control.

The post-1967 occupation continued along the lines set forth in the Oslo Accords, with the territorial administration divided between the PA and Israel. Israel continued to maintain several hundred roadblocks throughout the West Bank, which greatly hampered Palestinian mobility, and to exercise unrestricted authority to use force in the name of its security. In this respect Oslo has led to a partially collaborative relationship on security issues between Israel and the PA, including the training of internal security personnel in those parts of the West Bank under Palestinian control being undertaken with American financial and technical assistance. Especially in light of the conflict between the PA and Hamas, particularly after Hamas took control of the Gaza Strip in mid-2007 after a bloody struggle with Fatah, there has been no unified Palestinian representation for diplomatic initiatives. In the last several years, charges of abuse have been documented associated with both the PA's policies in the West Bank and Hamas' in Gaza toward their respective Palestinian political adversaries. The West Bank and Gaza moved in separate directions, with the West Bank seeking to develop state-like institutions despite the occupation, and Gaza increasingly cut off from the rest of occupied Palestine and enduring a punitive Israeli blockade. Such divisions further weakened Palestinian diplomatic capacity, a process definitely encouraged by Israel and the United States, as expressed by the insistence on treating the elected government of Gaza as a 'terrorist organization' rather than a political actor. This approach was reinforced with a comprehensive blockade on exports and imports initiated in 2007, widely denounced as a flagrant form of collective punishment in direct violation of Article 33 of the Fourth Geneva Convention dealing with belligerent occupation.

In 2004, Bush even went to the extreme of exchanging letters with Sharon, in their capacity as respective heads of state, in which it was agreed that Israel would have American support for the territorial incorporation of its unspecified large settlement blocs. It was an act of unsurpassed arrogance for an American president to purport to determine that settlements established in violation of international humanitarian law could be transferred to Israeli territorial sovereign control without even seeking Palestinian participation in reaching such a conclusion. Such an assertion also seemed to have been a unilateral modification of the reasonable expectations created by the Oslo Accords and reaffirmed by the Roadmap. It is true that in secret negotiations the PA seemed to accept the substance of what Bush had agreed to, but whether this would be acceptable to the Palestinian people seems doubtful (Swisher 2011). At the same time, it was Bush who clearly affirmed for the first time that a peaceful solution to the conflict would result in what was promised to be a viable Palestinian state.

Concluding Remarks

The present situation with respect to peace diplomacy is unacceptable. On the Israeli side is the offer of unconditional direct negotiations, but coupled with an insistence on the absence of preconditions, which is indicative of Israel's unwillingness to suspend, much less halt, the settlement process. On the Palestinian side, as formally represented by the Palestinian Authority and Mahmoud Abbas, is an insistence that such negotiations cannot go forward without an abandonment of settlement expansion, although not unequivocally incorporating in their demand the settlements in East Jerusalem. Both sides do not question the credibility of the peace process of the sort initially foreshadowed in the Oslo Accords but greatly undermined in credibility by several intervening developments: the split on the Palestinian side between Fatah and Hamas; the right-wing, pro-settler consensus governing Israel; and the expansion of the settlements, the construction of the separation wall, and the deepening of the Jewish presence in East Jerusalem. From these perspectives, the Oslo Accords/Roadmap should be pronounced finally as dead ends so far as peace is concerned.

But there are other issues present. Oslo did accord Palestinian self-government in relation to the majority of the Palestinian urban population in the West Bank. By the disengagement move of Israel in 2005, a similar result was achieved for the whole of the Gaza Strip. Despite the tribulations of this altered form of occupation, it has allowed a certain type of normality and autonomy to flourish in both the West Bank and Gaza, which is certainly preferable from the perspective of the Palestinian people to the type of direct military occupation that existed after the 1967 war and which lasted until the partial Israeli withdrawal arranged by way of Oslo. The effects of this post-Oslo arrangement are controversial, with many Palestinians contending that it undermined the will to resist by creating complex networks of quasi-dependence of the Palestinian Authority on Israeli financial and political cooperation and reinforced the disastrous Fatah–Hamas split. From the Palestinian Authority perspective, the road to statehood has been advanced recently by the November 29, 2012, vote in the UN General Assembly to confer on Palestine the status of 'non-member statehood,' an outcome surprisingly supported at the last minute even by Hamas. Such a Palestinian state seems valid under international law, but it is a far cry even from the Resolution 242 image, which is itself a far cry from the Resolution 181 conception. Each iteration of Palestinian statehood has been greatly reduced as compared to its predecessor (Quigley 2011).

At this stage, the sponsors of the Oslo approach, especially the United States and the other members of the Quartet, need either to explain how, in view of intervening developments, the realization of two states for two peoples can be achieved or to acknowledge that the approach is no longer politically attainable and that the pretension that it is has become morally unacceptable.

In many respects, Palestinian resistance hopes have shifted to the context of a legitimacy war, which depends essentially on a soft power global approach. Its current centerpiece is a growing campaign of solidarity, with the Palestinian struggle taking the form of boycott, divestment, and sanctions (BDS). This campaign is loosely modeled on the anti-apartheid campaign that was so effective in bringing a largely peaceful end to the racist regime in South Africa. Perhaps the time has come for civil society and world public opinion to switch its hopes and allegiances away from the Oslo/Roadmap approach and put its efforts solidly behind BDS and the logic of a legitimacy war.

Despite the passage of years, Edward Said's wise words written in 2000 still hold true, and remain as unheeded as ever: "My assumption throughout is that as a Palestinian I believe neither the Arabs nor the Israelis have a real military option, and that the only hope for the future is a decent fair coexistence between the two peoples based upon equality and self-determination" (Said 2000: xii).

Notes

1. It had long been believed that Israel launched a preemptive war in 1967 because of its reasonable apprehension that its Arab neighbors would attack it, which led to widespread support for the Israeli victory. For a convincing refutation of this bit of conventional wisdom regarding the 1967 war, see the well-sourced study by John Quigley (2013).

References

Abunimah, A. 2006. *One Country: A Bold Proposal to End the Israeli-Palestinian Conflict.* New York: Metropolitan Books.

Falk, R. 2005. "International Law and the Peace Process." *Hastings International and Comparative Law Review* 28 (3): 421–47.

Makdisi, S. 2008. *Palestine Inside Out: An Everyday Occupation.* New York: W.W. Norton.

Quigley, J. 2013. *The Six-Day War and Israeli Self-Defense: Questioning the Legal Basis for Preventive War.* Cambridge: Cambridge University Press.

_____. 2011. *The Statehood of Palestine: International Law in the Middle East Conflict.* Cambridge: Cambridge University Press.

Said, E.W. 2000. *The End of the Peace Process: Oslo and After.* New York: Pantheon.

Swisher, C.E., ed. 2011. *The Palestine Papers: The End of the Road.* Chatham: Hesperus Press.

8

A Legal Perspective on Oslo

John V. Whitbeck

The announcement on August 13, 1993, that secret Israeli–Palestinian negotiations, facilitated by the government of Norway, had produced the agreement which, exactly one month later, was signed between the State of Israel and the Palestine Liberation Organization (PLO) as the "Declaration of Principles on Interim Self-Government Arrangements" (the DOP) came as not only a surprise but also a shock to many people.

It should be recalled that the State of Palestine had been proclaimed on November 15, 1988, and rapidly recognized diplomatically by some hundred other states. Furthermore, official Israeli–Palestinian negotiations in Washington, D.C., which had been launched after the Madrid peace conference of October 1991 and in which Palestine was represented by a highly distinguished and competent team of Palestinian negotiators who were assisted by American law professor Francis Boyle and well-known Palestinian lawyers Raja Shehadeh and Anis Kassim, were still ongoing. It was widely reported that the members of the official Palestinian negotiating team were particularly shocked, both about their having been kept in the dark and about the terms to which the secret negotiators had agreed.

I was shocked, too. In an article published in the Washington quarterly journal *Middle East Policy* during the spring of 1993, I had written the following:

While a comprehensive Arab–Israeli peace is the formal goal of the current "peace process", the terms of reference for the Israeli–Palestinian bilateral talks effectively bar the Palestinian negotiators from even talking about peace. They may only discuss a restructuring of the administration of the occupation of the West Bank (excluding Jerusalem) and the Gaza Strip for a further period of at least five years. Unless one believes (or hopes) that Jordan, Lebanon, or Syria will agree to a Camp David-style 'separate peace' leaving the Palestinians out in the cold, one must now recognize that this Likud-imposed strait-jacket on the essential Israeli-Palestinian bilateral talks is preempting and preventing, rather than promoting, genuine progress toward peace . . . .

Accordingly [after an exposition of Palestine's state status under the applicable international law criteria], as a matter of customary international law, if not yet of international power politics or Western public consciousness, the status of the occupied territories today is clear and uncontested. The State of Palestine is sovereign, the State of Israel is the occupying power, and UN Security Council Resolution 242, explicitly premised on "the inadmissibility of the acquisition of territory by war", is the internationally accepted basis for terminating the occupation.

It is also absolutely clear that a territory cannot be 'autonomous' or 'self-governing' under its own sovereignty. Therefore, if the Palestinians were to accept a regime of 'autonomy' or 'self-government,' the ostensible goal of the Israeli–Palestinian bilateral talks, sovereignty would necessarily have to shift elsewhere—presumably to Israel. By agreeing to 'autonomy' or 'self-government,' the Palestinians would be acquiescing, for the first time, in the occupation and would, de jure, be renouncing their existing sovereignty over those portions of mandatory Palestine where they still constitute the overwhelming majority of the population. What could possibly induce them to do so?

In these circumstances, one may reasonably assume that, ever since Madrid, the Palestinians (as well as the Israelis) have been 'faking it' in the 'peace process' negotiations, concerned, above all else, with not being blamed for the inevitable breakdown of those talks when it comes. One may also assume that they will continue to 'fake it' until they, like the Jordanians, Lebanese and Syrians, are permitted to discuss with the Israelis what they want to discuss—*peace*, real peace, and how it could be structured to serve the needs and interests of both peoples. (1993: 63–65)

By agreeing to the terms of the DOP, those who secretly negotiated it made clear that they took Palestine's declaration of independence (still commemorated in occupied Palestine as Independence Day every November 15) less seriously than the other states, already constituting a majority of the world's states and encompassing an even higher percentage of the world's population, which had formally recognized the State of Palestine — indeed, not seriously at all.

The DOP was clearly a leap of faith—and a rather desperate one. Leaps of faith do occasionally produce happy landings, but the odds are against them. In this case, in light of the overwhelming asymmetry of power between Israel and Palestine, the nature of the landing depended almost entirely on the good faith and goodwill of the Israeli side in the negotiations which were to follow the famous handshakes on the White House lawn.

While the DOP in no sense fixed a 'two-state solution' as the agreed endgame of the contemplated five-year 'interim period' and three-year period of negotiations on 'final status,' which were not even to begin until two years into the 'interim period,' the Palestinians (and many others) chose to assume that this must surely be the common goal. Indeed, it may well have been the goal in the hearts and minds of Yair Hirschfeld and Ron Pundak, the Israeli academics who played an important role in initiating the secret talks which led to the DOP. However, once the document was signed, it passed immediately into the hands and effective control of Israeli politicians and generals (including politicians who had previously been generals), who, in the words of Uri Savir, Israel's chief negotiator with the PLO from 1993 to 1996, saw the DOP as "a new instrument for reaching traditional objectives" (Savir 1998: 96).

Those 'traditional objectives' combined the profound Israeli obsession with 'security' and the old Zionist goal of settling the 'Whole Land of Israel,' and the Israeli government rapidly took advantage of the ambiguities, omissions, and injustices incorporated into the DOP and amplified in subsequent implementing agreements to achieve a best-of-all-possible-worlds and cost-free (for Israel) situation in which the settlement project could continue unhindered (indeed, could accelerate and metastasize), in which 'security' in occupied Palestine was subcontracted to Palestinian 'security forces' that protected Israelis (including Israeli settlers) but not Palestinians, in which the costs of providing basic services to the occupied people (a legal obligation of the occupying power) as well as the costs of the Palestinian 'security forces' were miraculously borne by western friends of Israel, and in which any lingering concerns of the 'international community' regarding peace and justice were effectively anesthetized by a perpetual 'peace process' of never-ending negotiations, of which every 'failure' constituted a fresh success for Israel in maintaining this best-of-all-possible-worlds status quo.

It is important to recall that while Israel was represented in the secret negotiations that produced the DOP by Yoel Singer, a highly competent Washington-based lawyer who had been involved in all of Israel's important treaties since Camp David, Palestine had no legal representation whatsoever. I do not believe it to be unfair to characterize the absence of any legal representation on the

Palestinian side as reckless behavior on the part of the DOP's Palestinian negotiators. On every objective and practical ground, Palestine was at a huge negotiating disadvantage. To add to those unavoidable disadvantages the avoidable disadvantage of having an agreement of such fundamental importance to the Palestinian people, which was negotiated, drafted, and executed in the English language, negotiated and finalized exclusively by people with no legal training and for whom English is not a first language was a grave error that should never have been permitted.

My initial personal involvement in post-DOP negotiations involved serving as a legal advisor to the Palestinian negotiating team during the final week of the negotiations in Cairo, which produced the first post-DOP implementing agreement, the Gaza/Jericho Withdrawal Agreement, signed on May 4, 1994.

Until near the end of these negotiations, the only legal advisor taking part on the Palestinian side was an elderly Egyptian diplomat who was not, in fact, a lawyer. Shortly before my arrival, Nabeel Shaath, the future Palestinian foreign minister who was the chief negotiator in this round of negotiations, fortuitously ran across Palestinian-American lawyer Jonathan Kuttab, in Cairo on other business, and asked him to stay and help with the negotiations. Jonathan accepted but told Nabeel that he should also bring in one or more good native-English-speaking lawyers. Nabeel, who had previously invited me to Madrid to contribute ideas for the Palestinian speeches at the 1991 peace conference, called me, and I immediately flew from my Paris home to Cairo.

It was already very late in the negotiating day. In addition, the imbalance of legal talent was again overwhelming, with the Israeli side represented not only by the inevitable Yoel Singer but also by a half-dozen bright, young Jewish-American lawyers. Yoel was 'keeping the master,' the working draft of the future agreement to which the Palestinian side could only propose changes. In any negotiation, whether commercial or diplomatic, 'keeping the master" confers significant practical advantages.

By the time I arrived, the draft agreement already contained various provisions that could have been read as conferring implicit legitimacy on the occupation and as effectively renouncing the state proclaimed in 1988. Any suggestions of Palestinian statehood were rigorously rebuffed by the Israeli side. As proposed provisions passed back and forth, the Palestinian side would always refer to the "Palestinian National Authority" and the Israeli side would always cross out the word "National." The Israeli side was even adamant that postage stamps could not say "Palestine" but must say "the Palestinian Authority," which was a lot to squeeze onto a postage stamp.

To make it even more difficult to 'get to yes' in these negotiations, the Israeli side frequently presented its proposed provisions and revisions on paper headed 'Non-Paper,' a diplomatic term of art meaning that the proposal was not a true "offer" that, if accepted, would be binding on the party presenting it. Nabeel Shaath, who managed to maintain his wit and good humor even in the most frustrating of circumstances, broke new diplomatic ground by frequently presenting the Palestinian side's proposals to the Israelis on paper headed 'Non-Non-Paper.'

To make matters even worse, May 4 was President Hosni Mubarak's birthday and the Egyptian president had made it clear that he expected the agreement to be signed, with appropriate pomp and ceremony, on his birthday. Accordingly, blessed with this firm deadline, the Israeli side only needed to run out the clock, refusing to make any changes to the 'master' it was keeping that did not fully satisfy it. Indeed, the agreement was signed on Mubarak's birthday, in a packed auditorium, albeit only after an extraordinary hour's delay when Yasser Arafat, shocked by certain aspects of a map he was seeing for the first time, walked off the stage and had to be virtually dragged back by Mubarak to affix his initials to the offending map.

The only meaningful contribution to the text that I can recall making was securing the inclusion of Article XXIII(5), which was also included in subsequent post-DOP implementing agreements: "Neither party shall be deemed, by virtue of having entered into this Agreement, to have renounced or waived any of its existing rights, claims, or positions." This 'saving clause' was intended to ensure that the agreement could not, as a legal matter, be read as legitimizing the occupation or renouncing the state. If no 'final status' agreement could be negotiated during the contemplated five-year 'interim period' (extended by the Gaza/Jericho Withdrawal Agreement through May 4, 1999, the fifth anniversary of that agreement), then, as a legal matter, the status quo could—and should—have been restored.

Of course, as a practical matter, this did not happen. After five years a new status quo had developed, with a great many vested interests (notably including jobs, incomes, and, for the top leadership, privileges and an understandable sense of personal importance). Neither the Israeli side nor the Palestinian side, nor the 'international community,' had any incentive to point out that, as a strictly legal matter, the Palestinian Authority—indeed, the Oslo Accords in their entirety—had no basis for continuing to exist. Nonetheless, from a purely legal perspective, it would have been easier between May 4, 1999, when the 'interim period' ended, and January 3, 2013, when, pursuant to a presidential decree, the Palestinian Authority was formally absorbed and replaced by the State of Palestine, for a conscientious international lawyer to write a legal opinion that the State of Palestine existed than it would have been to write a legal opinion that the Palestinian Authority existed.

In addition to the cancerous spread of settlements in occupied Palestine (new settlement building not having been restrained in any way under the terms of the DOP), the collaborationist 'interim arrangements' were—and have continued to be—degrading and humiliating in innumerable ways. While such degradations and humiliations could have been tolerated for five years in the hope that the occupation would then end and true freedom be achieved, had the negotiators of the DOP presented these arrangements to the Palestinian people in 1993 as their people's 'final status' (something the negotiators could surely not have imagined in their worst nightmares), they would have been, quite rightly, lynched by their own people. Yet, these 'interim arrangements' (with those aspects even mildly favorable to the Palestinian people largely ignored by Israel) have, tragically, *become* 'final status.'

It is this catastrophic and claustrophobic cage from which Palestine's 'state status' initiative at the United Nations sought to extricate the Palestinian national movement and the Palestinian people.

In early 2011, the State of Palestine, never formally renounced but effectively consigned to a dark closet by the DOP and its subsequent implementing agreements, was brought out again into the light of day, dusted off, and polished up with a determined and highly successful effort, starting in South America, to add to the number of states extending diplomatic recognition to the State of Palestine. By November 29, 2012, when the State of Palestine was formally accorded 'state status' by the UN General Assembly, the number of states recognizing it had reached 131, more than two-thirds of the 193 UN member states, and these states, which included sixteen of the twenty largest states by population, encompassed well over 80 percent of the world's population.

On the sixty-fifth anniversary of the fateful General Assembly vote to partition Palestine into two states and on the annual International Day of Solidarity with the Palestinian People, the General Assembly voted, by 139 votes to 9, with 41 abstentions and 5 no-shows, to recognize the existence as a state "of the State of Palestine on the Palestinian Territory occupied since 1967." While 16 states that had extended diplomatic recognition to the State of Palestine abstained and 4 failed to vote, 28 states that had not yet recognized the State of Palestine (including Norway) voted yes.

The no votes came from an intriguing 'Gang of Nine': Israel, the United States, Canada, the Czech Republic, the Marshall Islands, Micronesia, Nauru, Palau, and Panama.

The Marshall Islands, Micronesia, and Palau, all former components of the US Trust Territory of the Pacific Islands, are 'freely associated states' of the United States, with US postal codes and 'Compacts of Free Association' that require them to be guided by the United States in their foreign relations. They more closely resemble American territories than genuine sovereign states and snuck into the UN in the flood of new members consequent upon the dissolution of the Soviet Union and Yugoslavia, when the previous standards for admission were effectively ignored.

Nauru, a tiny island of fewer than ten thousand people in the central Pacific, has, since the exhaustion of the phosphate deposits that briefly made it the country with the world's highest per capita income, had virtually no sources of income other than marketing its UN votes (reliably joining the United States in voting against Palestine) and diplomatic recognitions (joining Russia, Nicaragua, and Venezuela in recognizing Abkhazia and South Ossetia) as well as housing, in tents, aspiring illegal immigrants who had been hoping to reach Australia. It is a sad place, an isolated island with no beaches, the world's highest rates of obesity and diabetes, and no real alternative to diplomatic prostitution.

Accordingly, only three states of the slightest significance joined Israel and the United States in voting against Palestine and the 'two-state solution': Canada, the Czech Republic, and Panama. They will have to make their own excuses.

In population terms, those who opposed Palestine's 'state status' represented approximately 5 percent of the world's population, 370 million out of over seven billion. Of those, the United States accounted for 314 million. It follows that countries with less than 1 percent of the world's population supported the United States in this vote. By contrast, eighteen of the twenty most populous states (all except the United States and Germany) voted to support and confirm Palestine's 'state status.'

The European Union vote was fourteen yes, one no, and twelve abstentions. Aside from Germany, the Netherlands, and the United Kingdom, which abstained, all of the old 'western' members voted yes. All ten of the new 'eastern' members (the three Baltic states, formerly part of the Soviet Union, and the six former Warsaw Pact states and Slovenia) abstained or, in one case, voted against Palestine. These 'eastern' states have passed from domination by one empire to domination by another empire without ever daring fully to assert their independence. That said, all except the Czech Republic did at least dare to abstain.

It may take some time for the results of this vote to be fully digested. In the best of all possible worlds, one might hope that the United States would finally recognize that on the issue of Palestine, it is totally divorced and isolated from the moral and ethical conscience of mankind and must now stop blocking progress toward peace with some measure of justice, and step aside and permit other states with a genuine interest in actually achieving peace with some measure of justice to take the lead in helping Israelis and Palestinians to achieve it. (Perhaps the time is now ripe for Norway to resume a major role.)

Since we do not live in the best of all possible worlds, and since Americans persist in believing that they are the 'indispensable' nation, other states will need to make clear to the United States that its shameful vote against Palestine, the 'two-state solution,' and the overwhelming majority of mankind has definitively disqualified it not only from its prior monopoly control over the 'Middle East peace process' but also from any further role in it, and that its further involvement in the preeminent moral issue facing the 'international community' is no longer needed or wanted.

Notwithstanding all the disappointments and daily degradations and humiliations of the Oslo Accords for the Palestinian people, the process that began more than twenty-two years ago with the DOP did permit a governmental and administrative Trojan horse called the Palestinian Authority to be dragged into occupied Palestine and to start building the structures of a state that, until recently, dared not speak its name. The State of Palestine has now emerged from the belly of the Trojan horse, fully equipped to take its rightful place among all other states. The United Nations, with a resounding vote of endorsement and a prolonged standing ovation of support, has certified its existence as a current reality (albeit still under occupation), not simply as a future aspiration.

The State of Palestine is back. Whether its return is too late to make any meaningful difference on the ground remains to be seen but should be known reasonably soon. While a great deal of time has been lost, not all hope has been lost.

References

Savir, U. 1998. *The Process: 1,100 Days that Changed the Middle East*. New York: Random House.

Whitbeck, J.V. 1993. "Confederation Now: A Framework for Middle East Peace." *Middle East Policy* 43 (2): 63–68.

9

The Oslo Accords:
A Common Savior for Israel
and the PLO in Exile?

Petter Bauck

The breakthrough in the negotiations between Israel and the Palestinian leadership-in-exile, ending in the Oslo Accords, or the Declaration of Principles signed on September 13, 1993, is most often explained with the fact that Yasser Arafat supported Iraq's Saddam Hussein during the first Gulf War. As a consequence of this position, a number of Arab states terminated or drastically reduced their support to the Palestine Liberation Organization (PLO) and its main member Fatah. Transfers of money from Palestinians in the Gulf states were also substantially reduced (Bishara 2001: 100). The near bankruptcy of the PLO is used as an explanation for why the Palestinians were forced to engage in dialogue with Israel.

In this essay I intend to explore additional explanations for the negotiations resulting in the Oslo Accords. The dynamics within the Palestinian polity in general and in the Occupied Territories in particular changed dramatically after the Israeli occupation in 1967 and even more with the outbreak of the first Intifada in 1987. My question concerns the extent to which these developments had a substantial impact on the parties, not only the Palestinians but also the Israelis, leading them more actively to engage in dialogue.

I will also look at the possible outcome of these negotiations in relation to these changes in the Palestinian polity, not least for the Palestinian leadership. Its role as a guarantor for the security of Israel rather than the security of the Palestinian people has remained a paradox for the civilian population, victims of indiscriminate shelling and extensive house demolitions. A closer look at the elections of 2006 may broaden our understanding of these dynamics and how they developed in the aftermath of the accords.

An Election Well Overdue

The legislative elections in January 2006 had been well overdue. The Oslo Accords stated that a legislative council should be elected. In January 1996 the first election for the Palestinian Legislative Council (PLC) was organized. The term of the council was four years. Because of the Intifada erupting at the end of September 2000 and growing criticisms of Fatah among the electorate, and given Fatah's absolute majority in the first PLC and control of government, fresh elections had repeatedly been postponed. International pressure for elections grew stronger. After Arafat's death in November 2004 and the election of a new president in January 2005, internal Palestinian pressure for PLC elections, and a new government was reinforced.

A Divided Fatah

The run-up to the PLC elections grew rather traumatic, particularly for the dominant political force among the Palestinians for several decades, Fatah. Attempts to have 'primary elections' within the organization as a part of the nomination process did not succeed countrywide. This is said to be due to results being disputed or alleged raids on local party offices in Gaza, where election materials were stolen or destroyed. Often the Fatah leadership conducted the nomination to the electoral lists.[1]

That Fatah was (and is) divided was known. Before the second Intifada erupted in September 2000, its internal divisions came to the surface. During the Intifada, armed groups operated more or less independently from, and sometimes in contradiction to, the political leadership of the organization. Al-Aqsa Martyrs' Brigades are well known, but several others also emerged, often with links to one of the security organizations established under the Palestinian Authority, in particular Preventive Security.

The divisions within Fatah have a long history, which is also well known. Several analysts and researchers used the expressions 'old guard' and 'young guard' to characterize the two main trends in the organization (Shikaki 2002). Apart from age, these expressions refer to the Fatah leadership returning from exile as part of the Oslo Accords and the Fatah leadership emerging in the Occupied Territories before and during the first Intifada (1987–93).

Emergence of a New Leadership

Several changes of tremendous importance occurred on the Palestinian political scene after the Israeli occupation of the West Bank and Gaza in 1967. In Israel, there was a growing demand for an additional workforce. A short time after the occupation, a fast-growing number of migrant workers from the Occupied Territories entered the construction industry, the agricultural sector, and different service sectors in Israel. What is less known is that partly as a consequence of this migration of workers, soon to number 120,000 Palestinians, Israel managed to divert a substantial number of its own workers to the steadily growing military industry. Researchers point to this migration as decisive for the development of one of the biggest military industries in the world (Reiser 1989: 79).

In the Palestinian territories,[2] this extensive migration of workers led to a substantial number becoming wageworkers. Previously, most of them had been agricultural workers, often day laborers, or unemployed. The economy in Palestinian refugee camps and villages received a boost. A bigger part of the population was step by step relieved of the traditional relations that had remained for generations in Palestinian agricultural society between landowners and agricultural workers. At the same time, Israeli restrictions made the situation for Palestinian entities more difficult (Bouillon 2004: 41).

In 1972, the establishment of Palestinian universities began in the Occupied Territories.[3] In the past the offspring of landowners and others in the upper classes had sought higher education in other Arab countries, Europe, or the United States. Suddenly, youth from villages and refugee camps could follow the same route. A stratum of young people with higher education degrees developed in the Occupied Territories. They had a clearly nationalistic platform with the end of the occupation as a key demand. Within this group, what was to become the leadership and the backbone of the first Intifada emerged. Through its political performance, a new and different elite established a strong status in the population, replacing the traditionally influential families and the political leadership-in-exile (Robinson 1997).

New Challenges for the Occupier and the Palestinian Leadership in Exile

Through the first Intifada, the Palestinian exile leadership in the PLO — an organization dominated by Fatah under the leadership of Yasser Arafat, which moved its headquarters from Amman, Jordan (in 1970), to Beirut, Lebanon, and finally to Tunisia, Tunis (in 1982) — was challenged by a popular uprising opposed to the occupation. The leadership was not directly responsible for the uprising and in the beginning had little control over it. Even if Fatah was the main Palestinian organization in exile and the most important organization behind the Intifada, we can say, as Ghassan Khatib (2010) writes, that the two leaderships developed different views on the way forward and on key priorities. Centrally placed individuals within Fatah who traveled to Tunis during the first Intifada speak of the confusion of the leadership in exile and and the continuous questions then posed as to how the exile leadership should gain control of the uprising.[4]

According to Ghassan Khatib (2010), the leadership-in-exile and the emerging leadership in the Occupied Territories worked in solidarity with each other. He notes, however, that during the first Intifada the two leaderships developed different views on the way forward and key priorities. The exile leadership was focused mainly on recognition, statehood, and their related symbols , whereas the leadership in the Occupied Territories was focused on ending the oppression and exploitation arising from the Israeli occupation (Khatib 2010: 169).

Even if Khatib's assessment of the relationship between the exile and internal leaderships is correct, one could see the shape of a new political expression within the Palestinian polity, with the traditional leadership of the liberation struggle headed by Arafat being challenged from a leadership from within the Occupied Territories.[5] Khatib compares the negotiations in Madrid and Washington, in which Palestinians from the internal leadership participated as part of a Jordanian delegation, to the delegation participating in Oslo, which was recruited from the external leadership. The end of the occupation and all its atrocities competed with the symbols of recognition of the PLO in exile, its financing, and statehood with an authority at its head with all its symbols. According to Khatib, the absence of the exile leadership in Madrid and Washington and the absence of the internal leadership in Oslo "contributed negatively to overall Palestinian negotiating performance" (2010: 101).

The emergence of the new elite in occupied Palestine, which had strong support within the population, had the consequence that the traditional power networks among the landowning families, which often opposed the occupation but at the same time were ready to serve the occupier to safeguard their own interests, lost some of their influence. For any occupier, a relationship with these elite networks directly or indirectly eased their day-to-day administration of a hostile population. Israel, like the British and Ottoman empires, played on these networks, often coopting them into different positions. For Israel, the rise of a new elite meant new challenges regarding how to control the population and secure the availability of cheap labor. For the population, the new leadership in the Occupied Territories represented an alternative more uncompromising in the struggle to end occupation.

Common Strategic Interests?

At the beginning of the first Intifada, Israel has a positive attitude toward the establishment of an Islamic organization — Hamas (an acronym for 'Harakat al-Muqawama al-Islamiya') — in the Occupied Territories. Its hope was that Fatah, as the dominant organization, would be weakened (Robinson 1997: 143). Whether Israel could have aborted the rise of Hamas is doubtful. The movement was inspired by the Muslim Brotherhood in Egypt. However, the importance of Hamas becomes much more visible after the signing of the Oslo Accords, during the years leading to the outbreak of the second Intifada in September 2000 and after (Khatib 2010: 173).

Due to the changed position of Fatah/the PLO-in-exile and the changed position of Israel, it is tempting to ask what role the Oslo Accords played in relation to the new situation described above. The Oslo Accords made it possible for the PLO and Fatah leadership in exile to establish itself as an administration in the Occupied Territories, although with its authority limited by the occupier. This position allowed the leadership to challenge seriously the leadership of the first Intifada. For Israel, the Oslo Accords resulted in a Palestinian elite that would cooperate with it in administering the occupation.

No doubt, Israel and the exile leadership of the Palestinians (the 'old guard'), had joint interests in pushing the new leadership emerging in the Occupied Territories, or the 'young guard,' to the sidelines. The Oslo Accords made this possible.[6] Obviously, it is not only the support Arafat gave to Saddam Hussein during the first Gulf War and the consequent reduced economic support from several Arab countries that forced the Palestinian exile leadership to negotiate in Oslo and sign the Oslo Accords (see Khatib 2010: 90). The Palestinian leadership's own future role in the Occupied Territories was at stake.

Joint Interests and Different Visions

It is often suggested that the Oslo Accords explicitly mention that a Palestinian state is to be established in the territory occupied by Israel in 1967. The reality is quite different. The Oslo Accords are first and foremost a procedure aimed at searching for a settlement on a comprehensive peace agreement, or, as Marwan Bishara writes in his book, *Palestine/Israel: Peace or Apartheid*, it "shows even bigger problems, notably the continuation of overall Israeli control of the territories, and Israel's ability to manipulate the entire process according to its wishes and needs" (2001: 47).

For the Palestinians the vision has been one state within the Green Line with East Jerusalem as its capital. Their goal was clear: the end of occupation.

It soon became obvious that Israeli opinion was divided. Some wanted an agreement based on the 1967 borders, while others used strategic military concerns, security, religion, and history to argue for keeping control of extensive areas of the territory occupied in 1967.[7] Strong forces regarded Jerusalem as the "forever unified capital of Israel," rejecting any Palestinian claim to dividing the city. Palestinians living in East Jerusalem were to experience the Israeli policy of systematically reducing the percentage of Arabs in the area by rejecting the construction of new houses and confiscating Palestinian land. Several also had their residence permits in Jerusalem abolished (Cheshin, Hutman, and Melamed 1999). A widespread view in Israel was that the Palestinian territories should be kept under some kind of control in order to secure a cheap workforce and to corner a huge market for the Israeli consumer industry.[8] Different ideas on autonomy were debated. Israel still refers to the Occupied Territories as "disputed," a position clearly rejected by the International Criminal Court in The Hague in 2004 when it presented its recommendation on the Separation Wall.[9]

An outcome of the Oslo Accords that is more evident in recent years is how the Palestinian Authority, through its security organizations, became a guarantor for Israeli security rather than Palestinian security. After Fatah lost the elections in 2006, Fatah-controlled security organizations received direct training and equipment from the Americans, also to fight Hamas (Thrall 2010; Bishara 2001; Rose 2008).

Lack of Results and Extensive Corruption

The Palestinian leadership's return to the Occupied Territories as a result of the Oslo Accords gave rise to high expectations in the West Bank, in Gaza, and in the many refugee camps in other countries in the region. It was supposed to establish and head the administration of the geographical areas agreed upon with Israel, and to take over from Israel's administration within thematic fields, such as education and health, and in some areas even security. To fine-tune the transfer of responsibilities, the West Bank was divided into A, B, and C territories. The Palestinian Authority would hold responsibility for internal security as well as services in A territories. They would cater for services in the B territories, while Israel remained responsible for security. The C territories remained under Israeli security control with Israel responsible for rendering services also. The Gaza Strip was treated as an A territory from the outset.

It also represented a departure from what the local leaders in Gaza and the West Bank had mobilized people around during the first Intifada. Palestine was to change its status from being occupied to being a sovereign state like other countries in the world. The leadership was to be responsible for social services and securing positive economic development. At the same time, it was to proceed with the negotiations with Israel regarding a comprehensive peace agreement.

Nice words and visions proved more difficult to implement in real life. For the population in the Occupied Territories, the first years after the Oslo Accords were a continuous line of setbacks. New territories, in particular cities and other densely populated areas, came under Palestinian administration, but at the same time freedom of movement and the possibility of traveling internally in the territories and working in Israel were continually reduced. For long periods Gaza was more or less separated from the West Bank as well as the rest of the world. The West Bank became a web of military closures. The road toward a sovereign state seemed paved with unknown obstacles. This led to growing frustration toward the end of the 1990s, both with the Palestinian leadership and with the Israeli occupier. The economic situation did not improve before around year 2000. Problems with exporting agricultural products and the population's total dependency on imports from or through Israel remained an obstacle to development.[10]

During the negotiations leading up to the Oslo Accords and subsequent agreements, the Palestinian leadership received some 'good' advice from its Israeli counterparts, including proposals to establish different governmental monopolies in charge of importing petroleum products, tobacco, flour, and sugar. Histadrut, the Israeli labor organization, it was said, had 'good' experiences with such monopolies. The Palestinians took the advice and put it into practice. Several governmental monopolies were established. The population witnessed how centrally placed cadres in Fatah were put in charge, gaining huge economic benefits. Several are now under investigation.[11] Huge economic values were kept outside the control of governmental bodies, with a concomitant loss in taxes and profits. Only during recent years, partly because of strong pressure from the donor community but also because of critical voices among the Palestinians, have these monopolies been transferred to the Ministry of Finance or to the Palestine Investment Fund (PIF).[12]

Another growing criticism has been key Fatah members' close relations with Israel and the United States. During the first years of the second Intifada, questions were frequently raised concerning the extent to which key demands related to the establishment of a Palestinian state had been sold out. In particular, the demand for the right of return for refugees from 1948 and the demand for Jerusalem as the capital of the new state were of concern.

Election in the Shadow of Oslo

The parliamentary elections in January 2006 were strongly demanded by substantial parts of the Palestinian population and by the international community. Fatah, in control of the Palestinian Authority since its establishment in 1993–94, was the least eager to have elections. It knew that the election would challenge its dominance in Palestinian politics. What it did not know was that its loss to Hamas, its main challenger in the polls, would be so painful. For Hamas, the result was also surprising, and the international community was similarly shocked. A democratic election implemented under occupation, with mainly positive marks from international observers, resulted in a clear majority for an Islamist party. We know too well what followed, with the international economic boycott and political isolation of the initial Hamas government, attempts to form a broad national government to get international recognition,[13] and finally the fallout between Hamas and Fatah in Gaza, resulting in the division of Palestinian territory, with Gaza coming under the control of Hamas and the West Bank under Fatah's control.

Why did the election yield such as result? Some have explained it by way of the electoral system chosen by the Palestinians, with 'winner takes all' as the guiding principle. My question is whether the result should have been so surprising, regardless of the electoral system.

The Palestinian Legislative Council Elections in 2006

Fatah entered the 2006 elections under considerable attack for the lack of results in the progress toward a sovereign state, corruption, and the absence of any improvement in the health of the economy. It was criticized for allowing key officials to enrich themselves through the monopolies it had established and other economic activities. It also entered the election encumbered by internal divisions that had their roots in the years just after the 1967 Israeli occupation, and which reached their peak with the first Intifada.

The run-up to the elections can serve as some indication of the reasons for these attitudes toward Fatah. The PLC has 132 members. Half of them are elected through national lists and the other half through lists for the governorates. When the nominees for the national lists were to be drawn up, the Fatah central leadership to a large extent decided those nominations since primary elections did not take place as planned. The imprisoned Fatah leader Marwan Barghouti was the top nominee. In an open protest against the way in which the national list was composed, Barghouti and other key members of the leadership who emerged during the first Intifada released their own national list — the Future — also with Marwan Barghouti at the top of the list. Just days ahead of the election, the Fatah leadership succeeded in merging the two lists into one, headed by Barghouti (European Union 2006:7).

Regarding the governorate lists, experiences varied. In Rafah, a unified Fatah managed to conduct the nominations. That Fatah lost the municipal council elections in May 2005 to Hamas had been an eye-opener. In other governorates, the established leaderships of Fatah ruled and decided the composition of the lists. Popular leaders from the first Intifada were excluded. In reaction these leaders ran as independent candidates in several governorates (Tuastad 2006). According to the Carnegie Endowment (January 2013) similar experiences were drawn in the 2012 West Bank local election, where "Fatah members suffered defeat in many contests at the hands of breakaway Fatah members running on independent lists."[14]

The Election Results

We have heard it again and again: Hamas won the election! It did. Dissatisfaction with the governing Fatah party, including what was seen by the electorate as Fatah's readiness to compromise on Palestinian demands, was a key issue. Hamas was likely seen by many as less ready to sell out key Palestinian demands. It also had the struggle against corruption as a focal point in its election campaign. What has been less discussed is the possible importance of the split within Fatah.

On the national list, Hamas, under "The Party for Change and Reform," received 44.45 percent of the vote and twenty-nin seats. Fatah received 41.43 percent of the vote and twenty-eight seats. It was a close race. Looking at the governorate lists, we learn that Hamas in total won forty-five seats while Fatah only won seventeen. In Rafah, where Fatah lost to Hamas in the 2005 municipal elections,[15] Fatah managed to unite in support of one governorate list, achieving 53.23 percent of the vote and two out of three seats. In other governorates, Fatah did not manage to reach a unified list and instead had one or several independent candidates in addition. As a result, the official Fatah list received less support. In several governorates, the difference in support for Fatah and Hamas was negligible.[16] If the independent candidates originating from Fatah had joined the official list, the results might have been different. The split in Fatah ahead of the elections probably had a profound influence on the final outcome. Both parties could have come out with less than 50 percent of the seats in the PLC each.

A Challenging Future and Possible Stumbling Blocks

After the 2006 elections, Fatah faced a difficult task in developing an organization with an internal culture that took different trends and interests into account. Compromises still need to be reached. These tasks will not become easier considering how the international community now intervenes directly in Palestinian democratic life, favoring Fatah at the expense of Hamas, even if the latter won a democratic election. It was thought-provoking watching international attempts to get a favored party into office, without any concern for the internal split in Fatah or the fact that Hamas had won a majority of seats in free and fair elections. This would no doubt undermine the democratic trends emerging in Palestinian society post-1993. A unilateral election, such as the one conducted in the West Bank in October 2012, would have limited legitimacy among Palestinians.[17]

The international community's economic and political boycott of the Palestinian administration after Hamas peacefully took office in March 2006 and its focus on channeling any future support through the office of the president have given forces within Fatah the backing to step up the struggle against Hamas. As one Fatah leader in Gaza put it, "We have to build our military strength to show that they cannot do with us as they want."[18] The focus has changed from an urgent need for an internal clean-up within Fatah to the party-based militarization of Palestinian society, resulting in periodic fierce battles between Fatah and Hamas. This focus was strengthened by then US Secretary of State Condoleezza Rice's statements, during her visit to the region in October 2006, to the effect that the boycott against Hamas had been a success and should be continued and that the Palestinian people needed a government that could fulfill the demands of the international community.

President Mahmoud Abbas tried in the aftermath of the elections in 2006 to manage the growing international pressure on Hamas and at the same time force Hamas to adhere to the commitments the PLO had earlier in the Oslo-process accepted. In June 2006 he requested that Hamas adhere to the "Prisoners Document," or the National Reconciliation Document,[19] written by Palestinian prisoners held in Israeli jails, who were variously affiliated with Fatah, Hamas, Islamic Jihad, the Popular Front for the Liberation of Palestine (PFLP), and the Democratic Front for the Liberation of Palestine (DFLP), representing the entire spectrum of Palestinian political expression. Abbas threatened to call for a referendum if Hamas rejected this. The document focused on a Palestinian state within the 1967-borders with Jerusalem as its capital, the right of return of all refugees, and the release of all prisoners. Furthermore it envisaged Hamas and Islamic Jihad eventually becoming members of the PLO.

No agreement was reached on a coalition government and in December 2006 Abbas announced early presidential and legislative elections to end the stalemate between Fatah and Hamas.[20] The announced elections were overtaken by negotiations between Fatah and Hamas in Mecca, ending up in the PLC approving the National Unity Government in 17 March 2007.[21] The Hamas-Fatah Mecca Agreement proved to be short-lived thaw between two rivals. Disagreement over the control of national security forces, including the fact that Hamas in Gaza took control of the former Fatah-controlled security installations in June 2007, caused President Abbas to dissolve the Hamas-led government and declare a state of emergency,[22] indicating his readiness to call for new elections.

A number of attempts to reconcile Fatah and Hamas were launched. Egypt played a vital role in reaching an agreement signed May 4, 2011 in Cairo, outlining a technocratic national government, national elections for the presidency and the legislative council, and elections to the Palestinian National Council (PNC), the PLO-body representing Palestinians in both the Occupied Territories and in the diaspora.[23] PNC elections has been a stated condition for Hamas to join PLO.

Regardless of agreements reached between the two main parties, the progress toward implementation is slow or absent. President Abbas, with his newly won recognition as a nonstate member of the United Nations, is nevertheless walking a tightrope, with one eye to the Prisoners Document, which outlines the red lines of the Palestinian people and is important to the Fatah 'young guard' and for Hamas, and another eye to pressures from Israel, the United States, and others in the international community, which demand the resumption of negotiations for the achievement of a political settlement with Israel.

Ahead of the 2006 elections the message from the international community was clear: "Implement democratic elections." After the election the message changed: "Elect leaders we can accept." What needs to be pointed out is that as a consequence, the internal democratic process in Fatah (and the PLO) has been undermined. A minister in the Fayyad government told me on April 4, 2011 that the main threat to President Abbas and former (from April 2013) Prime Minister Salam Fayyad has not been Hamas but rather internal forces within Fatah. Are we once more going to experience what happened in 1993, when the Oslo Accords sidelined the popular leadership of the first Intifada? As time has passed it is observed that groups within Fatah voice opposition to President Abbas and the government in the West Bank, citing fear of reconciliation with Hamas as well as of the way Fatah used security forces to treat internal opposition. Some also see their economic interests threatened by reconciliation.[24]

Adding the goals outlined by economic circles in Israel—remaining in control of the cheap Palestinian workforce (to the extent that it is allowed to enter Israel) and the huge consumer market for Israeli goods in Palestine—the undermining of the legitimacy of the Palestinian democratic process through elections might have severe implications on the process ahead. Any weakening of the Palestinian struggle for independence will ultimately serve Israeli economic goals. And these economic goals clearly go hand in hand with military, strategic, and religious-historical arguments. The Oslo Accords did away with the Arab boycott of Israel and opened up international markets for the Israeli military and high-tech industries (Bishara 2001: 101).

Irrespective of what one thinks of Hamas and its political program and vision, I am not certain that the developments we have witnessed, in terms of the intervention of the international community in the democratic processes, will prove beneficial to the Palestinians and their struggle for a sovereign state and human dignity. When we add Israeli security as a key concern and responsibility forced upon the Palestinian Authority, the result of the Oslo Accords is an illegitimate Palestinian leadership unable to unite its people in the struggle against occupation.[25]

There's no doubt that national reconciliation between the main political forces in Palestine is urgent if the struggle to end occupation is to gain momentum again. Considering the developments that have taken place after the signing of the Oslo Accords, which have promoted a Palestinian society that is more and more fragmented, geographically as well as politically, it is perhaps time to ask if breaking with the Oslo parameters, the established conditions for a negotiated process between Israel and the PLO, is a necessity if national unity is to be attained. As shown in the essay "Palestinian Identity in the Aftermath of Oslo,"

Palestinians' national identity has been damaged. This is clearly a serious setback for the national project that the Palestinians — and the majority of nations worldwide — wish to realize.

Concluding Remarks

As much as they were a result of the first Gulf War and Arafat's politcal stance before and during that war, the the Oslo Accords negotiations succeeded because they were in the interests of both Israel and the PLO leadership-in-exile. With Arafat back in Palestine, and through the Palestinian Authority, the occupation continued, but with a softer cover of autonomy. The focus on Israeli security has remained a cornerstone of the political process involving Israel, Palestine, and the international community. For Israel, the accords in addition have meant that economic barriers internationally were lifted. This is in grave contrast to the steadily worsening situation for the Palestinian economy. As a result of the accords, the split within Fatah has been aggravated, which likely contributed to Fatah losing the 2006 election to Hamas. National reconciliation within the Palestinian polity continues to elicit nice words that lack substance from politicians. The Oslo 'peace process' and the twenty-two years since have laid the foundation for continued division in Palestine, within political organizations as well as the Palestinian polity. Respect for Palestinian democratic processes and a change in the treatment of Hamas will be needed to strengthen the Palestinians in their struggle for the end of occupation, national sovereignty, and dignity.

Notes

1. For the first time the Fatah leadership, in an attempt to democratize the organization, initiated a broad-based process to nominate candidates for the election, seemingly inspired by elections in the United States. The General Congress of Fatah, the organization's highest body, electing the Central Committee and the Revolutionary Council, has not been called since 1989 (Tuastad 2006).
2. 'The Palestinian territories' refers to the West Bank, East Jerusalem, and the Gaza Strip, territories occupied by Israel in the 1967 war.
3. Since 1967 the following universities have been established in the Occupied Territories: Al-Khalil University in Hebron (1971), Bethlehem University in the West Bank (1973), Bir Zeit University outside Ramallah (1972), An-Najah National University in Nablus (1977), Al Azhar University in Gaza (1991), Al Quds Open University (national) (1991), Al Quds University in al-Quds (1995), Arab-American University in Jenin (1996).

4. This is based on my conversations with Fatah members visiting Tunis during this period. Tveit (2005) also touches upon this issue.
5. Khatib (2010) notes that the Fatah leadership is mostly composed of middle-class professionals educated at Arab universities.
6. Tveit (2005) touches upon these issues several times. Among Norwegians working with the Oslo Channel, such arguments for making an agreement were discussed without focusing too much on them. The issue was discussed with several leaders in Fatah in Gaza in 2005, indicating their consent.
7. Apart from Sternhell (1998), more detailed analysis of different elements of the claims of the land of Eretz Israel is to be found in Alpher (1994). Regarding the Israeli position in the negotiations with the Palestinians, see Horowitz (1975), Na'aman (1986), and Bell (1978).
8. Bouillon (2004) studied the economic forces in Israel, Jordan, and the Occupied Territories and their role in the peace efforts. Regarding Israeli economic interests, he focuses on the desire to end the boycott of Israel internationally, to remain in control of a much-needed cheap workforce, and to keep control of a substantial consumer market. The first concern was solved a short time after the signing of the Oslo Accords. The remaining two relate to continued Israeli control of some kind in the Occupied Territories and over its population.
9. See the official statement of Israel to the International Court of Justice before its verdict on the separation wall in June 2004 and the rejection of key elements included in the court's argument. The court makes it clear that an area is occupied regardless of whether it was previously controlled by a sovereign state. This is also in accordance with several UN resolutions demanding Israeli withdrawal from the Occupied Territories.
10. Not least, the Paris Agreement between Israel and the PLO, signed in 1995, limits the freedom the Palestinian Authority, and private actors in the Occupied Territories have to establish economic cooperation directly and not through Israel.
11. Mohammed Daraghmeh, "Palestinian Attorney General Freezes Accounts of Dozens of Corruption Suspects," *Associated Press*, February 6, 2006. The Palestinian anticorruption organization MADAR has made similar claims.
12. It is important to distinguish between statements on corruption within the myriad monopolies and other economic activities established after the Oslo Accords with different affiliations to institutions established by the Palestinian Authority and statements on corruption related to development funds transferred from the international community. In relation to development funds, the World Bank, International Monetary Fund, and the European Union have undertaken investigations on extensive corruption without revealing the resulting information.
13. Among western countries, only Norway recognized this national unity government, which was in power for a short period in the spring of 2007.
14. See: http://carnegieendowment.org/2013/01/29/talk-of-reconciliation/f6tg

15. Fatah contested the results. Courts ruled in favor of Fatah in a limited number of districts and it was decided that the voting should be redone. This second vote was not been implemented, but it would probably not have changed the result for Rafah as such.

16. Jerusalem was 41.85 percent for Hamas, compared to 36.75 percent for Fatah; Tulkarem 43.52 percent, compared to 39.31 percent; Nablus 44.71 percent, compared to 38.24 percent; Salfit 35.41 percent, compared to 34.35 percent; Ramallah 42.24 percent, compared to 38.80 percent; and Northern Gaza 46.95 percent, compared to 41.41 percent. See Independent Election Commission, http://www.elections.ps/template.aspx?id=290. Fair Vote (2006) has an interesting analysis of the election results, touching upon some of these issues. It shows that in the governorate election in Tulkarem, where Hamas received 27.4 percent of the vote and Fatah 34.4 percent, Hamas won two seats and Fatah none. In Bethlehem, Hamas received 20.5 percent of the vote and Fatah 28 percent. Both won two seats each. In Nablus, Hamas received 38.2 percent of the vote and Fatah 36.5 percent, and Hamas won five seats and Fatah one of the six seats in the PLC.

17. These were municipal elections, which Hamas boycotted. Participation was around 50 percent.

18. Interview with former minister and centrally placed Fatah leader, Gaza City, 18 March 2010.

19. National Reconciliation Document: http://www.mideastweb.org/prisoners_letter.htm

20. The announcement was covered by CNN: http://us.cnn.com/2006/WORLD/meast/12/16/abbas/index.html

21. See: http://www.arabnews.com/node/296042; Norway was the only western country that recognized the Palestinian National Unity Government established after the negotiations in Mecca.

22. See: http://www.foxnews.com/story/0,2933,282195,00.html

23. See: 3P Human Security: http://3phumansecurity.org/site/images/stories/PolicyBriefs/ipcf_palestinian_reconciliation.pdf

24. See: Carnegie Endowment for International Peace: http://carnegieendowment.org/2013/01/29/talk-of-reconciliation/f6tg

25. See: "Assessment of Norwegian Support to Democratization and Strengthened Political Legitimacy in Palestine," Bauck and Skjæveland, Norad Report, June 2016, https://www.norad.no/om-bistand/publikasjon/2016/assessment-of-norwegian-support-to-democratization-and-strengthened-political-legitimacy-in-palestine/

References

Alpher, J. 1994. *Settlements and Borders. Final Status Issues: Israel — Palestinians*. Study no. 3.
Bell, R. 1978. *The Other Case for Defensible Borders*. Jerusalem: Carta.
Bishara, M. 2001. *Palestine/Israel: Peace or Apartheid*. London: Zed Books.

Bouillon, M.E. 2004. *The Peace Business: Money and Power in the Palestine–Israel Conflict.* London: I.B. Tauris.

Cheshin, A.S., B. Hutman, and A. Melamed. 1999. *Separate and Unequal: The Inside Story of Israeli Rule in East Jerusalem.* Cambridge, MA: Harvard University Press.

European Union, Election Observation Mission, *West Bank and Gaza Strip, Palestinian Legislative Council Elections, 25 January 2006* http://eeas.europa.eu/human_rights/election_observation/westbank/legislative/final_report_en.pdf

Fair Vote. 2006. *It's The Election System, Stupid: The Misleading Hamas Majority and the System that Created It.* Takoma Park, MD: Fair Vote.

Horowitz, D. 1975. *Israel's Concept of Defensible Borders.* Jerusalem: Leonard Davis Institute for International Relations.

Khatib, G. 2010. *Palestinian Politics and the Middle East Peace Process.* London: Routledge.

Na'aman, N. 1986. *Borders and Districts in Biblical Historiography: Seven Studies in Biblical Geographic Lists.* Jerusalem: Simor.

Robinson, G.E. 1997. *Building a Palestinian State: The Incomplete Revolution.* Bloomington, IN: Indiana University Press.

Rose, D. 2008. "The Gaza Bombshell." *Vanity Fair,* April.

Shikaki, K. 2002. "Palestinians Divided." *Foreign Affairs* 81 (1): 89–105.

Sternhell, Z. 1999. *The Founding Myths of Israel: Nationalism, Socialism, and the Making of the Jewish State,* translated by David Maisel. Princeton, NJ: Princeton University Press.

Thrall, N. 2010. "Our Man in Palestine." *New York Review of Books,* October 14.

Tuastad, D. 2006. "The Palestinian Election: Will the Victory of Hamas Renew Fatah?" *Palestina* 1.

Tveit, O.K. 2005. *War and Diplomacy: Oslo–Jerusalem 1978–96.* Oslo: Aschehoug.

10

Out of the Ashes of Oslo: The Rise of Islamism and the Fall of Favoritism

Ahmed Yousef

They asked me before the election if I'd honor [the Oslo Accords] .... I said I would, but [that] I'm going to interpret the accords in such a way that would allow me to put an end to this galloping forward to the '67 borders. How did we do it? Nobody said what defined military zones were. Defined military zones are security zones; as far as I'm concerned, the entire Jordan Valley is a defined military zone. Go argue.

—Benjamin Netanyahu[1]

The implementation of the Oslo Accords, or lack thereof, provided the greatest platform for the strengthening of Palestinian opposition groups in the Occupied Territories, at the same time weakening the Palestine Liberation Organization (PLO). Islamism in particular grew rapidly in the years that followed the 1993 signing. Organized political and militant Islamist groups first emerged in the early days of the first Intifada, which began in 1987. It was not until six years later, however, that they overshadowed the PLO in Palestinians' minds as the carriers of the torch of resistance. Thirteen years later that shift in allegiance was evident when Hamas, the Islamic Resistance Movement, won national legislative elections in 2006.

The Roots of Islamism

Palestinian Islamist activism began in the 1940s as a result of Muslim Brotherhood brigades coming from Egypt and Jordan to battle the Zionist militants of the Haganah, Stern, and Irgun. Although Arab guerillas were unable to prevent the establishment of the Israeli state, the Brotherhood's philosophy took root. Active members, however, numbered only in the hundreds by the time the Israelis occupied the West Bank and Gaza Strip from Jordan and Egypt, respectively. The Israelis ignored what they deemed an insignificant group, particularly as the PLO and its predominantly secular nationalist offshoots were causing the greatest disruption. The Brotherhood quietly grew through its social work, establishing charitable associations, mosques, sport clubs, and kindergartens. They followed a principle of 'societal correction' by advocating morality and ethics.

The group focused on education and grassroots aid rather than politics, a policy reflected in the establishment of the Islamic Society in 1973, the Islamic Association in 1976, and the Islamic University in 1978.

Politics, however, was unavoidable given the ongoing tensions. Initially, the Brotherhood's involvement took place largely via unions or multipartisan demonstrations. For example, its members took part in the doctors' strike of 1981. It also sanctioned members to participate in mass rallies denouncing the 1982 massacres in Sabra and Shatila, where Israeli troops enabled summary executions by sectarian Lebanese militants.

The unprecedented carnage in the refugee camps marked a turning point in Islamist strategy. Sheikh Ahmed Yassin, a leading Brotherhood figure, established a military arm named the Palestinian Jihadists in 1982. By 1984, the group had procured and stored large quantities of weapons, and in 1986, Sheikh Ahmed Yassin with Sheikh Salah Shehada established the security body, Magd.

It was not until the end of 1987, however, that the order to begin operations was issued. On December 8, an Israeli truck drove through a group of Palestinians, triggering the first Intifada. Three days later, seven senior leaders of the Muslim Brotherhood convened a council of elders, the outcome of which was the establishment of Hamas. On December 14, Hamas issued its first official communiqué, announcing it was the Muslim Brotherhood's representative in occupied Palestine. The declaration stated that Israeli army violence would be met with equal force, and thus began the first organized Islamist response to Israeli occupation.

The Oslo Accords: A Pyrrhic Victory

The Intifada galvanized global opinion in favor of the Palestinians, or at least in favor of finding a 'peace process' that would last. Numerous secret negotiations began at the 1991 Madrid Conference on Middle East Peace, sponsored by Spain, the United States, and the Soviet Union, and culminated in the Declaration of Principles on Interim Self-Government Arrangements or Declaration of Principles (DOP), commonly known as Oslo I, signed on September 13, 1993 (six months after the United States added Hamas to the State Department's list of foreign terrorist organizations).

The agreement, signed between Israel and the PLO in Washington, D.C., stipulated the establishment of a transitional, autonomous Palestinian body (known later as the Palestinian Authority) to be elected through a legislative council in the West Bank and Gaza. The parties agreed to postpone sensitive issues such as Jerusalem, refugees, settlements, security arrangements, borders, and relations with other neighbors. As per the agreement, the PLO's largest faction, Fatah, recognized Israel and disavowed its charter.

Palestinians were deeply disappointed; yet, initially there was hope among ardent PLO supporters that peace was possible. Although some cosmetic changes took place on the ground, however, there was little tangible evidence that Palestinians would soon be rid of Israeli occupation, let alone have their own state. By Oslo II, held in Taba, Egypt, in 1995, Palestinian opposition groups had began to question the accords more vocally. As the years passed and Oslo spawned more legal accords, such as the Hebron Protocol of 1997 and the Wye River Memorandum of 1998, issues critical to Palestinians were left unaddressed. Internal Palestinian tensions began to grow, with Hamas and Islamic Jihad joining ten other factions in opposing the terms of the Fatah–Israeli agreement.

The Second Uprising: The al-Aqsa Intifada

The PLO's leader, Yasser Arafat, joined US President Bill Clinton and Israeli Prime Minister Ehud Barak at Camp David in 2000, but the 'final status' issues of Jerusalem and the future of Palestinian refugees brought the talks to an impasse. Arafat could no longer placate Palestinian parties with promises of an equitable resolution. On September 28, 2000 mass protests began anew against the occupation, and some allege that Arafat himself encouraged Fatah as well as other opposition groups, including Hamas, to escalate the demonstrations.

The protests lasted five years, slowing after the death of Arafat in 2004. During that time, Hamas proved a formidable force through both its popular support and its armed military wing, the Izzedin Brigades. The result was a significant shift in public sentiment in favor of the Islamist movement.

Municipal Elections: An Islamist Triumph

In 2004 and 2005, Hamas entered the first municipal elections in the Palestinian territories and won a major victory of 65.25 percent of the vote. It also achieved major successes in student union elections. The Israelis disapproved of these developments and a propaganda campaign against the Islamist movement ensued. General Aharon Farkash Raesvi, the head of military intelligence, first coined the phrase 'Hamastan,' which was subsequently used by Israeli leaders in public statements. While Israeli efforts succeeded to some degree in convincing western allies of the dangers of Islamist governance, Palestinian popular support for the movement continued to grow.

Meanwhile, Fatah created droves of 'undecided' voters who increasingly referred to it as the "Party of Authority," a reference to the corruption and nepotism that had grown rampant in its ranks after Oslo. Even well-respected Fatah figures disappointed revolutionary stalwarts by continuing to support a 'peace process' that was perceived to give the Palestinians virtually no gains. Municipal elections are being repeated again in 2016 with much interest from locals as well as the West. Israeli security forces have warned that Hamas could win a majority again in the West Bank.

The Second Legislative Elections: Islamists Take Part

Hamas boycotted the first legislative elections held in 1996, in objection to the PLO's rapprochement with the Israelis, but the group decided to field candidates in the 2006 ballot. Hamas won 74 out of 132 seats, the largest number held by a single group. The victory made it possible for Hamas to form a government, and it imposed a new Palestinian political reality. Negotiating was no longer possible without reference to majority rule, represented by the Islamist party.

The movement asked Palestinian factions to join a government of national unity, but the offer was turned down. Seasoned politicians in Fatah felt Hamas was unlikely to last more than six months. President Mahmoud Abbas simply called on the new government to adhere to the agreements the Palestine Liberation Organization (PLO) had signed with Israel. Hamas formed its government, headed by Prime Minister Ismail Haniyeh, without the participation of opposition factions. Haniyeh delivered a list of his cabinet nominees to President Abbas on March 19, 2006, with little fanfare. The task of governing, however, was nearly impossible given not only the Israeli chokehold on the Occupied Territories but also internal attempts to undermine Hamas' authority, leading Haniyeh at one point to state, "We are in the government but we are not governing."[2]

Tensions continued to mount throughout 2006 between the institutions of the presidency and the government. This was reflected in the disputes over who held constitutional powers known as the "clash of wills." Security chiefs loyal to Fatah refused to deal with Hamas. As a result, Interior Minister Said Seyam established the Executive Force, loyal to the elected government. Random clashes ensued that ultimately led to the expulsion of Fatah officials from Gaza in early 2007. Two separate institutions were established, one to govern the West Bank and the other to govern Gaza.

The International Community's Dilemma

As it became evident that an Islamist authority would not be easily usurped, the Israelis escalated their efforts to isolate it, eventually imposing a mass siege on the entire Gaza Strip. Then Israeli Prime Minister Ehud Olmert declared that Israel would not negotiate with a Palestinian government that included Hamas and sought to persuade the international community to alienate Hamas and force it to renounce its war on the Israeli state.

The Israeli stance was bolstered by US President George Bush's view that Hamas could not be "a partner for peace" as long as it did not recognize Israel.[3] The European position was less dismissive at first, as evidenced by the views of European Commissioner for Foreign Relations Benita Ferrero-Waldner, who expressed a willingness to cooperate with Palestinian authorities as long as they sought to reach their goals in a peaceful manner. She stated, "It's not about political parties; it's rather about human rights, and the rule of law and democratic principles." European Union foreign policy representative Javier Solana somberly declared that the Hamas victory could put the EU in an "entirely new situation." The European Union, however, ultimately joined US ranks and placed Hamas on its list of terrorist organizations.

National Non-Consensus

The western nations' position created further fissures among the Palestinians. While some secular nationalists agreed with the western view, others emphasized the importance of unity. Palestinian prisoners of various parties released a document of reconciliation in early 2006. It resulted in the convening of a national dialogue conference on May 25, 2006. The effort, however, failed and tensions continued. Arab states, including Qatar, attempted to mediate but to no avail. By December 2006, President Abbas had called for new Palestinian Legislative Council elections, but a number of leaders of Palestinian factions in Damascus refused the call and the situation exploded again.

Saudi Arabia ultimately succeeded in bringing the two main parties, Hamas and Fatah, together. The leadership of the two movements signed the Mecca Agreement on February 8, 2007. The terms included ending internal fighting and the formation of a national unity government. Despite great optimism that tensions would be resolved, clashes continued in the weeks that followed the accord.

Hamas ultimately surrounded the headquarters of the Fatah-led preventive security service and, following the expulsion of senior officials, became fully in control of Gaza on June 14, 2007. As a result, Hamas lost some of the popular support it had gained, given that it was seen as attacking an institution of the revolution, Arafat's Fatah. Similarly, however, Fatah lost support in the West Bank, where its cadres were seen as undermining a popularly elected government. The situation did not deter President Abbas, who unconstitutionally, albeit symbolically, sacked the national unity government headed by Prime Minister Ismail Haniyeh and appointed Salam Fayyad as prime minister, who was later replaced by Rami Hamdallah. The result was two governments for a nation without an officially recognized state.

Al-Furqan War: Renewed Resistance while Reconciliation Lingers

Despite the internal schism, Palestinian activists continued to threaten Israel. Egypt played the role of broker between Fatah and Hamas that led to a ceasefire agreement in June 2008 that was intended to last six months. When the period passed, Israel officially stated it had no intentions of attacking Gaza; however, Foreign Minister Tzipi Livni stated from Cairo that "Israel will not allow a Hamas takeover of the Gaza Strip and will change the situation." Thus, on December 27, 2008 the Israelis carried out a preemptive attack on the Gaza Strip, deploying heavy artillery over twenty-two days during what Israel referred to as Operation Cast Lead, and which the Palestinians called al-Furqan War (meaning discernment, or a war to distinguish between good and bad). The human loss was significant, with 1,417 killed and about 5,450 wounded, in addition to major damages inflicted on infrastructure, healthcare facilities, and commercial and residential properties.

Although Fatah officials objected to the Israeli actions, there were no efforts to reconcile with the authorities in Gaza. The internal stand-off was to last an additional two years before President Hosni Mubarak's team presented "the Egyptian paper" to the warring factions in September 2009. Fatah expressed a willingness to sign but Hamas said it needed time to study the paper and asked for modifications. The Egyptian authorities rejected the request, which resulted in a further freeze on reconciliation efforts. Hamas had felt the terms were biased in favor of Abbas and the Fatah movement, given Mubarak's sympathies with the secular nationalists over the Islamist government.

Khaled Meshaal, Hamas' political chief, resumed discussions on the document with Omar Suleiman, Egypt's former chief intelligence officer, in mid-2010. This led to a preliminary Fatah–Hamas meeting in Damascus on November 9, 2010, which was meant to pave the way for concrete discussions in December. These were again delayed, with both parties accusing the other of disrupting efforts at a resolution.

Hamas: Resilient, Resurrected

Despite the continued tensions, the Palestinians agreed to an Egyptian-brokered prisoner exchange announced on October 11, 2011. The deal, locally known as Wafa al-Ahraar, or "loyalty to the free," included a Hamas agreement to release Gilad Shalit, an abducted Israeli soldier, while Israel released 1,027 Palestinians, including some activists sentenced to up to 745 years of imprisonment. The transaction was the largest ever concluded by the Israelis in exchange for a single soldier. Hamas declared a victory and enjoyed a renewed surge in popularity.

Hamas' fortunes were further bolstered by the onset of the Arab Spring in early 2011. Seeing Tunisians and Egyptians challenge their leaders galvanized the Palestinian public to take to the streets and call for a return to national unity. They organized a campaign of demonstrations and marches that began on March 15, 2011, in both the West Bank and the Gaza Strip. These efforts, driven by the youth, pushed both Hamas and Fatah finally to sign a reconciliation accord.

Hamas, whose popularity had waned since 2007, found itself once again hailed by many of its people as a stalwart resistor of the occupation, regardless of the tactics it employed, and yet a pliable force willing to compromise with its internal opponents.

With internal conflict quieted, Hamas focused on trying to alleviate the crippling siege of Gaza. The Israelis, however, were intent on escalating their efforts to topple the group, applying both military tactics, such as Operation Returning Echo, which began in March 2012, and starvation. In fact, the extent to which the Israelis planned the mass famine came to light in October when an Israeli court ordered the publication of a government report on minimum sustenance levels. The report calculated that Gazans needed 2,279 calories per day to stay alive and therefore recommended that Israel allow them the consumption of 1,836 grams of food per person, per day. This report played a significant role in the list of banned goods that would be restricted from the Strip.

The situation became intolerable by the end of the year. Militants, claiming the Israelis had increased attacks on civilians, launched numerous rockets on Israeli targets in what they called Operation Stones of Baked Clay (referring to a Qur'anic verse where stones were thrown on an ostensibly unbeatable enemy). The Israelis unleashed their own war machine in November during Operation Pillar of Defense, resulting in 170 deaths and substantial destruction of residential buildings and government installations. Israeli Interior Minister Eli Yishai is reported to have said, "The goal of the operation is to send Gaza back to the Middle Ages, only then will Israel be calm for the next forty years."[4]

At the end of the operation, however, the Islamists remained firmly entrenched. Hamas had launched an unprecedented number of rockets (approximately 1,500), several of which had reached further into Israeli areas than ever before. The group claimed victory, emphasizing that the Palestinian cause could not prevail from a position of weakness.

Twenty-two years after the signing of Oslo, Hamas has been able not only to survive but also to establish itself as an unshakeable part of the Palestinian political landscape. During these two decades, the Oslo Accords became defined, in Palestinian circles, as a security arrangement designed to favor Israeli interests and not as a peace treaty. It was, perhaps, a well-intentioned starting point, but there were no tangible efforts to grant Palestinians their inalienable right to self-determination, let alone independence. At first, it did provide a platform for Fatah and the Palestinian Authority to claim that they had pushed the cause forward. The Israelis, however, continued to expand settlements, conduct military campaigns, build a separation wall, and control borders and the flow of goods. They even retained control of the issuance of identity papers. As a result, the secular nationalists increasingly lost credibility with the general public, while Hamas stood its ground and provided ongoing social and charitable services.

Oslo's Failure, the Islamists' Gain

In effect, Oslo's failure was the Islamists' gain in three areas. First, as a faction-cum-political party, the movement has built a durable institutional network that allows it to govern political, military, security, economic, and social affairs relatively effectively, given the constraints on Gaza. It has consistently won elections of student councils, trade unions, municipalities, and at the legislative level. These gains were attained in part due to Israeli belligerence and a failure of other factions to fill the vacuum that the occupation and siege had created.

Second, at a national level, the movement's strategy has an elevated stature, not only its own stature but also that of the Palestinian cause's legitimacy. It has reinforced the ideological position that resistance is a necessary facet of the path to independence, particularly as it has demonstrated a deft response to Israeli attempts to choke it into capitulation through lengthy siege.

Finally, internationally, the movement has successfully kept the Palestinian issue at the forefront of regional politics, despite a tumultuous period of global financial devastation and political upheaval. Notwithstanding Israeli efforts at isolation, convoys and official delegations continue to stream into the Strip. In essence, Hamas has combined resistance and governance in an astute manner. Arab, Egyptian, and Turkish efforts increasingly refer to the Palestinian solution as one that must intrinsically include Hamas. Diplomacy, as practiced in Oslo, can no longer be deemed an effective path to peace. While negotiations are inherently more productive than violence, it is clear that the secular solution based on appeasement of one party to the conflict cannot produce a lasting settlement.

Notes

1. "Netanyahu in 2001: 'America Is a Thing You Can Move Very Easily," *Huffington Post*, July 16, 2010, http://www.huffingtonpost.com/2010/07/16/netanyahu-in-2001-america_n_649427.html
2. Ismail Haniyeh in Friday sermon, Gaza City, October 2007.
3. http://english.peopledaily.com.cn/200601/27/eng20060127_238687.html
4. http://www.aljazeera.com/indepth/opinion/2012/11/2012111912538816887.html

11

Hamas in Transition: The Failure of Sanctions

Are Hovdenak

Introduction

Since Hamas' electoral victory in 2006, Palestinian democratization has become heavily dependent on developments within Hamas, including its attitude to democracy, its policies toward Israel, and its international relations. The starting point of this analysis is the observation that Hamas, an acronym for Harakat al-Muqawama al-Islamiya (Islamic Resistance Movement), has undergone a rapid deradicalization process over a relatively short period of time. After having performed as a classical spoiler throughout most of the Palestinian–Israeli peace process during the 1990s (Malka 2005: 42), actively by its military operations against Israeli targets and passively by its boycott of the first Palestinian legislative elections in 1996, Hamas took on a very different role a decade later. Hamas declared, and respected, unilateral ceasefires toward Israel in 2003 and in 2005–2006. It decided to take part in the second elections of the Palestinian Legislative Council (PLC) in 2006, and, following its landslide victory, it took on its parliamentary responsibility by forming a government.

The democratic victory of the Palestinian Islamists took most observers by surprise and represented a major blow to the democratization strategy of the

European Union (EU), which was based on the assumption that the nationalist Fatah party of the Palestine Liberation Organization (PLO) would prevail as the leading political force among the Palestinian people. Among many elements of inconsistency in the EU's policy toward Hamas, the EU had supported Hamas' inclusion in the political process prior to the elections, while it refused to accept the outcome of the people's vote. In contradiction to its declared goal of promoting democratic principles in its European Neighborhood Policy (ENP) vis-à-vis its neighbors, the EU decided to join the rest of the Quartet (the United Nations, the United States, and Russia) in boycotting the Hamas government in order to force it to comply with three demands: recognition of Israel, renunciation of violence, and acceptance of past Israeli–Palestinian agreements.

Although Hamas rejected these demands, it went as far as granting the PLO and the Palestinian Authority (PA) president the mandate to conduct peace negotiations with Israel, accepting the goal of establishing a Palestinian state within the pre-1967 borders of the West Bank and the Gaza Strip, and, finally, agreeing to 'respect' previous agreements (Milton-Edwards 2007). These new signs of political moderation, here used in the sense of willingness to accept compromises at the expense of ideological dogmas and maximalist positions, were not easily reconciled with Hamas' long-held ideological purity, creating internal tensions between radical and moderate factions of the Islamist movement (Amayreh 2007). Rather than engaging in a gradual process of influencing Hamas by rewarding the pragmatic steps that had been taken, the EU decided to stand firm on demanding full compliance with the three principles of the Quartet.

How do the transformation process of Hamas and the international responses to Hamas' electoral success feed into the democratization process in the Palestinian arena? In a protracted conflict such as the Israeli–Palestinian one, the issue of democratization cannot be studied independently from the conflict itself. The 'democratic peace' literature suggests a direct, causal link between the presence of democratic structures and peaceful international relations, emphasizing the type of political system as a principal, explanatory variable for the prevalence of peace (Ray 1998). However, the causality in the relationship between democratic level and peace has been questioned by William Thompson, who argues that the relationship is reciprocal and that the creation of regional 'zones of peace' or 'cooperative niches' usually has "preceded substantial progress in democratization" (1996: 142). For obvious reasons, respect for basic human rights—the right to life, liberty, and security—that are the pillars of democratic rule suffer in the absence of peace. This observation makes it necessary to include the context of violent conflict when analyzing an ongoing democratization process for a people living under the constraints of military occupation.

In the Palestinian case, the domestic political climate and agenda have been completely dominated by the conflict with Israel. Although the question of democratic structures has been a point of dispute within the Palestinian national movement from time to time throughout its history, that topic has largely been overshadowed by the primary goal of national liberation and self-determination. The guerrilla warfare conducted previously by the PLO and its main component, Fatah, and more recently also by Hamas, necessitated a high degree of internal secrecy that clearly suppressed the growth of democratic practice.[1]

Acknowledging the prevalent interrelationship between domestic democratization efforts and external conflict, this chapter discusses the nature of the political transformation process that Hamas has undergone regarding, first, participation in Palestinian national elections and, second, regarding the issue of negotiations and compromise with Israel. Finally, it explores how the massive European and international pressure on Hamas for unconditional concessions toward Israel has affected the internal political dynamics of the movement. The underlying key question is whether the EU's failure to respond positively to the chain of conciliatory steps undertaken by Hamas in effect hampered the transformation process toward political moderation that was set in motion by Hamas' parliamentary participation. In other words, has the confrontational policy of the EU nurtured or quelled the potential for further moderation of Hamas policies?

The following empirical analysis is based largely on interviews conducted by the author with twenty-five Hamas leaders, including PLC members, Political Bureau members, and local leaders. The interviews were conducted in the Occupied Palestinian Territories (OPT), Syria, and Lebanon during March and August–September 2007. By focusing on the perceptions of the interviewees as expressed during interviews, the analysis attempts to bring to the forefront the reasoning behind Hamas' decision-making processes, as viewed and explained from within the organization. The sample of interviewees includes different segments of the Hamas leadership, representing different geographical areas, men and women, and 'hard-liners' and 'moderates,' but it is not claimed that the sample is representative in any statistical sense. Although the chapter focuses on the developments in the OPT, representatives of the Hamas leaders abroad are included, due to the central role of the Political Bureau of Hamas, operating from exile.

Gradual Steps toward Moderation

Hamas was born in 1987 with the first Intifada, the Palestinian uprising against the Israeli occupation of the West Bank and the Gaza Strip. Its creation was a result of a radicalization process within its parent organization, the Palestinian branch of the Muslim Brotherhood, at a time when the mainstream Palestinian nationalist movement, represented by the PLO and Fatah, was engaged in preparations for diplomacy, negotiations, and compromise based on the idea of a two-state solution. Thus, the radicalization process within the Muslim Brotherhood and Hamas happened simultaneously with the opposite trend, a process of deradicalization, within the PLO. With the failure of the PLO to secure, through negotiations, Israeli withdrawal from the OPT and the establishment of a Palestinian state on the liberated part of the land, the Islamist alternative to the PLO gained credibility and legitimacy among the stateless inhabitants of the West Bank and Gaza Strip, leading to the landslide victory of Hamas' electoral list, under the name 'Change and Reform,' in January 2006 (Abu-Amr 2007: 169; Tamimi 2007: 220).

The transformation process in Hamas did not, however, start with its entrance into parliamentary politics in 2006, but can be traced back to the mid-1990s, when Hamas started searching for political accommodation within the status quo of Palestinian society (Roy 2008: 294). The substantial changes the movement has undergone since that time can be observed at the ideological as well as at the behavioral level. At the ideological level, the evolution in the movement's main documents is illuminating. The 1988 Hamas Charter identifies the goal of the movement as "the liberation of Palestine" through the individual duty of jihad, leading to the establishment of an Islamic state "from the river to the sea."[2] The conflict with Israel is framed largely in religious terms, and the land of Palestine is called an Islamic *waqf* (trust), implying that no political leader will ever have authority to relinquish parts of it through peace agreements.[3]

It is noteworthy that the dogmatic and maximalist positions of the charter all disappeared in the Hamas election manifesto of the autumn of 2005. The election program aimed at limited goals, such as "resisting occupation" rather than liberating Palestine and achieving internal "administrative reform" and "combating corruption" within PA institutions rather than imposing Islamic laws.[4]

The moderation evident in Hamas' ideological documents (see Hroub 2006) was accompanied by moderation in behavioral policies along three dimensions. First, with regard to domestic political participation, Hamas developed from boycotting the first presidential and legislative elections in 1996 to participating in the legislative elections in 2006. Although Hamas cited contextual rather than principled reasons for its 1996 boycott (Butenschøn and Vollan 1996: 52–53), its entrance into the institutions of the PA created by the Oslo process was nevertheless a major shift in Hamas' political praxis.

A second dimension of Hamas' deradicalization process concerns the use of violence. Hamas developed the military tool only gradually, as the main focus during the first Intifada from 1987 to 1991 was mass mobilization in demonstrations and strikes in protest against the Israeli occupation, not the use of firearms (Andoni 2001: 212). A process of radicalization can be observed from 1992, reaching a first climax with a series of suicide operations against Israeli civilians from 1994 to 1996 and a second peak from 2001 to 2003, when Hamas' armed wing, the Izzedin al-Qassam Brigades, took a lead in the militarization of the second Intifada on the part of the Palestinians. But from 2003, Hamas leaders actively sought to deescalate the conflict with Israel by declaring, and keeping, unilateral ceasefires (Tamimi 2007: 204, 212).

However, in the domestic arena, the picture was somehow different. While Hamas tried to reduce tensions with Israel, conflict intensified internally between Hamas and Fatah following the former's election victory in January 2006. Although Hamas in the past had repeatedly asserted that it would "not cross the red line to civil war" (Hroub 2002: 56), bloody clashes erupted frequently in Gaza during 2006–2007, ending with a five-day battle and the subsequent military takeover of the entire Gaza Strip by Hamas forces in June 2007. In other words, deradicalization on the Hamas–Israel frontier was accompanied by a radicalization of Hamas' position toward its long-term rival, Fatah.[5]

Finally, a third important dimension is Hamas' attitude to negotiations with Israel. Hamas leaders appear unified behind the tenet that Israel's 'moral legitimacy' as a Jewish state cannot be recognized. However, Hamas leaders have, since the early 1990s, suggested that Hamas would be prepared to accept a *hudna*, an Islamic concept for a long-term truce, as an alternative to a full peace agreement (Tamimi 2007: 158). Following its election victory, Hamas has displayed further flexibility, most notably by accepting the PLO president's mandate to conduct peace negotiations with Israel, as mentioned earlier (Milton-Edwards and Crooke 2004: 45).

The EU has generally failed to respond to these developments within Hamas in a dynamic way that would facilitate further reconciliatory steps on the part of Hamas. Rather, EU policy toward Hamas has evolved within the context of internal differences between member states on the one hand and the challenge of establishing a policy independent from that of the US on the other.[6] From the

late 1990s, European diplomats began to argue that Hamas could not be eliminated by force and should be included in the political process. EU officials
engaged actively with Hamas representatives until 2003, when the EU, at the
height of the second Intifada, classified Hamas as a terrorist organization (International Crisis Group 2006a: 22). Following the local elections in 2005, several
European governments reestablished de facto contacts with elected Hamas officials at the municipal level, but this contact was suspended later the same year.
The frequent shifts in European policy and practice toward Hamas left an impression of ambivalence rather than one of a firm strategy for how to implement the
EU's stated goals in the visionary democratization schemes within the framework
of the 1995 Euro-Mediterranean Partnership (EMP) and the 2003 ENP. In 2004,
the PA and the EU approved an action plan within the ENP framework that
emphasized the goals of "political dialogue and reform" and "building the institutions of an independent, democratic and viable Palestinian State."[7] Several initiatives within these frameworks explicitly call for strengthening engagement with
Islamist organizations (Emerson and Youngs 2007: 5). The contradiction
between declaratory support to the integration of Islamists into the political
sphere and the practice of denying Hamas such a role represents a basic inconsistency in the EU's democracy promotion in the Palestinian case.

Hamas and Democracy

During the course of fieldwork interviews conducted for this study, Hamas leaders consistently emphasized that the movement envisions a pluralistic and democratic society within an Islamic framework. A recurring argument in response to
western pressure for democratization was that political pluralism and respecting
the choice of the people are not a western construct but rather one deeply rooted
in Islamic tradition, implying that building a Palestinian democratic system is not
necessarily a result of political influence from Europe or the US. Mashhour Abdel
Halim, Hamas' leader in the Burj al-Barajneh camp in Beirut, referred to the *shura*
(assembly) system as described in the Qur'an to illustrate that the idea of a people's assembly is not foreign to Islam. He noted, "It is crystal clear according to a
verse in the Holy Qur'an that within the system of *shura* Islamic decision makers
must respect the view of the majority."[8] Furthermore, Abdel Halim explained
that Hamas belongs to a tradition within the Islamic movement that accepts that
there is room for *ijtihad*, that is, interpretation of the Holy Scripture, which is
important for Hamas' appearance as a politically flexible movement with high

capabilities to adapt to rapidly changing circumstances and conditions (see Pace 2008).

In contrast to this harmonious view of Islamic democracy, some secular critics, Palestinian as well as foreign, distrust the sincerity in Islamists' adherence to democratic rules and claim that Hamas would use elections as a vehicle to obtain power and, thereafter, never leave power voluntarily. Ahmad Yousef, the political advisor of Hamas Prime Minister Ismail Haniyeh, dismissed such allegations as unfounded polemics. The basic problem is, according to Yousef, that "unfortunately, nobody is prepared to test the Islamists' intentions to see whether they really will get stuck in power by offering them a fair chance to complete their four-year term in power without external interference."[9] Yousef viewed the international boycott of Hamas as another missed opportunity to let an Islamist party handle the challenge of political power and responsibility.

Hamas members claim to practice democracy internally by applying the Islamic principle of *shura* (consultation) as an important element in its decision-making process. Given the circumstances of occupation and war, which require a certain degree of secrecy and limitation on transparent structures, Hamas actually demonstrates a relatively advanced culture of including the rank and file in policy discussions.

Geographically, the Hamas movement is divided into three sections: Gaza, West Bank, and exile. A fourth branch is the political prisoners currently jailed in Israeli prisons. In addition, there is the military branch, the Izzedin al-Qassam Brigades, which has its own internal structure and leadership. Each section of Hamas is divided into smaller subunits, down to local neighborhood committees led by a political leader with the title of *amir al-mantiqa* (prince of the neighborhood). An anonymous *amir al-mantiqa* in the Zaytun neighborhood of Gaza City explained that important policy questions are being discussed at seminars at the local level and that local and regional leaders communicate opinions expressed within their area further up in the organization. The highest decision-making body is the Majlis al-Shura, which is an elected assembly, while executive powers rest with al-Maktab al-Siyasi, the Political Bureau, with some ten to twenty members.[10] While members claim they have a voice in the movement's policy-making process, they tend to be loyal to the outcome once a decision is taken, as few will publicly voice opposition to official positions. Interestingly, this practice appears to be an Islamic version of the communist doctrine of democratic centralism.[11]

Moreover, the *amir* explained that all PLC candidates on the Change and Reform list were first elected in a three-stage primary election process within

Hamas. From each level, five candidates continued to the next level, until the final list was fixed.

Local Hamas leaders in exile confirmed the practice of organizing local conferences from which policy input is conveyed to the leadership. A Hamas leader in the Burj el-Barajneh camp in Beirut explained that, "usually, for the important decisions, the leaders consult all the local leaders." This practice reflects the traditional, Islamic ideal of rule through consultation and consensus, representing an idealized model for Islamic democracy. Asked about the procedures for registering the opinions expressed at the camp level, he explained,

> We organize big meetings, for instance here in Burj, where members can express their views. For some important issues — such as that of participating in elections and about the Prisoners' Document — there have been questionnaires distributed among local leaders, who will base their answers on the views expressed by the members.[12]

The display of such a level of internal democracy among the Palestinian Islamists makes it timely to raise the issue of who are the driving forces for democratization among the Palestinians. Knowing that the main secular rival, Fatah, has for years resisted internal demands for reforms that would end the autocratic structures that dominate the backbone of the PLO, it is a remarkable paradox that European funds for democratization still target the secular 'liberals' while bypassing Hamas-affiliated civil society organizations.[13]

Consequently, European fear of Islamic influence and the exclusion of Islamists may in reality represent major obstacles to democratic progress.

From Boycott to Participation

Hamas' decision to boycott the 1996 elections was taken after a prolonged internal debate. A range of Hamas leaders, mostly from inside the OPT, considered a tactic of 'opposition from within' the PA. From his prison cell, the late Sheikh Ahmad Yassin wrote a series of letters arguing that Hamas' participation in professional and municipal elections since the early 1990s had set a precedent for participating in PA elections (Milton-Edwards 1999: 163). Despite the apparent ambivalence within the organization, Hamas announced in November 1995 that it would boycott any forthcoming elections for the presidency or the legislative council of the PA (Milton-Edwards 1999: 165).

Hamas leaders consistently separate the question of accepting democratic principles from the issue of under which conditions Hamas should accept to run for elections. They reject the interpretation that Hamas' shift from boycotting the 1996 PLC elections to participating in 2006 represented a change in the movement's attitude toward pluralism and democracy. They cite a range of contextual reasons for their decision to boycott the 1996 elections, including opposition to the peace process, the continued Israeli occupation of the Palestinian territories, and the autocratic rule of Yasser Arafat. Mahmoud Zahar, one of the founding members of Hamas, stated,

> We have never been against elections as a principle. We boycotted the 1996 elections because they were held within the framework of the Oslo Agreement, which we were against because it provided nothing to us Palestinians, and because the administration of the PA apparatus was completely in the hands of Yasser Arafat. He cheated and fabricated results in the 1996 elections.[14]

The deputy leader of the Political Bureau, Musa Abu Marzuq, explained that Hamas refused to participate in the first PLC elections "because we didn't want to provide the Oslo Agreement with any legitimacy at that time" and because Hamas would not give up the right to resisting the occupation.[15]

It is noteworthy, though, that Hamas actually applied a 'light' boycott, which implied refraining from participating but without trying to have the elections canceled. Abu Marzuq claimed that Hamas had no intention of spoiling the election process. "We didn't want to make any obstacles for these elections and we didn't call people to boycott. We simply didn't participate," said Abu Marzuq, who explained this carefully calibrated protest position by a wish on the part of the Hamas leadership to see what the participation of the people would be.

This reasoning was reiterated by Hamas' representative in Lebanon, Osama Hamdan, who said that the policy of boycotting on the one hand and refraining from sabotaging the process on the other rested on Hamas' positive attitude to the principle of elections. In spite of all its shortcomings, Hamdan viewed the 1996 election as a step in the right direction, as preparation for building a democratic system. "If you want to build a political system you have to choose whether you want a dictatorship or a democratic system. Our choice was, from the beginning, the democratic option," said Hamdan.[16]

The leadership also tactically considered the possible negative effects of a boycott on Hamas' public standing. The elections were at the time widely understood as a referendum on the peace process, which had solid backing, according to opinion polls.[17] Abu Marzuq reasoned that "if we called the electorate to refrain from voting and people still voted, it would be interpreted as if they voted against Hamas and, if people stayed away from the ballots, it would appear as a measure of Hamas' strength."[18]

The turning point for Hamas' entrance into the political arena came with a series of meetings hosted by the Egyptian government between the main Palestinian factions in 2004 and early 2005. The talks were held in an atmosphere of historical change following Arafat's death in November 2004 and prior to the announcement of unilateral Israeli withdrawal from the Gaza Strip.[19] The talks in Cairo produced what has been known as the six-point Cairo Declaration of March 2005, which succeeded in having thirteen Palestinian factions endorse a common platform on elections, a ceasefire with Israel, and reforming the PLO. One of the participants, Abu Marzuq, maintained that the agreement was made possible as the newly elected President Mahmoud Abbas realized that any agreement with Israel needed Hamas' acceptance for implementation and that he could not move on the political track without talking to Hamas.[20]

Furthermore, Hamas' successful participation in the municipal elections held in late 2004 and early 2005 boosted the organization's confidence. Hamas won the majority of seats in many of the main cities, both in the West Bank and in the Gaza Strip. Participation in local elections was never a contested issue within Hamas, as municipalities were not part of the institutions created by the Oslo peace process.

According to Ghazi Hamad, a former Hamas government spokesman, the local elections showed "that people were looking for an alternative, due to the corruption and mismanagement among Fatah people. Hamas understood that people wanted them as the alternative."[21] This massive popularity was also felt as a sort of political obligation that Hamas could hardly shirk: "It was the people that pressured Hamas to participate, because they wanted Hamas to be represented and they wanted the elections to reflect the true will of the people."[22]

The entrance of Hamas into municipal elections represented an early opportunity for the EU to reorient its policies and adapt to the reality of Hamas as an important political player. The fact that Hamas throughout 2005 largely kept its commitment to a unilateral ceasefire toward Israel presented the EU with another good reason for normalization of relations. This opportunity was not taken, however, although some contact was established for a brief period between EU governments and Hamas members at the municipal level. On the contrary, the EU, along with the US, renewed its ban on contact with Hamas and its classification of Hamas as a terrorist organization in October 2005 (International Crisis Group 2006a: 23–28).

Finally, the context of the Intifada also played a role in Hamas' desire for entering elections. The uprising broke out following the collapse of the final status negotiations between Israel and the PLO in 2000. Despite the heavy human losses on the Palestinian side during the Intifada, the unilateral withdrawal, or 'disengagement' in Israeli terms, of Israeli troops and settlers from the Gaza Strip, which was carried out in mid-2005, was widely celebrated by the Palestinians as a victory of the resistance in general and of Hamas in particular. The lesson that was repeatedly preached by Hamas leaders was that "what Fatah and the PLO failed to achieve by negotiations, Hamas managed to take by force."[23]

Although Hamas was apparently militarily weakened by the Israeli assassination campaign against dozens of its top and medium-level leaders, the fact that the movement's leaders suffered no less than its rank and file activists provided the movement with a degree of popular sympathy and political legitimacy that probably outweighed any military losses. By running in the 2006 elections, Hamas showed it was prepared to harvest the political fruits of its military resistance at a time when it was most convenient to downplay the military option anyway.

However, the main political argument applied by Hamas to justify entering the institutions of the PA was the interpretation that the Oslo Accords and the peace process were 'dead' and that, thus, electoral participation no longer implied any commitment to the outcome of the failed peace exploration of the 1990s.[24]

Hamas' view that the Oslo Accords were no longer a valid reference was supported by the fact that the stipulated five-year interim period expired already in 1999, and that Israeli Prime Minister Ariel Sharon in 2002 publicly retracted Israel's commitments to the signed agreements with the PLO.[25] The Israeli move facilitated Hamas' claim that the PA institutions were now detached from the Oslo process, paving the way for Hamas' entrance. Furthermore, the apparent conformity in opinion between Hamas and Likud in rejecting the validity of the Oslo Accords displayed one of many unbalanced positions of the EU and the Quartet. While the Sharon government acted decisively on its anti-Oslo stance by violating or ignoring past Israeli–Palestinian agreements without attracting more than rather mild criticism from Europe, the Hamas government was put under sanctions to alter its view on the same agreements.

Hamas' wish to improve its standing in the international society may also have been a factor supporting democratic participation. "We decided to participate in the political game to show the world that we are not a terror organization," said Jamal Iskaik, PLC member in Gaza, hoping that this would "give the international society a chance to understand our conflict through dialogue."[26] Iskaik admitted that international pressure did have an impact on Hamas' moderation:

> We have an Arabic saying that what you take by force you have to return by force, meaning that the occupied land can only be returned from Israel by force. But we have come to be more realistic, as we realized that we could not fight all the great powers. So we decided to be more moderate and to participate in elections to gain at least something.

Other Hamas leaders, however, upheld that the relationship with the rest of the Arab and Islamic world plays a more significant role in Hamas' geopolitical orientation than that of the West.

In sum, the explanations reviewed above regarding a pressing 'need' or 'obligation' for Hamas to enter politics reflect a growing desire within Hamas for political power based on pragmatic considerations of its opportunities within that sphere of Palestinian life.

The Burden of Victory

The process leading up to the 2006 elections constituted just the first phase of the transformation that Hamas was to go through. The second phase, the period following the election victory in January 2006, was even more challenging for the movement. Hamas won 74 out of 132 parliamentary seats and was left with the obligation to form a government.[27] The leadership admitted that it was taken by complete surprise by the victory and that it was not prepared for the scenario of forming a government alone. "When we decided to participate in elections, we considered two options: either to participate in a national unity government or to be a strong opposition; nobody talked about forming the government," claimed Osama Hamdan.[28] The express journey from a guerrilla movement to government went apparently faster than the leadership could handle. Ghazi Hamad described an atmosphere of confusion and tension among the members following the election victory:

> Most Hamas members had, until the elections, considered their movement primarily as a military organization fighting the occupation. But when they woke up one morning and found that Hamas had won the majority of the parliament and was to form the government, everything was changed. Just two days earlier, all the members had been against joining the government; they just wanted to be a big

opposition in the parliament and monitor the politics of the PA. The leadership tried to accommodate this new situation and to convince its members that it was an obligation to move along this track. But inside Hamas it was not easy to spread a culture of political visions because the mindset was always built on resistance and martyrdom.[29]

Hamas tried to relieve the burden of governmental responsibility by inviting Fatah to join a unity government. But Fatah had no interest in coming to Hamas' rescue and refused to accept the humiliating position as the minor party in a Hamas-led coalition (International Crisis Group 2006b: 9).

Eventually, Ismail Haniyeh formed the first Hamas government, which, from the first day, faced formidable challenges at all levels. Not only were the movement's cadres inexperienced in parliamentary and governmental work, but at the domestic level it also faced a fully uncooperative Fatah, which had a hard time accepting its electoral defeat and showed little interest in helping the Islamists to achieve any success whatsoever. This had dramatic implications for the internal security situation, as the Fatah-loyal security forces refused to obey orders from the Hamas interior minister, although the Palestinian Basic Law prescribed a coordinating role on internal security to the Interior Ministry.[30] A key point in this context is that it was the Quartet that initiated a security reform process in the first place as part of the 2003 'roadmap' peace initiative. The goal at that time was to strip Yasser Arafat of his powers by transferring control over the security apparatuses from the president to the government (Hovdenak 2003: 505). However, with Hamas controlling the government in 2006, the EU in fact supported a reversal of the prescribed security reforms in order to prevent the Hamas government from gaining control over the security sector. This maneuver of the EU and the Quartet clearly exacerbated the tension between the Hamas government and the security forces loyal to the Fatah opposition and to President Mahmoud Abbas, opening the stage for the bloody strife that was to develop over the following year, eventually leading to the violent takeover of the Gaza Strip by Hamas-controlled forces in June 2007 (International Crisis Group 2007a: 7–9).

On the economic front, the main obstacle to the Hamas government's functioning normally was the international sanctions applied by the US-led Quartet, which suspended all economic aid and diplomatic contact with the Palestinian government. In addition, Israel continued its practice of withholding taxes on goods imported into the Palestinian territories via Israel, which Israel collects on behalf of the PA (Sayigh 2007: 17–19). The Quartet established alternative channels for its increasing humanitarian aid, donated through nongovernmental organizations, UN organizations, and the President's Office while bypassing the government and the ministries. The boycott thus had a major paralyzing impact on all governmental structures of the PA and it hurt governmental employees, most of whom were Fatah loyalists, whose salaries were not paid for a period (Tocci 2008). The paralysis of Palestinian local industry led to a dramatic shift from development assistance to humanitarian assistance, the latter increasing from 16 percent of all aid in 2005 to 56 percent by late 2006.[31]

It would be safe to say that the boycott had the unintended effect that people lost the chance to judge Hamas from its record in power. Hamas could, and did, blame all its shortcomings on the external hostile environment (Brown 2007). Thus, as an experiment in showing what Hamas could contribute to Palestinian democracy, the output was meager.

The boycott applied by the EU and the rest of the Quartet left the Hamas leadership with a very concrete dilemma. On the one hand, resisting unified international pressure would apparently lead to political isolation, economic recession, and the institutional collapse of PA structures. On the other hand, complying with the Quartet's demands would imply a capitulation on Hamas' most basic ideological doctrines. The movement, which had vested so much political prestige as well as human sacrifice in the struggle to 'save' the Palestinians from what was seen as a disastrous peace process, could obviously not suddenly surrender on its core tenets without risking a serious internal crisis. According to a leading scholar on Hamas, Ali Jarbawi, the leadership of Hamas could probably not have complied with the Quartet's demand of recognizing Israel without causing a full split in the organization.[32]

Consequently, Hamas had to choose between risking the complete disintegration of PA institutions if it rejected the Quartet's demands and a split within Hamas if it accepted these demands. Seen in this light, the choice of the Islamist leadership to preserve the unity of the movement rather than giving in to the Quartet's ultimatum appears fully rational.

Hamas' Approach to Israel

In spite of the fierce criticism that Hamas has voiced against the Quartet's three demands, few Hamas leaders reject them outright on principle. Many Hamas leaders would rather link their opposition to specific Israeli positions or to circumstances that may change in the future. This is another observation of key importance because it implies that Hamas' position is not fixed but may be revised if and when circumstances allow. In the words of Musa Abu Marzuq, "We are against these demands, but we are willing to talk about them. We asked the Americans to mediate, to make a dialogue, not to boycott the Palestinian people."[33]

A main objection frequently raised by Hamas leaders is linked to the lack of reciprocity in the Quartet's approach, as the three demands with which Hamas was pressured to comply were not required from Israel. This point was summed up accurately by Hamas legislator Jamal Saleh from Gaza:

> The international community asks us to stop using violence, but Israel doesn't stop [using violence]; it asks us to recognize the Israeli state, but Israel doesn't recognize our right to a state. It asks us to comply with previous agreements, but Israel violates them every day. We would respect it if the Quartet had asked us both to comply with these demands, but they are demanding it from us, the weaker party, only.[34]

The message to the Quartet is clear: if the great powers took a balanced approach and applied the same measures to Israel as to the Palestinian side, Hamas would likely respond with flexibility on a range of topics.

The most difficult point of the Quartet's demands appears to be the one concerning recognition of Israel, which contradicts the most basic tenet, in Hamas' view, of the State of Israel as a foreign implant on Palestinian soil. Hamas leaders consistently claim that the issue of recognition is not on the table for the time being, while referring to Hamas' official position regarding a *hudna*, a long-term truce, between a Palestinian and an Israeli state as a pragmatic alternative. A *hudna* is, according to the spokesman for the Hamas bloc in the PLC, Saleh Bardawil, "the best and most practical solution for everyone as long as Israel is not ready to recognize our Palestinian state now — and we are not ready to recognize Israel. Then we leave the issue of recognition for the next generation to decide."[35]

Hamas' restrictive approach to the issue of recognition reflects the fact that the movement is not politically ready for such a dramatic, symbolic step. However, there may also be tactical assessments underpinning the position. Ahmed Yousef admitted that he considered the issue of recognition to be a valuable asset for the future:

> This is one of our cards in our hands, and we are not going to give it for free. So we are not addressing this issue now, until the ending of the occupation, then we can talk about what is going to be the future relation between the Israelis and the Palestinians. I know that if I say I recognize Israel it will not lead to anything in return

from Israel . . . . There are certain factors they [the Quartet] have to address before they push Hamas to recognize Israel.[36]

This tactical assessment is important as it reflects a long-term strategy in which Hamas is positioning itself in preparation for any upcoming negotiations. Far from being contradictory to negotiations, such positions may, in fact, be a component in Hamas' preparations. The EU has failed to appreciate and to act on such crucial political signals representing an opening for creative diplomacy. Instead, the EU has pursued its narrow and short-term focus on the issue of immediate formal recognition of Israel.

Hamas leaders claim to have learned a lesson from what is judged as Yasser Arafat's strategic mistake of offering Israel recognition at the outset of peace negotiations. In the words of Mahmoud Zahar, "Arafat's and the PLO's recognition of Israel was not reciprocated by an equivalent Israeli recognition of a Palestinian state or national rights. It was a dirty game, and we are not going to repeat it. When in history did any occupied people recognize its occupiers?"[37] Although such a statement may appear as an expression of militancy, it does not preclude the option of recognition in the future. Rather, it may be interpreted as yet another signal emphasizing that Hamas' flexibility depends on Israeli actions. At this point, Hamas is basically advocating respect for international law and the implementation of UN resolutions.

The Quartet's demand of renouncing violence is also dismissed by Hamas as another fundamentally unbalanced demand. In Hamas' reasoning, the use of violence is, even more than the question of recognition, linked to Israeli policies, pointing to Israeli military operations or to the occupation itself as the two main driving forces behind the resistance. Although Hamas in its ideological documents emphasizes armed resistance as the main tool to liberate Palestine, leaving the impression of an offensive strategy behind its warfare, the military ambitions expressed by its leaders appear far more modest. Hamas officials generally describe the military activities of the Izzedin al-Qassam Brigades as defensive in nature and usually initiated as direct responses to specific Israeli military operations. PLC member Mushir al-Masri claimed that all the big waves of violence from Izzeddin al-Qassam have been set off by Israeli actions:

Remember that the first Palestinian martyr operations, in 1994, were preceded by the Massacre of Baruch Goldstein in Hebron; the attacks in 1996 came after the Israeli assassination of [Hamas operative] Yahiya Ayyash; and the renewed martyr operations from March 2001 came after hundreds of Palestinians were killed in the preceding six months of the second Intifada.[38]

Both actions and statements of Hamas in this regard illustrate the extent to which the pressure of the Israeli occupation is keeping Hamas preoccupied on the military front, while at the same time narrowing the political options at hand for the policy makers in Hamas, including that of pursuing the path of democratization.

Hamas' Receptiveness to External Pressure

Hamas politicians were partly provoked, partly surprised, and certainly disappointed by the European role in the Palestinian democratization experiment. While most Hamas leaders would easily admit that they had no expectations for a balanced policy on the part of the US, they did expect the EU to take a different stance. The deputy prime minister in Haniye's first government, Nasr al-Din al-Sha'er, offered this analysis of the difference in American and European perceptions:

> There are two ways of thinking—the American and the European. The American way is dealing with the Palestinian issue without Hamas; they would like to kick Hamas out of the political picture altogether. But I feel that a lot of Europeans prefer to talk with the whole Palestinian people. And they prefer an agreement to be signed by all Palestinian factions, including Hamas. They see that if there is an agreement without Hamas, it will not work.[39]

The widespread frustration within Hamas about the EU's attitude toward the Palestinian election process in 2006 indicates that the policy of sanctions has backfired and weakened the political stature of the EU in Palestinian eyes. "They defended democracy everywhere, but when democracy brought Hamas to power, they changed their position," complained ex-Refugee Minister Atef Adwan, who believed the Palestinian people understood well that the guilty party for the sanctions was the western world, not Hamas. In addition, Adwan claimed that the boycott was obviously counterproductive: "The aim of the siege is to weaken Hamas and pressure it to withdraw from its positions. Instead, Hamas hardened their stance on many things."[40]

The claim that Hamas will not be changed by coercion is illustrated well by the attitude of Izzat al-Rashaq, who said that "Hamas stood up against this embargo, which did not achieve its goal of changing Hamas."[41] Apparently, it became a point of prestige for the Political Bureau, then based in Damascus, to resist western pressure and the sanctions.

One of the more visible effects of the boycott was that it caused increased internal tension between and within Palestinian groups. Hamas became divided over how to respond to the demands. Fatah was also ambivalent about how to deal with the isolation of Hamas. Hamas blamed Fatah for instigating strikes in the Ministry of Education and the Ministry of Health. "The goal of these strikes was to oust Hamas from the government," claimed Hamas legislator Muna Mansour.[42]

Eventually, Hamas decided to move closer to international demands. There seemed to be a genuine attitude among Hamas legislators and political leaders that Hamas indeed made some historical decisions by signing the National Conciliation Document of the Prisoners[43] in June 2006 and the Mecca Agreement[44] in February 2007.

The Mecca Agreement marked the peak of moderation in the sense of signaling willingness for compromise over its previous positions on the part of Hamas. The leadership expected to be rewarded for its willingness to establish a National Unity Government (NUG) and for its promise to 'respect' previous Israeli–Palestinian agreements — diplomatic steps which had been taken only with the cost of increased internal tension within the movement. Hamas leaders strongly recommended, almost begged, the western world to respond. "Hamas is a flexible movement, responding to international community claims. This should be a good opportunity for the international community to communicate with Hamas," claimed legislator Mushir al-Masri a day after the inauguration of the NUG.[45]

Although the NUG was welcomed as a positive development by European governments, it failed to cause the sanctions to be lifted (see International Crisis Group 2007a). Only non-EU states Norway and Switzerland established diplomatic links with the NUG, a step that was highly appreciated by Hamas. However, according to diplomatic sources, several EU states, including France, were in a process of reassessing their policies and might have recognized the NUG if it had survived longer.[46] Without the materialization of the expected rewards from the compromises reached at Mecca, internal frustration rose within Hamas.

With the sanctions in place, the unity government collapsed within three months amid a bloody showdown in which Hamas overran PA security forces and established full control over the Gaza Strip. Hamas claimed that its military offensive was triggered by secret collaboration between Fatah-loyal security forces and the US preparing to crack down on Hamas.[47] The failure of the

Quartet to reward the achievement of the NUG and the direct US intervention in internal security affairs seems to have contributed directly to the chaos and violence that followed in Gaza.

Hamas' military takeover of Gaza marked the end of democratic and constitutional rule in both the Gaza Strip and the West Bank, cementing the political division between Hamas and Fatah with a territorial division of the OPT.

Within the ranks of Hamas, an atmosphere of bitterness spread following the political breakdown, which they saw as a direct outcome of the boycott of the Quartet. In hindsight, Nasr al-Din al-Sha'er claimed that a historic opportunity was lost when the Quartet failed to appreciate those steps taken by Hamas up to the Mecca Agreement:

> There was a big chance for the whole world, for the Palestinians — and every single person in this region — when Hamas offered the opportunity and authority to President Abbas to go and negotiate with Israel and to give him a security network that never happened before, even for [late President] Arafat. But unfortunately, they spoiled this opportunity.[48]

Nasr al-Din al-Sha'er, Ahmed Yousef, and Ghazi Hamad were all leaders who had invested much of their personal and political capital in convincing the movement to accept the compromises aimed at securing international recognition. When this strategy of moderation failed, the militant forces took the lead on the ground, while the moderates were sidelined. Ghazi Hamad resigned as Hamas spokesman, while political advisor Ahmed Yousef admitted that his influence was radically reduced:

> Yes, my position is weakened. In internal discussions, people tell me that "we followed you for a year and a half, but you failed; we trusted your assurances that the Europeans would change their mind once Hamas forms the unity government and accepts the previous agreements or renounce terrorism." But nothing changed. This weakened my argument, and I am no longer a credible source for any political change.[49]

Illustrative of the apparent fragmentation between moderates and militants in Hamas is the fact that all political leaders interviewed for this study consistently claimed that the military takeover of the Gaza Strip was neither planned nor approved by the top political leadership. This indicates a serious weakening of the whole political leadership in a movement that generally has been considered very disciplined.

One underlying message that can be read out of all these frustrations cited above is increased resentment against the west and against Europe more specifically. This resentment may well lead to the opposite result than the declared goal of compliance with western wishes. Several Hamas leaders expressed the fear that pressure on Hamas would not result in bolstering Fatah and President Abbas but rather in more militant forces than Hamas. In the words of Izzat al-Rashaq, "The Americans have to know that if they don't deal with Hamas today they will have to face al-Qaeda in the future. If you neglect our rights and the west continues to boycott Hamas, I am afraid this ideology will grow in the region."[50] Nasr al-Din al-Sha'ir feared, furthermore, that even Hamas itself would move its policies in that direction as a consequence of western pressure: "I'm afraid that Hamas itself in Gaza, if the whole world makes a lot of pressure, might choose a policy that seems close to that of al-Qaeda, even though they are not really al-Qaeda. But the pressure makes the political person very weak and the militant person very powerful."[51]

Paradoxically, the European strategy aimed at supporting liberal democrats apparently became a liability for those voices in Hamas who tried their best to push the political line in a moderate direction.

Conclusion

The apparent inconsistency between the EU's rhetoric and its actual policies in regard to democracy promotion is, as correctly interpreted by Hamas politicians, a display of European double standards. The counterproductive consequences of this misguided strategy are not limited to the obvious regress in the process of democratization, institution building, and economic development within PA structures. Even more serious is the devastating impact this policy has had on internal Palestinian politics, as it has weakened political moderates within Hamas and strengthened the more militant factions of the movement. It has also fueled the strife between Hamas and Fatah that led to the division of the West Bank and the Gaza Strip into two separate political units, a situation that will paralyze any diplomatic efforts toward renewed final status negotiations. Finally, the EU has seriously discredited itself in the eyes of not only Hamas supporters but also larger segments of the Palestinian public with its misguided policies. The failure of the EU to honor a democratic election in the Arab world seems also to have backfired in the sense that the EU's democracy promotion agenda itself has lost much of its credibility and legitimacy.

At the heart of the EU's democratization failure lies the strategy of demanding that Hamas abandon its militancy toward Israel as a precondition for accepting Hamas as a legitimate actor in Palestinian parliamentary politics. However, the three conditions that the US-led Quartet applied went far beyond a demand for nonviolent behavior and adherence to democratic principles, and had dubious relevance for Hamas' right to fulfill its governmental responsibilities after having received the confidence of the Palestinian electorate. In addition, the demands appeared clearly biased in the sense that Israel was not required to comply correspondingly.

The interviews with Hamas leaders presented in this study document that Hamas presents pragmatic positions on key issues in the domestic field as well as with regard to Palestinian–Israeli negotiations. The EU's strategy of forcing Hamas to accept an ultimatum rather than to encourage gradual steps in the right direction has clearly not succeeded in nurturing the apparent potential for further moderation and compromise on the part of Hamas. The main Palestinian Islamist party has demonstrated that it should not be seen as an obstacle to democratization. To the contrary, any successful democratization as well as peacemaking in Palestine depends on Hamas' contribution as a key political player. The EU's refusal to accept such a role for Hamas has contributed significantly to the failure of the EU's democratization agenda.

Notes

1. For the organizational development of the PLO and Fatah, see Sayigh 1999.
2. For an English translation of the Hamas Charter, see Appendix 2 in Hroub 2006.
3. However, the militant language of the charter, which had little space for political visions, was already, from the first years, contradicted by pragmatic signals from top leaders. For instance, the idea of entering a *hudna* with Israel as an interim solution was brought up by several top Hamas leaders from the early 1990s (see Tamimi 2007).
4. For an English translation of the Hamas election manifesto, see Appendix VI in Tamimi 2007.
5. The tension between Hamas and Fatah loyalists was further exacerbated by the reasserted role of traditional clan allegiances (see International Crisis Group 2007b).
6. FRIDE, "Europe and Palestinian Democracy," 2006, http://www.fride.org/publication/168/europe-and-palestinian-democracy
7. See discussion on the content of the EMP and the ENP in Pace 2009.

8. Interview, Mashhour Abdel Halim, Hamas leader, Burj al-Barajneh Camp, Beirut, September 2007.
9. Interview, Ahmed Yousef, political advisor of Hamas Prime Minister Ismail Haniyeh, Gaza, August 2007.
10. Due to the need for privacy/secrecy, the exact number of members of the Political Bureau is not known. For more on the organizational structure of Hamas, see Mishal and Sela (2006).
11. Inspiration from Leninist organizational structures has influenced several modern Islamist organizations, for instance Hezbollah in Lebanon (see Abu Khalil 1991: 390–403).
12. Interview, Mashhour Abdel Halim.
13. Interviews, Islamic civil society organizations, Gaza, March 2008.
14. Interview, Mahmoud Zahar, foreign minister in Hamas' first government), Gaza, March 2007. However, the international observer delegation to the 1996 elections concluded that "the elections can reasonably be regarded as an accurate expression of the will of the voters on polling day" (Butenschøn and Vollan 1996: 128).
15. Interview, Musa Abu Marzuq, deputy leader of Hamas Political Bureau, Damascus, August 2007.
16. Interview, Osama Hamdan, Hamas representative in Lebanon and member of Hamas Political Bureau, Beirut, September 2007.
17. Of the Palestinians in the Occupied Palestinian Territories, 78 percent supported the peace process, according to a poll in December 1995. See the collection of polls on Palestinian attitudes to the peace process in Jerusalem Media and Communications Center (1998).
18. Interview, Musa Abu Marzuq.
19. The death of Arafat represented, in the words of Osama Hamdan during our interview, "a new chapter and a new era in Palestinian politics."
20. Interview, Musa Abu Marzuq.
21. Interview, Ghazi Hamad, ex-spokesman of the Hamas government, Gaza, August 2007.
22. Interview, Mashhour Abdel Halim.
23. Interview, Ghazi Hamad.
24. Interview, Izzat al-Rashaq, member of Hamas Political Bureau, Damascus, March 2007.
25. In an interview with Israeli newspaper *Ma'ariv* on September 6, 2002, Sharon declared that "Oslo doesn't exist anymore, Camp David doesn't exist, neither does Taba . . . . We will not return to these places." BBC, "Sharon Calls for New Palestinian Security," September 8, 2002.
26. Interview, Jamal Iskaik, Hamas legislator, Gaza, August 2007.
27. Final election results released by the Central Elections Commission Palestine, http://www.elections.ps/template.aspx?id$^1\!/_4$291

28. Interview, Osama Hamdan.
29. Interview, Ghazi Hamad.
30. See the Palestinian Basic Law of 2003, http://muqtafi.birzeit.edu/mainleg/14138.htm
31. S. Erlanger, "Aid to Palestinians Rose Despite an Embargo," *New York Times*, March 21, 2007.
32. Interview, Ali Jarbawi, professor at Birzeit University, Birzeit, March 2007.
33. Interview, Musa Abu Marzuq.
34. Interview, Jamal Saleh, Hamas legislator, Gaza, March 2007.
35. Interview, Salah Al-Bardawil, Hamas legislator and spokesman for the Hamas bloc in the PLC, Gaza, March 2007.
36. Interview, Ahmed Yousef.
37. Interview, Mahmoud Zahar.
38. Interview, Mushir al-Masri, Hamas legislator, Gaza, March 2007.
39. Interview, Nasr al-Din al-Sha'er, deputy prime minister and education minister in Hamas' first government, Nablus, August 2007.
40. Interview, Atef Adwan, minister of refugee affairs in Hamas' first government, Gaza, March 2007.
41. Interview, Izzat al-Rashaq.
42. Interview, Muna Mansour, Hamas legislator, Nablus, March 2007.
43. For an English translation of the National Conciliation Document, see http://www.mideastweb.org/prisoners_letter.htm
44. For an English translation of the Mecca Agreement, see, http://www.jmcc.org/Documentsandmaps.aspx?id=690
45. Interview, Mushir al-Masri.
46. Interview, Norwegian diplomat in the Middle East, September 2007.
47. On the collaboration between PA security forces and the US against Hamas, see, D. Rose, "The Gaza Bombshell," *Vanity Fair*, April 2008.
48. Interview, Nasr al-Din al-Sha'er.
49. Interview, Ahmed Yousef.
50. Interview, Izzat al-Rashaq.
51. Interview, Nasr al-Din al-Sha'er.

References

Abu-Amr, Z. 2007. "Hamas: From Opposition to Rule." In *Where Now for Palestine? The Demise of the Two-State Solution*, edited by H. Jamil, 167–87. London: Zed Books.
Abu Khalil, A. 1991. "Ideology and Practice of Hizballah in Lebanon: Islamization of Leninist Organizational Principles." *Middle Eastern Studies* 27:390–403.
Amayreh, K. 2007. *Hamas and al-Qaida: The Prospects for Radicalization in the Palestinian Occupied Territories*. Beirut: Conflicts Forum.

Andoni, G. 2001. "A Comparative Study of Intifada 1987 and Intifada 2000." In *The New Intifada: Resisting Israel's Apartheid,* edited by C. Roane, 209–18. London: Verso.

Brown, N.J. 2007. *The Peace Process Has No Clothes: The Decay of the Palestinian Authority and the International Response.* Washington, D.C.: Carnegie Endowment for International Peace.

Butenschøn, N. and K. Vollan. 1996. *Interim Democracy: Report on the Palestinian Elections, January 1996.* Oslo: Center for Human Rights.

Emerson, M. and R. Youngs. 2007. *Political Islam and European Foreign Policy: Perspectives from Muslim Democrats of the Mediterranean.* Brussels: Center for European Policy Studies.

Hovdenak, A. 2003. "Middle East: More Need for Traffic Police than Road Maps." *Security Dialogue* 34:503–10.

Hroub, K. 2006. "A 'New Hamas' through Its New Documents." *Journal of Palestine Studies* 35(4): 6–27.

_____. 2002. *Hamas: Political Thought and Practice.* Washington, D.C.: Institute for Palestine Studies.

International Crisis Group. 2007a. *After Gaza.*

_____. 2007b. *Inside Gaza: The Challenge of Clans and Families.*

_____. 2006a. *Enter Hamas: The Challenges of Political Integration.*

_____. 2006b. *Palestinians, Israel and the Quartet: Pulling Back from the Brink.*

Jerusalem Media and Communications Center. 1998. *Palestinian Public Opinion since the Peace Process.*

Malka, H. 2005. "Forcing Choices: Testing the Transformation of Hamas." *Washington Quarterly* 28:37–54.

Milton-Edwards, B. 2007. "Hamas: Victory with Ballots and Bullets." *Global Change, Peace and Security* 19:273–91.

_____. 1999. *Islamic Politics in Palestine.* London: I.B. Tauris.

Milton-Edwards, B. and A. Crooke. 2004. "Elusive Ingredient: Hamas and the Peace Process." *Journal of Palestine Studies* 33:39–52.

Mishal, S. and A. Sela. 2006. *The Palestinian Hamas: Vision, Violence, and Coexistence.* New York: Columbia University Press.

Michelle, M. 2009. "Paradoxes and Contradictions in EU Democracy Promotion in the Mediterranean: The Limits of EU Normative Power." *Democratization* 16 (1): 39–58.

_____. 2008. "A 'Modern' Islamist Democracy? Perceptions of Democratisation in Palestine: The Case of Hamas." Paper presented at the University of Birmingham's Department of Theology and Religion, March 18.

Ray, J.L. 1998. *Democracy and International Conflict: An Evaluation of the Democratic Peace Proposition.* Columbia, SC: University of South Carolina Press.

Roy, S. 2008. *Failing Peace: Gaza and the Palestinian–Israeli Conflict.* London: Pluto Press.

Sayigh, Y. 2007. "Inducing a Failed State in Palestine." *Survival* 49:7–39.

_____. 1999. *Armed Struggle and the Search for State: The Palestinian National*

Movement, 1949–1993. Oxford: Oxford University Press.

Tamimi, A. 2007. *Hamas: Unwritten Chapters*. London: Hurst and Co.

Thompson, W.R. 1996. "Democracy and Peace: Putting the Cart Before the Horse?" *International Organization* 50:141–74.

Tocci, N. 2008. "The International Dimension: Western Policies towards Hamas and Hezbollah." In *Domestic Change and Conflict in the Mediterranean: The Cases of Hamas and Hezbollah*, edited by A. Elshobaki, K. Hroub, D. Pioppi, and N. Tocci. Lisboa: EuroMeSCO.

12

Palestinian Prisoners from Oslo to Annapolis

Sufian Abu Zaida

Introduction

The issue of Palestinian prisoners in Israeli jails is considered one of the most sensitive for the Palestinian people. It is central to all of the different Palestinian organizations, their supporters, and their social and national bases. The issue started with the creation of Israel in 1948 and became a central part of the conflict after the Israeli occupation of Palestinian land in 1967.

Since then, according to statistics provided by the International Committee of the Red Cross (ICRC), which has been tracking the issue of prisoners for decades, the total number of Palestinian prisoners has reached more than 650,000. According to Palestinian estimates, the number has reached more than 800,000.[1] The Palestinian political definition of a prisoner in an Israeli jail, as stated in the Palestinian prisoner law of 2005, is all Palestinian or Arab prisoners arrested by Israel due to their resistance to the Israeli occupation.

Before the signing of the Declaration of Principles (DOP) in Oslo in 1993, the number of Palestinian prisoners in Israeli jails and detention centers was around twelve thousand. When the peace process collapsed after the Camp David II negotiations and after the outbreak of the so-called second Intifada in

September 2000, 1,850 prisoners were left in Israeli jails. Of these, 450 were detained before Oslo and the rest were arrested later.

The reduction in the number of prisoners between the signing of the DOP and the collapse of the peace process in 2000 was due to many reasons: the end of the prison terms of some prisoners, a decrease in the number of arrests after the end of the first Intifada, the continuation of negotiations, and the release of thousands of prisoners as part of confidence-building measures or as a visible part of the benefits of the peace process.

However, the Palestinian approach to the prisoner issue was based on the view that an injustice was being done to those who remained in captivity and their families, especially those who were arrested before the Oslo Accords and who had been identified as 'old prisoners.' Palestinian public opinion was that the negotiators did not give the issue sufficient and appropriate attention in Oslo, given the status of the prisoners among all Palestinians.

Apparently, from the beginning, the Palestinian leadership did not realize the sensitivity of this issue. It dealt with it as one of the important issues to be postponed to final status negotiations, along with issues such as Jerusalem, refugees, borders, and water. The DOP did not include a section on prisoners or even mention the issue in the context of confidence-building measures that should be taken by each party. The Palestinian leadership explained its lack of insistence on the release of all prisoners as an attempt to find a foothold for the Palestine Liberation Organization (PLO), which had been suffering from an economic and political blockade after the first Gulf War (1991).

This was a shock for the prisoners in Israeli jails, particularly those who had been imprisoned for long time, some for more than twenty years. After the agreement was signed and the PLO recognized Israel, and Israel recognized PLO as the legitimate representative of the Palestinian people, staying in jail was meaningless and illogical for the prisoners. This had a negative impact on them and on their families.

This chapter focuses on all aspects of the issue of Palestinian prisoners in Israeli jails in the period between the signing of the DOP and the Annapolis negotiations that stopped in 2008. It also focuses on the Israeli position on this issue and how the state has dealt with it over almost two decades of negotiations, as well as the position of the Palestinian Authority (PA) and the Palestinian negotiators. I discuss how the prisoners have been affected by these negotiations, as well as how the prisoners' cause has impacted Palestinian–Israeli negotiations. The chapter is based on my personal experience as a former prisoner. I spent twelve years in Israeli prisons and was a spokesman for the prisoners for many years.

I was a member of the negotiations committee for prisoners from the negotiations in Eilat and Taba in 1995 until the negotiations in Annapolis in 2008. I am also a former minister for prisoners' and ex-prisoners' affairs in the Palestinian Authority.

Palestinian and Israeli Perspectives on the Prisoner Issue

There has been no agreement on how to define who is a Palestinian prisoner, as the Palestinians and the Israelis disagree on almost all aspects of the prisoner issue. First, there is disagreement on naming, as Palestinians call Palestinian prisoners in Israeli jails prisoners of freedom, or freedom fighters, as they were arrested for those reasons, regardless of the charges against them, their actions, or the time they must spend in jail. The Palestinians consider these prisoners their best sons and the elite of the Palestinian people, who have sacrificed their future, their youth, and their personal freedom for the freedom of their people. Israel, meanwhile, deals with the prisoners as it would with terrorists and saboteurs who have committed security crimes. They are seen as the biggest threat to the security of the state and therefore cannot be dealt with as having political rights. They are judged only from a security perspective.

Second, Palestinians do not distinguish between the prisoners in terms of political affiliation, their place of residence when they were arrested, or why they were arrested. Israel, on the other hand, does not treat the prisoners equally, distinguishing between a prisoner accused of killing Israelis, or wounding or planning to kill Israelis, and other prisoners. Israel also distinguishes between prisoners on the basis of their place of residence. Palestinian prisoners from inside Israel (known as the Arabs of 1948 or Israeli Arabs) are seen as Israeli citizens. Palestinian negotiators have never been allowed to talk about them. Israel also distinguishes between prisoners from Jerusalem and elsewhere because it considers Jerusalem to be under Israeli sovereignty and thus argues that Israeli law applies to these prisoners.

Third, the Palestinian side, especially since the Taba negotiations, has considered the prisoner issue an essential part of the negotiations that should be a central part of any agreement to be signed. The negotiators have made it clear that they will not sign any final agreement before all prisoners are released without discrimination. Israel, on the other side, deals with the issue of prisoners as part of confidence-building measures, especially when there are negotiations or they perceive progress in these negotiations.

Fourth, the Palestinian position is that the issue of prisoners is a political issue primarily linked to the Israeli occupation. In this view, the prisoners have been arrested because of their struggle against the occupation and, according to international law, should be considered prisoners of war and be released, not only as part of confidence-building measures but also as part of the political merit of the peace process. Israel, on the other hand, deals with the prisoners as terrorists who represent a risk to Israeli security. In this view, the Palestinian territories are not occupied but disputed areas. The matter of releasing the prisoners is linked to security considerations rather than the political situation and negotiations.

As will be seen later in this chapter, the dispute over the definition of prisoners and their political and legal position, as well as Israel's distinguishing among them, has overshadowed the peace negotiations for the last two decades. Ironically, the Israeli position has not developed over time but rather regressed. Instead of improving conditions of detention in prisons, Israel has allowed the prisoners' conditions to become worse.

The Israeli Position during Negotiations

In the Oslo negotiations, Israel succeeded in avoiding any mention in the DOP of the release of Palestinian prisoners, even if related to confidence-building measures to be taken by each party. Israel was thus free from any legal obligation. The prisoners' fate was left to Israel's evaluation, made contingent on the progress of the negotiations and, most important, on the security situation prevailing after the agreement.

Both criteria that Israel put forward did not help in achieving substantial progress toward meeting Palestinian ambitions. To the contrary, with the passage of time, the Israeli position became tougher in many respects, as did its procedures for releasing prisoners. The security situation was also used throughout the period of negotiations by Israel as a pretext for not releasing prisoners.

During the negotiations, from Oslo to Annapolis, there was some development in the Israeli position in terms of realizing how important the release of the prisoners was for the Palestinians. The release of prisoners became important for the Palestinian leadership just as it became more complicated and harder. The prisoners' conditions inside Israeli jails became more difficult, especially after the collapse of the peace process at Camp David II.

The Israeli shift in dealing with the issue of prisoners happened in two phases: first, after the victory of the Israeli right in the 1996 elections, which were held after the assassination of then prime minister, Yitzhak Rabin, and which

Netanyahu won, and, second, after the collapse of the peace process at Camp David II, the start of the second Intifada, and the subsequent deterioration of the security, military, and political situation that led Israel to reoccupy the West Bank.

This shift manifested itself in a number of ways. First, before the Oslo Accords, the release of Palestinian prisoners before their sentences came to an end was simple. The Israeli military governor of the area or the military commander of the southern or central region had the authority to release any number of prisoners he wanted without reference to the Israeli government or even the defense minister. After the Oslo Accords, the process became more complicated. The release of any Palestinian prisoner or the number of prisoners needed the approval of the Israeli government and became part of the political bargaining with the Palestinian leadership.

Second, restrictions as a consequence of Israeli classification of prisoners according to their sentences and acts became more complicated. In 1997, the Israeli government introduced the concept of prisoners with "blood on their hands." Before then, according to the Israeli definition, prisoners who had killed or injured Israelis (Jews) were not considered for release. In 1997, the Israeli government decided that a prisoner who had injured or planned to kill any Israeli, whether Jew, Arab, or a collaborator with the occupation, should not be considered for release. This reduced the number of Palestinian prisoners who could be candidates for release in relation to negotiations.

Third, through the negotiation process and with the passage of time, especially after 1996, the Israelis distinguished between prisoners on the basis of their place of residence at the time of arrest. Israel had never discriminated in the past between a prisoner from Gaza, West or East Jerusalem, and Arabs who hold Israeli identity cards. Over time, Israel restricted the release of any prisoner from Jerusalem and Arabs holding an Israeli identity card. The Israelis even refused to speak to the Palestinian negotiators about these prisoners. Israel justified this shift by claiming that they are Israeli citizens and residents of Jerusalem, for whom Israeli law applies.

Fourth, Israel also distinguishes between prisoners based on their organizational affiliation, differentiating those belonging to PLO factions who recognize Oslo and support the peace process from those who belong to organizations opposed to the peace process and who are struggling to make it fail, such as Hamas and Islamic Jihad. In fact, Israel did not release one prisoner from Hamas or Islamic Jihad during the negotiations from 1996, just as they did not release any prisoner from Jerusalem or any Israeli Arab.

Fifth, as a result of pressure from the Israeli right, the Knesset passed a law committing the Israeli government to publishing the names of prisoners to be released at least forty-eight hours beforehand, regardless of whether the release was part of political negotiations or an exchange of prisoners, in order to allow any Israeli to appeal to the Supreme Court to stop the release process. This law has not prevented the release of any prisoner so far, but the goal is to impose more restrictions on the Israeli government.

Sixth, Israeli laws and conditions not only reduce the number of prisoners that could be freed as part of the negotiations, but also include restrictions on prisoners inside Israeli jails as well. In the Knesset, members of the Israeli right have passed laws to deprive prisoners of many privileges and rights, such as education in Israeli universities, television, and regular visits from family members — all measures designed to oppress the prisoners inside Israeli jails.

The Palestinian Position on the Prisoner Issue

During the negotiations in Oslo, the issue of prisoners was not central for the Palestinian negotiators, as the DOP did not include clear text on the release of Palestinian prisoners or even a timetable and identifiable steps for the release process — something the prisoners, their families, and the Palestinian people were expecting.

There is more than one explanation for why the issue of prisoners was not addressed at that time. The most important is that the Palestinian leadership was concerned with reaching a political agreement to save the PLO from political and economic ruin and to end its political isolation. As a result, not only were prisoners not included in these negotiations, but also other important issues, such as settlements. The Palestinian negotiators agreed to postpone negotiations on the final status issues: borders, security, refugees, Jerusalem, and water. Later on, prisoners were added to this list.

This order of priorities was not understood by the prisoners, their families, and the Palestinian public. They agreed that the Palestinian leadership did not act as it should have on the prisoner issue, arguing that it should not have signed any agreement that did not include the release of all prisoners or most of them, with a timetable for the release of the rest.

The shock was hard for the prisoners, especially prisoners from the PLO. They had believed that the signing of the DOP would ensure their release within a short time. They were very happy, hugged each other, handed out candy, and gave away personal items they thought they would no longer need to their prison colleagues. Their families began to prepare to meet their children, especially after receiving assurances from Palestinian leaders that their children would be released soon.

This optimism and joy turned into curses on the Palestinian leadership, which was accused by the prisoners and their families of abandoning them. Although in Israeli jails, the prisoners considered themselves under the custody of the Palestinian leadership, which they felt had not done enough to release them. They could not imagine how Israel could have changed its policy toward the Palestinian leadership, giving them VIP cards, while the prisoners who were ordered by this leadership to resist Israel remained with their status unchanged and no chance of release.

This situation has created a big gap between prisoners who have not been released and their families on the one hand and the Palestinian leadership on the other. The leadership has struggled in the years since to correct its mistake. This became clear when it introduced procedures that reflected a changed attitude among the leaders in general and among the Palestinian negotiators in particular. I will outline the most important of these measures.

First, as a direct consequence of the leadership's previous mistake, the issue of prisoners has been reflected in all negotiations and in every agreement since Oslo, including the Gaza–Jericho agreement in 1994, the Taba agreement in 1995, and the Annapolis negotiations in 2008. This will be elaborated on later.

Second, unlike the Israelis, Palestinian negotiators do not distinguish between the prisoners. They have sought to release them all without exception. Given their greater power, the Israelis have directed all the negotiations and not allowed the Palestinians to impose conditions except for in a few cases; hence the results were also modest, both in terms of the negotiated terms of release and the actual release of prisoners.

Third, with the passage of time, the Palestinian leadership has become more sensitive to the pulse of the Palestinian street, including on the issue of prisoners. As a result, the file of negotiations on the issue was given to former prisoners. Since 1995, the negotiators have been Hisham Abdel Razek, who spent more than twenty years in Israeli jails, Qaddoura Fares, who spent almost twelve years in jail, and myself, who also spent more than twelve years in Israeli prisons.

Fourth, the Palestinian leadership tried to show concern for the prisoner issue by responding to prisoners' demands to form a Ministry of Prisoners' Affairs in 1997 and appointing a minister to monitor all aspects of the issue, including participation in negotiations for their release. The Palestinian Legislative Council has also enacted a law that aims to support those remaining in captivity and to help former prisoners overcome various challenges after their release. What is most important with this law is to provide allowances for prisoners inside prisons that are commensurate with their years in detention and to give priority to former prisoners in who have been reintegrated into society.

Fifth, the Palestinian leadership has committed itself to not signing a final peace agreement without a comprehensive and complete release of all prisoners from Israeli jails without discrimination. It has also indicated readiness to resume the negotiation process after the release of prisoners, especially old prisoners who were arrested before the signing of the DOP. After the Shalit deal, these were about a hundred and thirty-five in number.

Sixth, through the various stages of negotiations, the leadership has been able to achieve some breakthroughs in relation to prisoners that Israel considers have "blood on their hands," such as the release of Salim Alzeriei, who spent more than twenty years in Israeli jails and was released in 1994, Khalil al-Raee, who was released following the Taba negotiations after spending nearly twenty-three years in jail, Ahmed Jabara (Abu al-Sukar), who was released in 2003 after spending twenty-seven years in Israeli jails, and Saeed al-Ataba, released in 2008 after spending more than thirty years in jail.

Seventh, due to the sensitivity of the issue of female Palestinian prisoners, the Palestinian negotiators were able to secure the release of all of them without exception in 1997 as part of the Taba agreement. At that time they numbered thirty-one. Among them were female prisoners accused of killing Israelis, such as Lamia Marouf, who holds Brazilian citizenship and has since emigrated to Brazil.

The Prisoner Issue in the Gaza-Jericho Negotiations

After ignoring the prisoner issue in the Oslo negotiations, the Palestinian leadership, at least from the Palestinian public's perspective, started gradually to show interest in it from the Cairo agreement in 1994 until the negotiations in Annapolis in 2008. This was despite the fact that Israel released nearly two thousand prisoners from the West Bank and Gaza in 1994, the vast majority of them with only days or months left in their sentences. This was not considered a positive step by the Palestinians but a move to mock them.

The agreements that followed included clear text on the release of prisoners, but this was not sufficient to compel Israel to implement an unconditional release of all prisoners. This happened despite the fact that talk about prisoners was an essential part of any negotiation. No longer could any Palestinian official talk about the peace process or sign any agreement without mentioning the issue of prisoners.

Thus, with the Cairo agreement (Gaza-Jericho), Israel released about 4,450 prisoners. Five hundred and fifty were released to Jericho city. Nearly three hundred and fifty were criminal prisoners. The Israeli government did not release the agreed-upon number. Israeli officials explained the reason to be that hundreds of prisoners refused to sign a pledge document stating that a prisoner will not return to the practice of 'terrorism' or hostilities.

The Prisoner Issue in the Taba Agreement

In the Taba negotiations, the prisoners were considered one of the fundamental issues for the Palestinians. The result was substantial achievements, as can be seen from the text of the signed agreement. Most notable was the agreement to release of all female prisoners in Israeli jails without discrimination, implemented after a delay of one and a half years.

When the Taba agreement was signed, the number of Palestinian prisoners was about six thousand. Article 16 of the agreement, on confidence-building measures, states, "Israel will release or transfer to the Palestinian side detainees and prisoners from the West Bank and the Gaza Strip; the first stage will release prisoners and detainees when we sign this agreement, and the second stage will be ahead of the election day, and there will be a third stage of the release of detainees and prisoners."

The agreement included details about prisoner categories, and the most important thing was the release all female Palestinian prisoners, as well as sick and elderly prisoners and those who had served two-thirds of their sentence or spent more than ten years in captivity. Israel was reluctant to release a number of female prisoners accused of killing Israelis. Ezer Weizman, the head of the Israeli state at the time, did not approve their release. The reaction was that the female prisoners refused to be released individually. As a result, their release was delayed until the signing of the Hebron Protocol on January 17, 1997. This protocol did not mention prisoners, focusing on the redeployment in Hebron, but it was launched with the release of all thirty-one female prisoners.

The Prisoner Issue in the Wye River Negotiations

Contrary to the Taba agreement, the Wye River the negotiations resulted in a memorandum that was considered a real setback. It did not discuss the issue of prisoners: it simply mentioned that Israel should release three hundred prisoners in three phases with American warranty.

The memorandum did not include any written text regarding the release of Palestinian prisoners in general. Instead it just mentioned that Israel should release 750 Palestinian prisoners in three stages over three months, with 250 prisoners each month, with American warranty.

Indeed, on November 20, 1998, the Israelis released 250 prisoners, including 94 political prisoners with low or medium sentences who were coming to the end of their prison terms, as well as 156 criminal prisoners.

The Palestinians believed that the Israeli government went back on its promises twice, first when it released criminal prisoners who were not supposed to be part of the agreement and second when it did not release the next two rounds of prisoners. They felt that Israel had insulted the Palestinian people and returned to the lack of seriousness experienced with the Netanyahu government.

The prisoners in Israeli jails declared a hunger strike. The Palestinian public expressed its anger in different ways and not only accused Israel of stalling the process but also the Palestinian leadership of deceit, as it did not include in the negotiations any member of the negotiating committee for prisoners.

The Prisoner Issue in the Sharm al-Sheikh Agreement

Because of the harm inflicted on Palestinian prisoners through the Wye River negotiations and the frustration dominating the prisoners, their families, and the Palestinians, the Palestinian leadership focused on the need to release old prisoners during the Sharm al-Sheikh negotiations. It agreed in detail on prisoners' characteristics and number. The agreement stated that the Israeli government would release Palestinian prisoners who had committed violations of laws before September 13, 1993, and who were arrested before May 4, 1994. The two sides formed a joint committee to follow up on the release of Palestinian prisoners and agreed on the names of the prisoners to be released in the first and second stages.

Israel committed itself as part of this agreement and released hundreds of prisoners, but it did not release all those who were in jail before the DOP. About 135 prisoners were left in jail after the signing of the Shalit deal between Israel and Hamas in October 2010, a deal considering the most important Palestinian demands.

The Prisoner Issue after the Collapse of the Peace Process at Camp David

Following the collapse of the peace process at Camp David in 2000 and the outbreak of the second Intifada after Ariel Sharon entered al-Aqsa Mosque in September of that year, and until the resumption of negotiations between the Palestinian and Israeli sides in 2008, there was no serious negotiation between the parties on prisoners or any other issue.

Attempts to revive the negotiations did not stop. There were many initiatives and plans, with the most important being the launch of the roadmap. During this phase, there were several releases of Palestinian prisoners, but all came under the pretext of strengthening trust and an expression of goodwill by Israel. The number of prisoners released between 2000 and 2008 is about 2,100, the vast majority near the end of their sentences or who had served at least two-thirds of their sentence.

Concluding Remarks

More than twenty-two years after the signing of the DOP in Oslo, the matter of prisoners is still considered one of the central issues in any future negotiation. The official Palestinian position has become to give attention to the release of prisoners and to insist that no political agreement is acceptable to the Palestinians without including full and complete release without any discrimination of all Palestinian prisoners in Israeli jails, especially old prisoners who were arrested before the signing of the DOP.

Despite all of Israel's postponements and delays, despite the fact that Israel has only been dealing with this issue as a part of confidence-building measures and expressions of good intentions, and despite the fact that the Palestinian leadership was late in becoming aware of this issue, since the signing of the DOP more than 12,000 Palestinian prisoners have been released. The total number of remaining prisoners today is 4,500 nearly all arrested after the signing of the DOP. There are only 135 old prisoners. The Palestinian leadership insists on the release of them all without exception before it can resume negotiations with Israel.

Notes

1. http://www.addameer.org/arabic.php; http://www.freedom.ps/

13

Some Gaza Impressions, Over Two Decades after Oslo

Mohammed Omer

We are entering a third decade since the Oslo Accords and the sole responsibility for the Palestinian people has supposedly shifted from the Israeli occupation forces to the Palestinian Authority (PA), which now is tasked with the functions of healthcare, education, civil administration, and all the accounting, economical processes of the Palestinian population in both the Gaza Strip and the West Bank.

A forty-two-year-old Palestinian nurse working for the PA walks into a supermarket in Tal al-Hawwa, Gaza City. He has been waiting two months for his monthly pay and has just received half of it. Now he has to find a way to budget the money, feed his family, and buy basic necessities. He does not blame the PA for not being able to deliver the wages of 130,000 public service employees; rather he blames what he calls the "shameful Oslo Accords" as he picks out a bag of macaroni, tomato sauce, and washing detergent. "It is Oslo which forces Palestinians to depend on Israel — our jailer — to channel aid to the PA's budget, after we've paid our taxes to Israel," he says.

The accords provided for the creation of a Palestinian interim government represented by the PA, which would be responsible for administrating the land.

The Oslo Accords called for withdrawal of the Israeli administration from both West Bank and Gaza.

"We would be better off without Oslo—just to leave it to occupying Israel to take care of the captive Palestinian population," says the nurse. He is unaware that the anniversary of the Oslo Accords is entering a third decade, but like many other shoppers in the supermarket he agrees that Oslo imposed more complications and restrictions on Palestinian life, whether deliberately or accidentally.[1]

Who Is to Blame?

Abu Wissam Mahdi, a former trade union employee, says the culprits are the original architects of the agreement, Palestinian and Israeli, and the international community thereafter, which refused or neglected to intervene to "stop the intimidation and punishment of the Palestinian people as a whole civilian body."

When the Oslo Accords were first published, Abu Wissam was asked to translate some of its articles. As he says, "if the general principles of Oslo agreement were followed, we would have had a viable, contiguous Palestinian state ten to fifteen years ago. But Israel refused to commit with honor, to the agreement, and the international community didn't challenge Israel, so the Oslo agreement collapsed." He goes on to list all the violations by the Israeli occupation forces. "The only recognizable element left from Oslo is the title of the 'Palestinian Authority,'" he adds.

Abu Wissam is convinced that Israel is not, and never has been, sincerely interested in mutual, equitable peace or establishing a Palestinian state with pre-1967 borders side by side with the Israeli state originally assigned by the partition plan.

When the Oslo Accords were signed, Abu Wissam, like many others, was among those who cheered for it. But he has long lost hope, or trust, in the Oslo plan. "Look at this cell phone SMS I am receiving," he says, holding his cell phone, "It says the PA is offering to pay half the wages owed to Palestinian taxpaying public servants. It is disgraceful that Oslo brought us to such a low level—where we have to wait for Israel to channel our own, earned salary to us, like charity."

He compares Israel to the United Nations Relief and Works Agency for Palestine Refugees in the Near East (UNRWA), calling them both just channels of basic support to refugees. Whether through UNRWA or the PA via Israel, the aim is to channel just enough rations to survive on, but not enough to develop, thrive, or prosper.

Withholding such human rights is tantamount to contrived attrition and collective punishment, or, as Israeli officials call the plan, "a diet." These actions have not received international recognition as blatant war crimes against a captive civilian population.

Future of Negotiations

As to where the future is headed, it remains to be seen whether all negotiations are doomed to absolute failure by Israeli conditions, caveats, and loopholes, especially now, after Israel's latest wars in 2014, 2012, and 2008–2009, which left more Palestinians believing in armed resistance against Israel's occupation and illegal intimidation.

Abu Wissam does not seem to view negotiations as a solution either, noting that "any broker or negotiator who is weak will gain nothing." It is very apparent that most Palestinians believe negotiations have failed, because there was never an impartial broker willing to exercise rule-of-law power over Israel's breach of international laws or to hold Israel accountable to international laws, conventions, statutes, treaties, or United Nations General Assembly expectations.

Abu Wissam says there is only one option: "Through popular resistance, Palestinians will have our voice heard and get our human rights back." Abu Wissam is one of the many who believe that Palestinian President Mahmoud Abbas, also known as Abu Mazen, "needs an honest, strong and impartial power beside him to broker a viable, contiguous Palestinian state."

The majority of Palestinians in Gaza blame the failure of negotiations not only on Israel but also on Palestinian leaders. Abu Wissam concurs with this majority opinion. For him, "Palestinian leaders are preoccupied with their own personal or political interests."[2]

Blame also lies with the United States government, which blocks every possibility of mutual peace through its bias toward Israel. In addition, it lies with pressure, and criticism, from Israeli lobbyists every time the US tries to take a step toward mutual peace based on international laws, as with the example of freezing or dismantling illegal settlements and preventing the annexation of Jewish-only outposts on Arab occupied or open rural land, as stipulated in United Nations resolutions and required by the Geneva Conventions.

Since American involvement in the Israeli–Palestinian conflict has for decades been unhelpful and, some say, designed to prevent the end of the occupation, and since any achievement of positive, mutual peace with a fair measure of justice has not occurred, this 'peace process' constitutes unmitigated bad news for all who genuinely seek the end of the occupation, peace, and "life, liberty and the pursuit of happiness" with some measure of humanity and justice.

If the US administration, which robotically puts Israeli and Zionist desires ahead of America's own interests and professed principles, continues successfully on this craven and impractical course, the three alternatives to the dead-and-buried two-state solution can only be those cited by Stephen Walt (2011): democracy in a single state, another round of ethnic cleansing, or some form of apartheid.

The European Union has taken on a subordinate role, focusing on and funding only secondary projects — temporary charity — for Palestinians and footing the bill for the damage caused by Israel, while wealthy Arab states pledge aid but are too busy with their own affairs to appear concerned about Israel's destruction of a pluralistic Holy Land, all of which directly and indirectly affects them as well. Israel's policies of segregation and its prime focus of a Jewish-only state encompassing Jerusalem, Bethlehem, and so forth also threaten to isolate and offend many Christians worldwide.

None of these peripheral approaches challenge the root cause of the conflict, which is the illegality of the Israeli occupation, as well as the blockade of Gaza, which is now entering its second decade, the increasing number of Jewish-only settlements and outposts, the growth of existing blocs of annexed Palestinian land, and water access rights. Peripheral 'balms' do not cure the root cause, which is the total avoidance, by all parties, of the resolution of 'final status' issues with the aim of creating a positive, mutual, legitimate peace.

Unbalanced Equation

Samira Abdel Aleem, a trade union leader as well as a community leader, says Oslo ignored the struggle of the Palestinians under occupation and "indiscriminately equated the oppressor with the oppressed."

For her, the legacy of the twenty years post-Oslo is only an anniversary of more theft of land, loss of rights, and Palestinian struggle. "It is not that we are against peace, but it must be a peace that is just, mutual, and welcome," she says.

Looking back on the Oslo Accords, Abdel Aleem insists that the whole process achieved nothing for Palestinians, whether in terms of security, economic growth, or overall development. The only visible evidence of it is more discord. She blames this on the fact that Palestine and Israel are not treated as equals at the negotiation table. Many people also view US brokers as unwilling to offer any solutions that are not approved by ultra-conditional Israel first.

"The Palestinian economy is controlled by Israel, and therefore controls Palestinian lives," Abdel Aleem says, explaining the structure of the siege, checkpoints, walls, and discrimination against Palestinians as ongoing proof of the Oslo Accords' failure. Israel is wealthy and powerful with a thriving independent economy by comparison. Yet, it still receives US annual foreign appropriations, foreign military financing, direct foreign aid, numerous US loans (rarely fully paid back), military grants, and subsidies (with special exemptions) for research, education projects, infrastructure, and Jewish-only settlements, to the tune of $3–10 billion per annum. Israel receives this aid despite being legally barred under international and US law from receiving US tax-exempt financing, including incentive subsidies to Israeli Jews to populate Jewish-only settlements in the Occupied Territories. These generous subsidies may appear to US tax payers as an abuse of US taxes, considering the bad economy, foreclosures, and unemployment within the United States itself.

This ongoing US aid is not needed by wealthy Israel, and it bolsters the occupation of the Palestinian territories to the detriment of a just and mutual peace for all, not to mention damaging US integrity and foreign relations worldwide due to obvious double standards and bias toward injustice.

Abdel Aleem sees complicity with crimes against Palestinians on multiple levels: from the international community, Israel, and the Palestinians who signed the Oslo Accords. They all have "committed a crime against the human rights of the Palestinian people."[3]

Gazans Still Doubt

Among the nearly 2 million Palestinians in Gaza, the average person believes that Arab resistance was the reason for Israel's unilateral disengagement from Gaza in 2005. The general Palestinian public also believes, however, that Israel was never serious about dismantling Jewish-only settlements in the West Bank and Jerusalem and that Israel's disengagement was merely a demographic strategy by then Prime Minister Ariel Sharon (embraced by President George W. Bush as "a bold courageous step") to wreck all 'roadmap' negotiations and put the "political process with the Palestinians" in "formaldehyde."[4]

Palestinians suspected, quite prophetically, that Israel would even accelerate the Jewish-only settlement program in the long term by building more illegal settlements and annexing them to existing ones. This suspicion is now a visible fact at such a critical moment in the Middle East. More Palestinians express their disappointment and outrage that Oslo was little more than "ink on paper," containing no valid instruments to make Israel take the legal steps expected under international laws and universal human rights.

Palestine is a multiparty confederation and although initially Fatah loyalists were in support of the Oslo Accords, few, including Abdel Aleem, remain so. Hamas, Islamic Jihad, and the left-wing Popular Front for the Liberation of Palestine (PFLP) have all expressed frustration and objections to the agreement because they are unwilling to accept the presence of Israel's military or Jewish-only occupation on legitimate Palestinian land.

Since the failure of Oslo, the majority of Gazans, including Hamas members, refer to the Oslo Accords and its architects negatively as "the clique of Oslo." Others refer to the accords as the "agreement of shame" and "Oslo Discords." Some Palestinian academics have started to name and shame those supporting the PA's line of negotiations, arguing that these "futile negotiations" are pushing the "Osloization of the Palestinian mind" while Israel pushes the Judaization of all of Palestine.

PFLP leader Jamil Mezher describes this general feeling in saying that Palestinian leaders almost reached the horizon on the Palestinian national project and then it all but vanished under the threat of Israel's practices. On the other hand, Dr. Faisal Abu Shahla, a member of the Palestinian Legislative Council for Fatah, says Oslo initially had some positive points, represented by the return of tens of thousands of Palestinians homes, the broadening and strengthening of the PA, and improved living conditions for Palestinians who were under occupation for twenty-seven years. It is easy to see why Palestinian views are divided on how to move forward, even though they are not on how this problem began.[5]

Oslo Good for Some

Of course, in Gaza there are still a few who see Oslo as a line of survival. Among them is Abuelabed Younies, a twenty-nine-year-old Palestinian who prefers to see the positive side of the Oslo Accords because he and his family were refugees in Egypt whose entry to the Gaza Strip was denied at the time. They were among the very first families to return to Gaza after Oslo. After "living displaced, in a refugee camp outside, when we arrived we saw people who were keen on the Oslo agreement. But this enthusiasm began to vanish as the reality of time passed by," he recalls as he sits next to his father in their pharmacy. "The Nakba was, of course, intolerable," he says, "and it's not that Gaza is a paradise."[6]

In 1993, many Palestinians went to the Egyptian border at Rafah to welcome those allowed to return home. They carried banners and slogans stating Palestine would be "self-governed" at last. However, Israel only dismantled its Gaza settlements and disengaged in 2005. Many say this was merely to increase the Jewish-only demographics via growing settlements in West Bank and to hermitically seal off Gaza as an open-air prisoner-of-war camp. Whatever the reason, life under Israeli occupation or blockade by land, sea, and air is more restricted than ever before. People have condemned the Oslo Accords, calling them biased and that attempt at mutual peace a ploy or farce.

Abu Wissam says that despite having some positive points, Oslo was not enough. The aspirations of the Palestinian people were never fully achieved due to Israel's procrastination and hard conditional policies built on constantly evading, deferring, and distracting from 'final status' agreements that would open the door to the chance of establishing a self-determined Palestinian state. Oslo was doomed to failure by all its methods. It was a deal that even many Israelis said they would not have accepted were they in Palestinian shoes.

Hamas, meanwhile, according to its spokesman, Fawzi Barhoum, is sure that the Oslo Accords almost destroyed the Palestinian people because of the agreement's main focus on Israel's security alone, with drastic economic and political consequences for Palestinians. He says, "The way Oslo was implemented has been very fruitful to the Israeli occupation, but has caused massive cost to Palestinian land, progress, and human rights." His movement sees the only rational way out to be the creation of a new Palestinian-Arab strategy that focuses on the new Palestinian-Arab reality on the ground, to face all challenges now and ahead.[7]

The Oslo Accords stated that both Israel and the PA would cooperate in promoting a development program for the region, including in the West Bank and the Gaza Strip, to be initiated by the G7 countries. Abdel Aleem sees that particular article as impossible to realize, considering that Israel still controls Gaza.

Palestinians barely discuss the issue of the one-state or two-state solution, as neither solution is offered by the occupying power. Instead, people in Gaza are left to cope with daily life, power outages, shortages of water, unemployment, restrictions on mobility, border closures, and the constant fear imposed by Israeli jets and drones flying overhead. However, some academics in Gaza clearly see the two-state solution as dead and beyond resuscitation.

If the two-state solution is a dead end, the question is what the Palestinian president and state secretaries would say if asked about an alternative to present options, stalemates, the process that is "frozen in formaldehyde," and the 'roadmap' to nowhere but discord.

Sadly, based on the record of recent decades, it is barely conceivable that any American government would either have the courage to restrain Israel's disrespect for international laws and United Nations resolutions or publicly display a genuine conviction to support democracy and "Equal Justice under Law," as carved in stone above the entrance to the US Supreme Court.

Western support of democracy in Palestine has always been selective and limited to funding either local PA projects or nongovernmental organizations to make only minimal improvements to the lives of Palestinians, deferring any serious attempt to address the major legal issues that block the road to an economically viable, contiguous, self-determined Palestinian state on all land previously allocated to the Palestinian people by the partition plan. The aid comes in different formats, with different canards, so that the PA, for example, is not even allowed to produce locally a valid Palestinian passport but rather must have it imported blank from France or Germany with the relevant data to be added on in Ramallah.

As twenty-two-year-old journalist Hala Elalami says, "If we look at Oslo from the perspective of profit and loss, we only achieved a Palestinian passport which does not allow us to travel, except to a few countries. The same passport is issued by a weak authority on crutches, which was hobbled out of Israel's fake disengagement, and we still live in the big prison and the siege continues."[8]

Anesthetization for Palestinians

Wherever the blame for the failure of Oslo lies, be it Israel, the United States government, or the Palestine Liberation Organization (PLO), the tragedy, as stated by Rashid Khalidi (2006), is the "lamentable error of accepting a series of flawed accords with the Israelis beginning with the 1993 Oslo agreement."

Elalami says that Oslo failed to deliver much to Palestinians during a time when "the security of the Zionist entity was returned, but with nothing, including security, given to the Palestinians." Many young Gazans are fully aware of and engaged with politics, which affects their daily lives. Long after the Ben-Gurion agreement stated in 1948 that "we must do everything to insure they [the Palestinians] never do return," David Ben-Gurion assured his fellow Zionists that Palestinians will never come back to their homes and that "the old will die and the young will forget."

When Elalami is asked about the Oslo Accords, she cannot help but ask when the time will come when she can finally return to her original land, and home, in Jerusalem. She is very aware that Israel has swallowed three-quarters of the land

and is still "bargaining for the rest by using all method of defense to distance the idea of giving way and returning the land."

She admits that Oslo failed because it tried to "anesthetize the Palestinian people and leadership." However, there are signs of a youth awakening in Palestine, with voices in Gaza becoming more radical in terms of not giving away their rights as well as being openly critical of the peace process and negotiations. Elalami no longer views the word 'peace' in this context with any trust. As translated to her during a lifetime of conflict since her birth, "peace is a word that lost its meaning for me." She notes, "How can they call Oslo, a 'peace' agreement while in my entire life I have never felt safe within my land—experiencing the last two Israeli attacks on Gaza Strip, which killed innocent men, women, and children, and destroyed the lives of the survivors, among an infrastructure around them that was left in bombed-out rubble? What kind of peace is that?"[9]

Broken infrastructure is not a new problem for many Palestinians, who since 1947 have been forced to be born and live in broken-down, bombed out, or temporary shanty-like dwellings or tent cities, never knowing what it is like to reside in the strong, solid infrastructure of the permanently owned properties their families had before, whether in rural villages or towns.

Inexperienced Palestinian negotiation teams and negotiations being monopolized by the PLO also receive criticism from Palestinian youth. "Look at the period from 1993 to 2013, Israel has several negotiation teams and whenever they feel embarrassed by, or annoyed with, Arab demands they immediately replace these teams, delaying any further negotiations," says graduate student Mohammed Ghunniem in Gaza City.

Saeb Erekat has been a negotiator for the Palestinian side since 1991, in comparison to the ever-changing Israeli negotiators. Ghunniem notes that Israel keeps changing the heads of negotiation teams and experts as a way of maneuvering, delaying, avoiding, and skirting final decisions and repeatedly "starting all over again from the beginning," thus never reaching the final agreement. He provides a clear example on the issue of water, recalling that "for negotiating water, Israel sent an expert with masses of documents on water, while we could only send a professor of biology who lacked the minimum understanding specific to water issues and only had a thirty-page research paper to compete with an Israeli negotiator who had piles of documents and more experience as back-up." Ghunniem is critical of a PA that has never paid attention to changing or improving Palestinian negotiation teams by giving a chance to the younger, more educated generations.[10]

Counterpart to Failure

The growing frustration among Palestinian young people is clear, particularly with the inter-Palestinian division most recently started with the Fatah–Hamas military conformation in 2007, with Palestinians blaming both Hamas and Fatah for their failure to bridge the gap, while still being aware of the bigger failure of Oslo. With more calls for national resistance in all its forms, while Gaza youth sit passively and observe the situation first, the majority, including Elalami, fully understands and describes the situation as "the cancerous expansion of settlements in West Bank . . . forcing Palestinians to live in canton-like enclaves with the loss of geographical concept and living instead only with the remains of a historical concept."

This same historical concept still lives in the spirits of millions of Palestinians forced to observe the "facts" that have changed on the "ground" as a result of Israel's illegal occupation in the Palestinian territories. But, despite the empty 'process' of 'peace,' the same stalwart spirit keeps Palestinians present and has not succeeded in forcing them completely from their homeland, history, culture, or ancestry. Whether as second-class citizens of Israel, refugees in Gaza and the West Bank, or out in the diaspora, this spirit unites Palestinians, becomes more determined, and focuses on 'home,' at the same time as more of the global consensus recognizes and applauds that righteous resistance in the pursuit of equitable and mutual peace.

For many in Gaza there is no final Zionist solution, just a final irony that Israel cannot conveniently 'process' mutual 'peace' like Swiss cheese.

In conclusion, Elalami quotes Palestinian-American literary theoretician Edward Said by saying, "Oslo has been 'an instrument of Palestinian surrender, a Palestinian Versailles'"; however, Palestinians are still here and are not going anywhere.

Notes

1. PA employee serving as nurse in local hospital, interview with the author, Tal al-Hawwa Supermarket, Gaza City, 20 February 2013.
2. Abu Wissam Mahdi, interview with the author, in Mahdi's home, Gaza City, January 13, 2013.
3. Samira Abdel Aleem, interview with the author, Rafah, January 8, 2013.
4. Sharon's then senior adviser Dov Weisglass quoted in Ari Shavit, "Top PM Aide: Gaza Plan Aims to Freeze the Peace Process," *Haaretz*, October 6, 2004.
5. Jamil Mizher, in interview with *Elnasra*, "Da'wa li-tashkil istratijiya badila," September 2012, http://www.elnashra.com/news/show/522373/

6. Abuelabed Younies, interview with the author, Rafah, January 30, 2013.
7. Fawzi Barhoum, in interview with *Elnasra*, September 13, 2013, http://www.elnashra. com/news/show/522373/ع ب
8. Hala Elalami, in interview with the author, March 10, 2013.
9. Hala Elalami, in interview with the author, March 10, 2013.
10. Mohammed Ghunniem, in interview with the author, Gaza City, April 1, 2013.

References

Khalidi, R. 2006. *The Iron Cage: The Story of the Palestinian Struggle for Statehood*. Boston: Beacon.
Walt, S.M. 2011. "Eldar: 'The Oslo Process Is Over.'" *Foreign Policy*, July 6.

14

The Shattered Dream

Gideon Levy

I, too, fell for the oh-so-promising sweet trap: the Oslo Accords worked like magic on me. The previously unthinkable handshakes on the White House lawn, Yasser Arafat shaking hands with Yitzhak Rabin and Shimon Peres, President Bill Clinton standing between them, and then the similarly dramatic scenes when the Palestinian Authority entered occupied Palestine, Arafat's festive helicopter landings in several cities, and both sides' mutual obligation to forge a final agreement within five years. Compared to all we had known up to then, these events were unprecedented and mesmerized me. Still, the element that worked the spell on me and many other Israelis was the completely new spirit that took hold, from Gaza to Jenin, and among huge portions of the Israeli public. It was no less than the sound of the Messiah, the true sounds of peace, the sounds of the end of the occupation. That's what we thought, that's what we believed, naive and desperate as we were.

I saw events unfold and I reported from several of the West Bank cities at the time that they were seemingly being liberated. I'll never forget the sight of Yasser Arafat descending from the sky in his Russian-made helicopter, flying in the skies of al-Halil and Gaza that up until that moment rained mostly bombs and fear; the masses that awaited him on the ground, excited and emotional, just as the Jews will be when the Messiah finally comes. The Jewish Messiah will come riding on a white donkey, the Palestinian Messiah landed that day in a white helicopter. Young Palestinians sported shiny uniforms, already sensing pride in their soon-to-be state and soon-to-be army. Palestinians that were mercilessly interrogated in Shin Bet facilities walked into the evacuated sites where they had been tortured and told their children and grandchildren stories of their experience in these very cells. People returned and rehabilitated houses that were sealed up for years. All banned flags were now openly raised and flown with pride.

And then, one day, on the ruins of the Ansar 2 detention camp, not far from the Gaza shoreline, an Uzbek circus troop erected a tent, the first circus ever to perform in Gaza. True, the whole circus could fit into one small truck, bears, acrobats, clowns, and all, but still, emotional parents, including many ex-prisoners, came to watch the amateurish show with their children, whose excitement knew no limits. The first circus in Gaza on the ruins of a notorious detention and interrogation camp — what could possibly beat that as a promising beginning, a sign of the most amazing transformation? It truly seemed that the occupation was about to be relegated to the past.

And there was one, personal, particularly theatrical moment. It happened long ago, somewhere in the mid-1990s. After many years of visiting, working in, and learning to love Gaza, we stood there at the Erez Crossing — Bassam Eid, the Palestinian human rights activist, Miki Kratsman, my devoted and brilliant photographer, and I — leaving Gaza after another day of festive documentation. Those were the drunken Oslo days, and we believed it was all over, that Gaza's occupation was over, that Gaza was free, liberated, and finally independent. We believed that we would no longer return, at least not in the role of Sisyphus, the role we took upon ourselves for years, informing the Israeli public what was being done in their name to Gaza's two million residents, telling Israelis about things they did not wish to hear, see, or know. After fifteen years of heartbreaking visits to Gaza, in one unforgettable moment, we turned to look back at the view of Gaza's impoverished homes, and with one spontaneous and dramatic gesture, seemingly taken from a Hollywood film, we waved goodbye to Gaza. Goodbye, Gaza, we will never meet again, at least not to document your fields of destruction and death. We will not enter your gates again, visit your towns and villages, homes and fields, in order to document the occupation, the bloodshed, the ruins and destruction. We will hear no more stories of humiliations, impoverishment, and brutality carried out by the Israeli occupiers. Gaza first, remember? Gaza was embarking on a new road, we believed, on our way home, to Tel Aviv, the most distant point on earth from Gaza, only an hour's drive away. This theatrical gesture was soon revealed to be a false start, as reality sunk in. We were soon to return to Gaza, the same Gaza, to the same brutal occupation, the same terrifying and bleeding images, to the same stories of life and death. The occupation didn't end, and still hasn't ended to this very day, even if its form evolved in the West Bank and even more so in Gaza after the disengagement of 2005. Even today, Gaza is still the largest prison in the world, because after the Israeli warden left, he took the key with him, still imprisoning its residents from the outside.

And the warden hasn't even begun to leave the West Bank. The Israeli occupation, twenty-two years after Oslo, is the same occupation, sometimes crueler, sometimes less cruel, but it was and remains criminal, inhuman, racist, and intolerable. No state in the world recognizes it, not even Micronesia, and there isn't one moral and honest person in the world who is willing to accept it.

But in the Oslo days we believed it would be different, naive and stupid as we turned out to be. Maybe it was the desperation following twenty-five years of occupation, maybe we clung to the Oslo dream as people who found a treasure — there was nothing else around. We believed it was only the beginning when it was actually the end; the end of hope, the end of illusions. Israel has since tripled the number of settlers, and the occupation has completely ceased to trouble Israeli public opinion. It is a nonissue. Few deal with it, nobody of any significance seems troubled by it, not morally, not legally, not even from a purely practical or economic point of view.

And the wall was erected, the 'separation wall,' partially on Palestinian land, locking the Palestinians behind it, allowing the Israelis to create a new bubble of reality, even more remote than in the pre-Oslo days. Up until then, the two peoples still had a chance to meet face to face. Palestinians came to work in Israel, to sweep its streets, build its houses, and work in its fields. And Israelis still entered the occupied areas to buy cheap goods, fix their cars and their teeth. It was on uneven and unjust grounds, but it was nonetheless a form of interaction. This interaction ended with the second Intifada, which was cruel to both peoples. Most Israelis, who have never met a Palestinian in their lives, now conceive of the Palestinians as suicide bombers. For Palestinians, the only image of Israelis is that of the armed soldier barking orders, storming into their houses at all hours of the night, arresting them brutally, often for no reason. Twenty years after Oslo the word 'peace' has become extinct in Israeli discourse. Twenty years after Oslo, reality is even more depressing than it ever was, without even one ray of hope.

But at the time, 1990s romanticism filled the air. We traveled to peace conventions, spent exciting evenings in Ramallah, and were positive that a new era was underway. It felt like a completely new beginning after a hundred-year conflict. Only years later would I realize how deceptive and misleading that feeling was. Yes, there were some worrying signs at the time, but they didn't seem that severe. For example, the agreements did not include evacuation of even one settlement, not even a symbolic evacuation, not one settlement, not one house, or even a balcony. This fact should have raised suspicions as to Israel's true intentions. An agreement, any agreement with the Palestinians that does not include settlement evacuation, even in the most scaled or miniscule manner, is not worth the paper it's written on or the time wasted. This is the *only* litmus test for true Israeli intentions. Anything else is *klam fadi*, empty words. The Palestinians, exhilarated as they were, did not understand it at the time, and some Israelis, also exhilarated, didn't understand it either. This was the basis for the huge deceit of the Oslo Accords. What came after was the rest of the breaches of the agreements, mostly by the Israelis, the 'redeployments' Israel was committed to but never carried out, the prisoners who weren't released, the evacuations that never happened, the Israel Defense Forces (IDF) incursions into the Palestinian-controlled 'A area' that continue to this day, and all that followed. What is left of the Oslo Accords is no more than documents and intentions that now one may doubt were ever really good to begin with, and the three Nobel Prizes awarded to three men who probably didn't deserve them. But the Original Sin was already evident, even then in the gay 1990s: the Palestinians didn't insist and Israel did not evacuate even one settlement. Today, with the perspective of two decades, this truth is loud and obvious.

Still I travel back in the time machine to those wonderful hopeful days. My book, *Twilight Zone: Life and Death under the Israeli Occupation*, a compilation of stories from the Occupied Territories published in 2004, takes me back to those days. Here is what I wrote on January 5, 1996: "The Jadua family from the al-Am]ari refugee camp near Ramallah returned to the home that had been sealed by the IDF. The family lived for four years in unbearable crowded conditions in a tin shack in the yard, exposed to the cold and heat, and now the Palestinian governor of Ramallah came and unsealed their house." This act played on my emotions at the time. Some family members were still imprisoned in Israel, a fact that spoiled the occasion, but still, there was joy. Hundreds of houses sealed by Israel were unsealed, due to the agreements, and that, too, counts. The head of this long-suffering family, Faraj, said to me at the time, "Suffering should be forgotten, but for us this will happen only when true peace arrives. We still have settlers on our lands and boys in prison. Only when two states come into existence will I be relieved of all the pressure and forget the suffering."

And there you have the story of the Oslo Accords in a nutshell. Three months later, in April of the same year, reality struck us again in the face. I then published my first story about a woman who lost her baby at the roadblocks. Sadly I've reported many similar stories since, but I cannot forget Faiza Abu Dahuk, the woman from Nebi Samuel who was forced to give birth at a checkpoint after soldiers at three different checkpoints refused to allow her to go through to the hospital in her brother-in-law's car, forcing her to carry her newborn baby on foot, in the cold and rain, until the baby arrived dead at the Augusta Victoria hospital in East Jerusalem. She reminded us of the Oslo deceit. There you have the dream and its shattered pieces within two months.

I now read the reports I published, telling of Palestinian suffering under the occupation: there is no difference between the pre-Oslo and post-Oslo features. In both eras I met parents whose children were shot, children whose parents were shot, terrifying stories of arrests, torture, and cruel interrogations. In both periods I found myself among the ruins of houses demolished as a result of draconian decrees or 'punitive measures.' I walked between uprooted olive trees, spoke to farmers banished from their lands. I saw soldiers beat up and humiliate people. I watched settlers impose a rule of terror. I met the deportees, the homeless, the tortured, parents who lost their children, children who lost their parents, invalids, and prisoners detained for years without trial. Nothing has changed.

Nothing is new under the sun of the Israeli occupation. Oslo was a scam, perhaps the biggest deceit in the history of this bleeding occupation, and even now, in 2013, as I write these lines, the end of this occupation is still, sadly, nowhere in sight.

15

Palestinian Identity in the Aftermath of Oslo

Ahmed Abu Rtema

The Palestinian Created by Oslo

Palestinian sociology professor Shokry al-Hazil describes the Palestinian created by Oslo as a negative, dependent being who is oblivious to national causes and whose perception of the world is personal and materialistic.[1] He or she is indifferent to the condition of his or her home and people. The culture of the aftermath of Oslo is that of the salary, the job, and indifference.[2]

This is the 'new' Palestinian, as described by former US Security Coordinator for Israel and the Palestinian Authority (PA), Keith Dayton,[3] whose role was enchanced after Hamas was elected in 2006 and whose "mission was not only to coordinate with Israel but to lead Palestinians, security bodies in particular, in a way that would push them to implement programs that ensure the security of Israel."[4] The new Palestinian according to Dayton is the same Palestinian former Mossad chief Efraim Halevy hoped to produce with instruction based on Dayton's training of the security forces in the West Bank, as he stated, "Israel does not think of transferring security responsibility to the West Bank in the near future and if this should happen, we have to wait for at least two years for the establishment of ten Dayton forces formed by the new Palestinians produced."[5]

This is the Palestinian Israel wants, the Palestinian willing to offer security services to Israel without demanding any national rights.

Along the path of the Palestinian cause, Oslo represented a turning point the consequences of which went beyond the political sphere to the Palestinian individual. The Oslo Accords were the first official agreement signed between Israel and the Palestine Liberation Organization (PLO). The accords included the establishment of a Palestinian interim self-government and an elected Legislative Council for the Palestinian people residing in the West Bank and the Gaza Strip, thus excluding the Palestinian diaspora. Fundamental issues, including Palestinian refugees, Jerusalem, settlements, and borders, were postponed to final status negotiations.

Regarding security, the accords urged the establishment of a strong Palestinian police force to secure general order in the West Bank and the Gaza Strip. The Oslo Accords also provided for Palestinian–Israeli coordination for mutual security purposes that would be detailed later. However, it was implicitly indicated that this security coordination meant pursuing 'terrorists' in order to eradicate all that might constitute a threat to Israel, not Palestine.

Oslo and the Abortion of the First Intifada

The Oslo Accords were an Israeli attempt to marginalize the first Intifada, which erupted in 1987 and lasted six years. This uprising has been the most prominent for the Palestinian cause, as it won the Palestinians unprecedented international solidarity.

The Intifada's leadership invested in the media to influence and win public opinion to the side of its just cause and to create a counterpoint to Israeli media discourse at the international level. Those televised scenes of Israeli oppression, such as those of Israeli soldiers breaking the hands of Palestinian youth with massive stones, contributed to increasing sympathy for Palestinians. The Palestinian keffiyeh became a revolutionary icon and Palestinian literature represented by the novels of Ghassan Kanafani, the poetry of Mahmoud Darwish, the cartoons of Naji al-Ali, and the books of Edward Said gained an international following.

For Israel, the Intifada was evidence of the futility of a military solution and the necessity of a political settlement with the Palestinians. The Madrid Conference offered a prospect for bilateral peace negotiations between Israel and Arab countries. Secret negotiations were carried out between Israelis and the leadership of the Palestine Liberation Organization (PLO) in Norway that led to the signing of the Oslo Accords, resulting in the gradual redeployment of Israeli occupation forces in Palestinian cities, starting with Gaza and Jericho in 1994.

The agreement was also Israel's perfect means of burying the Intifada, minimizing the Palestinian cause, freeing itself of the embarrassment caused by its oppression of the Palestinians, and engaging the Palestinian negotiators in an endless maze. Israel was not serious about offering any genuine political concessions. Twenty years after the signing of the accords, the facts on the ground speak to the lack of any genuine political settlement. Moreover, with the PLO's decision to go on with secret negotiations without reference to the Palestinian people, the organization marginalized several movements that opposed such a settlement. The PLO leadership promoted the agreement as a transitional stage, arguing that this first step, which came in the frame of political pragmatism, was necessary to establish a Palestinian independent state with Jerusalem as its capital.

The master of the accords was Israel, the stronger party militarily and politically, directing Oslo to fit its own interests. The weaker of the two parties, the PLO, was negotiating without means of pressure or sufficient public representation. Soon enough, it was clear that any talk of the achievements of Oslo for Palestinians was a façade.

Israel did not abide by the Oslo Accords, as its withdrawal processes have not been fully carried out and there is little prospect of the establishment of a Palestinian state. The vision current Israeli Prime Minister Benjamin Netanyahu is promoting is one of economic peace. Economic peace, according to Netanyahu, stands for replacing the 'land for peace' principle with that of developing the economy and improving Palestinian livelihoods under an authority, an administrative council, and self-government.

Israel's unwillingness to offer any genuine concession confirms that it holds to what former Israeli Prime Minister Golda Meir claimed: that there is no such thing as a Palestinian people.

Oslo has presented Palestinians with several forms of sovereignty, including raising the Palestinian flag, playing the national anthem, and laying down the red carpet. The PA leadership has obtained VIP cards that enable it to move through the checkpoints in the West Bank. Palestinians have also been given the right to administrate their civil affairs and now bear the responsibility of paying the salaries of around 160,000 government employees, of whom 60,000 are employed in policing and security services. Israel had no problem with handing Palestinians the responsibility of managing their daily lives and decreasing the cost of its occupation, but that is all Israel has to offer.

Therefore, Oslo enabled Israel to preserve its control and occupation of the Palestinian people while ornamenting the image of the occupation and decreasing its economic, security, and political costs.

According to one commentator,

> After Oslo, Israel has successfully tripled the number of settlements. The number of settlers in the West Bank including Jerusalem has risen to 650,000 settlers. There is still a three-year-plan to increase the number of settlers to a million, continue the construction of the separation wall, and achieve an advanced stage in the Judaization of Jerusalem. However, one of the most dangerous consequences of Oslo was the ability to reshape the form, function, and role of the Palestinian Authority to bring it closer to the Israeli perspective so that it would become an agent of the occupation in administrating the security, administrative, and economic sectors instead of leading the Palestinian people to end occupation and achieve national independence.[6]

Oslo's Damage to National Identity

Those who argue that the Oslo Accords were a success state that the agreement and the system it established have played a significant role in strengthening national identity through the establishment of the PA on Palestinian territories, the election of a legislative council, and the founding of economic, social, and public institutions, ministries, and organizations in the territories. If we examine these perspectives, however, it is clear that what Oslo has achieved is the complete opposite. One of Oslo's gravest outcomes is its threat to Palestinian identity.

On how Oslo has threatened Palestinian identity, Palestinian researcher Wesam Rafidi states:

> Oslo has actually drained the PLO of its content and marginalized its role, creating an empty dysfunctional body with no real influence on Palestinian politics. This was not only manifested in the dysfunctional organizations it created but by the cancellation of the comprehensive Palestinian National Covenant which is an embodiment of Palestinian rights and one important component of the identity of the Palestinian people and their vision of their history. The collective body of the PLO, which represented Palestinians as a unified nation inside the occupied territories and in the diaspora was thus liquidated and replaced by a modernized system of customs.[7]

By 'system of customs,' Rafidi meant tribal, familial, and sectarian divisions, which were reinforced during the Oslo years, affiliations which had been denounced during the Intifada as antithetical to nationalist loyalties.

In addition, recognizing Israel means that the 1948 Palestinians, a million and a quarter people, were excluded from the Palestinian agenda, and therefore from the legitimate pursuit of a unified identity for the Palestinian people despite their geographical fragmentation — a pursuit the PLO had begun through its covenant, subsequent struggle, and the agendas of its various factions.

On the system of customs created by Oslo, Rafidi adds:

> It is not strange that all bodies which were marginalized prior to Oslo would be active in the aftermath of Oslo. Those bodies were tribal, familial, and even sectarian, and they spread as fast as fire in few years. Tens of similar recently established bodies are dotted along villages, camps, and cities. The ideologies behind such bodies often promote backward perspectives that are opposed to the construction of personal and national identity.[8]

The PA's continuing attempts to weaken opposition to any kind of normalization of the Israeli occupation is another threat to Palestinian identity that Oslo created. Some leading lights in the PA have sponsored activities that target some of the most important sectors in need of protection from normalization, such as youth and children. "Seeds of Peace" was one such collaborative normalization project initiated in the late 1990s between the PA and the occupation forces. The Ministry of Education and Higher Education would send children for normalizing activities as part of the program.

The danger of normalization lies in the way it changes cultural and psychological terminology for Palestinians to urge them to accept the occupier colonizing their homeland and to surrender to the occupier's power. This weakens their willingness to struggle and distorts their construction of a Palestinian identity. No national identity can be built from either the feelings of inferiority that support the occupier's supremacy or from a submissive belief in the unwillingness to defy oppression.

The Cancellation of the Palestinian National Covenant

The cancellation of the Palestinian National Covenant, adopted by the PLO in 1968, was one of the most prominent concessions made by the Palestinian leadership in its implementation of the Oslo Accords. This took place in Gaza on

December 14, 1998, during a visit by US President Bill Clinton, when members of the Palestinian National Council (PNC) ratified the cancellation of twelve articles from the covenant and the erasure of parts of sixteen articles, leaving only five articles unamended.

One of the articles deleted from the covenant was Article 5, which stated that the stage the Palestinian people are living in now is the national struggle to liberate Palestine. Therefore, the disparity between Palestinian national factions is secondary, as it stands in opposition to the main struggle between Zionism and colonialism on the one side and the Palestinian Arab nation on the other. Palestinians, whether within or without the diaspora, whether as part of an organization or as individuals, should form one national front that works to liberate Palestine through armed struggle.

Oslo and the Right of Return

What about the right of return, which is considered the fundamental issue in the struggle, as the Palestinian cause in its essence is the cause of a nation displaced from its original villages and cities and still holding on to the right to return home, which is a right adopted by UN General Assembly Resolution 194?

According to one commentator, "The PLO recognized 'Israel's' right to exist on the land occupied in 1948, which constitutes 78 percent of the land of Palestine, which was therefore left outside the frame of the struggle. This means Palestinian refugees who left Haifa, Jaffa, Safad, Saforia and other villages and cities are not entitled to return."[9]

There is no reference, whether direct or indirect, in the Oslo Accords to the right of return. The issue of Palestinian refugees was left to later 'final status' negotiations, which means that refugees are negotiable and can be the subject of a political settlement.

If the refugee issue could be settled by direct bilateral negotiations, and if direct bilateral negotiations are subject to the power balance on the ground, Oslo has certainly served the strategic Israeli stance in its refusal of the return of Palestinian refugees.

Israel perceives the return of Palestinian refugees as a threat to its ethnocracy. Recently, Israel increased its blackmailing of Palestinians by not only demanding recognition of the State of Israel but also demanding recognition of the Jewishness of the state, so that it can completely destroy the right of refugees to return to their homes and raise its legitimacy by claiming to have more than a million and a quarter Palestinians living within its borders.

Oslo's Institutionalization of Division

The Oslo Accords were one of the causes of the internal division from which Palestinians are still suffering. During the first Intifada, the dominant feeling among Palestinians was that they were all targets and thus partners in the cause and destiny that strengthened national unity. Palestinians were strongly unified by the commonality of their struggle. Their solidarity was like a paradise and Oslo is the forbidden fruit Palestinians tasted and then descended from the heaven of agreement and solidarity to the earth of disagreement and misery.

Oslo has managed to transfer the economic burden of the occupation from Israel to the USA and the donor European countries. Israeli journalist Amira Hass explains that the 900 million dollars which were pledged to the Palestinians by the United States and other, European donor countries in the Sharm al-Sheikh Conference to reconstruct Gaza after the Israeli aggression of 2008–2009 should be seen as part of the United States' reguar aid to Israel. As an occupying power, Israel is, according to international law, obliged to assure the well-being of the population under its control. But Israel harms that population instead, after which the United States (like other countries) rushes to compensate for the damage.

Hass adds:

> During the 1990s it was still possible to describe donations to the Palestinians as an expression of confidence and hope in Israel's readiness to free itself of the occupation regime it had created. But not in 2009. Support for Israeli policy — this is the only way to understand the fact that other countries keep pouring in hundreds of millions of dollars meant to put out the fires set by this policy, without extinguishing the source of the blaze.[10]

The reason behind the current rifts in the Palestinian political arena is a division between two projects, one that obtains its legitimacy through heroism and national rights and another that derives its legitimacy from false pragmatism. Therefore, genuine national unity has to be regained through liberation from Oslo and a return to the basic principles that represent the sole commonality that can reunite Palestinians.

Oslo and Economic Dependency

The Oslo Accords caused damage not only to Palestinians' political life but also to their economic life. The accords failed to establish an independent Palestinian economy and, throughout the past twenty years, the substance of the economy overseen by the PA has been donations and international aid.

After Oslo, the economic and social burden was transferred from the Israeli occupation to European and American donors. These donor countries have contributed to the economic dependency of the PA and the Palestinian people in the Occupied Territories by establishing policies that only cover financial crises and fund the expansion of administrative and security bodies. These policies depend upon giving charity instead of helping Palestinians to build an infrastructure for development. Amira Hass describes the donor countries as those who give Palestinians fish instead of giving them the fishing rod.[11]

Another manifestation of Oslo's contribution to economic failure is the unilateral merging of the economy and customs of the Palestinian territories with the Israeli economy. Given the lack of any seaport or airport in the Palestinian territories, Israel is considered its semi-sole gate to the world. According to the Paris Protocol, Palestinian trade has first to pass through Israel, and Israeli authorities are unilaterally responsible for imposing fees on imports by the PA. The Israeli occupation has also imposed the Israeli shekel as the official currency in the Palestinian territories. In brief, the economy is built on an unequal relationship between an industrial, technologically developed economy and an agricultural economy that depends on money transfers and international aid. The occupation has created this state of economic merger, dependency, and disparity as weapons with which to blackmail Palestinians for more political and security concessions.[12]

Oslo's Weakening of National Belonging

The most dangerous impact of Oslo has been its influence on the Palestinian individual and its creation of a 'new' Palestinian whose national belonging, which was once the main strength in times of severe power imbalances in favor of Israel, is fragile.

During the Intifada, Palestinians' living conditions contributed to strengthening values of heroism, sacrifice, martyrdom, patience, and steadfastness. Palestinians no longer viewed death as a finite loss but as a martyrdom of eternity and glory. The scene of a mother greeting the news of her son's martyrdom with joy became a familiar one. At martyrs' funerals, coffee was replaced with juice, which symbolizes happiness and indicated that martyrdom had acquired a fundamental meaning in Palestinian culture.

In addition, prison became an icon of struggle, honor, and dignity that deserved pride because the imprisonment of Palestinians for struggling against the occupation was more common than imprisonment for criminal activities. I personally am unable to imagine that prison might symbolize anything negative, such as a crime. When I left Gaza for the first time for Egypt after the withdrawal of the Israeli occupiers in 2005, I was surprised to hear some of my relatives in Egypt denounce a prisoner jailed for a crime in an Egyptian prison. In Palestine, prison is synonymous with struggle, honor, and dignity.

Before Oslo, heroic scenes, such as that of Palestinians with their faces covered with keffiyehs so that Israeli occupation forces would not recognize them, were celebrated, and such icons became both mythical and holy. The stones Palestinian children hurled at Israeli soldiers became a symbol of steadfastness and persistence in a hugly unequal confrontation. Thousands of Palestinian national songs were sung for martyrs, prisoners, and exiled Palestinians. These songs inspired the public, enhanced Palestinians' sense of revolution, and glorified sacrifice, heroism, and martyrdom. Leaflets and graffiti on walls functioned as local media for reinforcing steadfastness in Palestine during the first Intifada. All these scenes represented a heroic state that strengthened Palestinians' sense of national belonging.

When the sin of Oslo was committed, Palestinians descended from heaven in their greed for statehood, settlement, and progress. After years of exhaustion through the Intifada, Palestinians were like a drowning man who is willing to cling to a straw. They hoped that Oslo, as promoted by the PA, was just a prelude to national sovereignty and economic prosperity. The years under the PA and all the corruption that followed its establishment deepened feelings of frustration among Palestinians. Oslo weakened Palestinians' national belonging and distracted the Palestinian people from the fundamental battle of liberation and self-determination with false illusions. Therefore, the 'new' Palestinian neither preserved the status of heroism and unity nor achieved the dreams of statehood or prosperity.

The Oslo Accords led to the absence of a Palestinian national agenda or an actual liberation agenda through all forms of struggle. They also resulted in the absence of a leadership that could move the national struggle forward from the status quo to a transitional stage of struggle in order to reach a national dynamic that included all sectors of the Palestinian people.

Today Palestinians are in a state of loss and disarray. This is mainfested in various ways, the most prominent of which is the presence of an impotent PA that waits for futile American and western solutions to its problems.

A Social Failure

Internally, Oslo failed to establish democratic governmental or civil society organizations. It also created an alternative leadership sunk in corruption, bribes, and wealth. The PA's governmental institutions suffered from an expansion in employment and the absence of organization, which created a financial burden and institutionalized manifestations of bureaucracy and underemployment. Employment was often based not on professional standards but on family connections, interests, or bribes. In addition, a large number of employers lacked effective monitoring systems. The Palestinian government has not provided a vivid and certified structure for ministries and governmental organizations.

Oslo also created corrupt security bodies that are accountable to no one. One of the manifestations of this corruption was an increasing number of armed confrontations between different sectors of the security forces, such as those that took place between the intelligence agency, the police, the military intelligence, and the preventive security forces in some parts of the West Bank and the Gaza Strip.

The corruption developed a dominant state of fear, violence, and lawlessness, and some Palestinian cities were turned into arenas for infighting through which many institutions of the PA were attacked. Security threats have also reached some personnel in the PA and led to kidnappings of leaders of some security bodies and workers in government institutions. Assassinations and assassination attempts, such as the attempt on Palestinian Minister Nabil Amro's life and the assassination of former head of intelligence Musa Arafat, were carried out.

On the other hand, the Legislative Council had little effect in its practice of legislative authority and monitoring because it was devoid of independence from the executive.

Civil society organizations have not constituted a better alternative. Their most prominent problem has been that the political prevails over the civic in their pursuit of support and funds from political factions. Civil society has not performed its role in developing Palestinian society and changing its conventionality. In addition, security bodies have interfered in the monitoring work of civil society organizations, hindering their activities. The judiciary has no monitoring control over these organizations. They are also largely dependent on international aid from donor counties or Arab and Islamic groups and countries, rather than on aid obtained from their own social networks or which they have raised themselves in order to remain independent (Abrash 2006).

The Osloization of the Palestinian Mind

The severe impact of Oslo on Palestinians led Palestinian academic and activist Haidar Eid to coin the phrase "the Osloization of the Palestinian mind" to describe the way Oslo penetrated Palestinian consciousness and deformed the Palestinian educational process. In his article, "Security or Education," Haider states,

> In any analytical reading of the accords, we are faced with the importance it connects to security at the expense of other basic rights of the colonized. This is the way the Osloization of the Palestinian mind started, through the reformation of priorities so that education is no longer a priority and is no longer an important weapon. With the rise of unemployment and the decline of income, young Palestinians are faced with two choices: whether to join one of the security bodies or join the universities within the Palestinian Territories. Universities graduated groups of students with no knowledge of the basics of their major.

The integration of security considerations into the academic system has led to the deterioration of educational standards in Palestinian universities. Eid explains that in some universities there were even offices set aside for the various security bodies. The transparency and integrity of academic institutions became compromised and universities became hostage to political interests as "several workers of security bodies were university students only for the sake of improving their status in the body. Several leaders of those security bodies sought to obtain higher education for the sake of the title and prestige." Academics working at those universities, which should offer an atmosphere of freedom and professional appreciation, were drawn into an endless political struggle.

The process of constructing the Palestinian and his liberation is no longer a priority. Under the pretext of Oslo, security, even under occupation, colonization and apartheid, is the most important component of an independent state.[13]

Oslo's Damage to the Revolutionary Spirit

The impact Oslo had on Palestinians was grave. Palestinians did not win political sovereignty, a stable national economy, or independent civil society organizations. All Oslo did was to imprison them with restraints they cannot escape.

In a recent article, journalist Ben White asks why there has been no Palestinian Spring despite the eruption of revolutions in several Arab countries, including Egypt, Tunisia, Libya, and Syria. White argues that the Oslo Accords froze the Palestinian struggle for return and decolonization. He identifies several factors that restrain the Palestinian revolutionary spirit, including the checkpoints established by the Israeli occupation, the strategic planning of Israeli settlements, and the 'separation wall' that closes off Palestinian cities. White also notes that Oslo has shaped the behavior and direction of key political actors in the Occupied Territories who marked the shift from a revolutionary focus to that of 'interim' autonomy. The PA's leadership role has been constrained and disconnected, even from those over whom it governs, let alone the outside world.[14]

There Is Still Hope

It is true that Oslo has caused damage to the Palestinian revolutionary spirit, but this inclination is still present. It is Israel that enhances the inclination and keeps it alive with its oppressive policies. The Intifadas and the intermittent confrontations witnessed in the last twenty-two years are evidence that Oslo has hurt the Palestinians but has not killed them yet.

On May 15, 2011, the sixty-third anniversary of the displacement of the Palestinian people, hundreds of thousands of Palestinian refugees from Gaza, the West Bank, 1948 Palestine, Jordan, Syria, and Lebanon conducted a peaceful sit-in at the borders of their homeland, chanting for return. Such demonstrations continue today and are likely to continue, as this is their only way to express their discomfort over their alienation and that they are living in refugee camps.

This scene is an indication, among many others, that years of political agreements signed by the Palestinian leadership without the representation and consent of the people within the current state of imbalance in favor of the occupation is not sufficient to make the Palestinian people forget their historical rights.

Notes

1. This chapter was translated from the Arabic by Sameeha Elwan.
2. S. al-Hazil, "'Ajz wa daya': al-qadiya al-filistiniya ila ayn?" *Majallat al-wa'i al-'arabi*, http://elw3yalarabi.org/modules.php?name=News&file=article&sid=12841, Dhu al-Hijja, 17, ah 1433 (November, 2, 2012 ce).
3. K. Dayton, "The Making of the New Palestinian," speech at Soref Seminar, Washington Institute for Near East Policy, May 7, 2009.
4. Q. Abdelsattar (2009) "Dayton: za'im Filistin," *AlJazeera.net*, July 1, 2009, http://www.aljazeera.net/home/print/6c87b8ad-70ec-47d5-b7c4-3aa56fb899e2/6194b9bf-edf3-4061-9145-f6d33726238d
5. E. Hlevy, "Abu Mazen's Weakness: The New Palestinian," *Ynet*, May 24, 2009, http://www.lnn-press.net/modules.php?name=News&file=print&sid=1683

6. K. Shaheen, "19 Years for Oslo: The Independent Palestinian State Is an Illusion," *al-Hal*, September 8, 2012.

7. W. Rafidi, "al-Hawiya al-wataniya al-filistiniya ba'd Oslo," *BADIL*, 2011, http://www.badil.org/en/haq-alawda/item/1706-art5

8. W. Rafidi, "al-Hawiya al-wataniya al-filistiniya ba'd Oslo," *BADIL*, 2011, http://www.badil.org/en/haq-alawda/item/1706-art5.

9. M. Abu Laila, "Ittifaqiyat Oslo wa athariha 'ala qadiyat al-laji'in al-filistiniyin fi Libnan," *Palestinian Return Community*, 2012, http://www.wajeb.org/index.php?option=com_content&task=view&id=10578&Itemid=125

10. A. Hass, The Israel Donors Conference," *Haaretz*, March 4, 2009, http://www.haaretz.com/print-edition/opinion/the-israel-donors-conference-1.271385

11. A. Hass, "Palestinian Farmers Are Being Treated Like Criminals, *Haaretz*, January 21, 2010, http://www.haaretz.com/weekend/week-s-end/amira-hass-palestinian-farmers-are-being-treated-like-criminals-1.261871

12. F. Tarabulsi, "Oslo al-iqtisadi: al-istitba' siyasiyan," *Filistin*, September 20, 2010, http://palestine.assafir.com/article.asp?aid=276

13. H. Eid, "al-Amn amm al-ta'lim?," *Wakalat ma'n al-ikhbariya*, August, 2, 2012, http://maannews.net/arb/ViewDetails.aspx?ID=509321

14. B. White, "Why Has There Been No 'Palestinian Spring'? One Word: Oslo," *Guardian*, June 11, 2012, http://www.theguardian.com/commentisfree/2012/jun/11/palestinian-spring-oslo-accords

References

Abrash, I. 2006. *The Role of the Authority: An Orientalist Perspective to a State Authority.* Birzeit: Birzeit University Development Studies Program.

16

Israeli Impunity

Mads Gilbert

A former Israeli soldier is to serve forty-five days in prison on charges in connection with the deaths of a Palestinian mother and daughter who were shot while waving white flags during the three-week war in Gaza in 2008–2009. The ex-soldier, who has not been named, agreed to a plea bargain under which he was convicted of shooting without permission, and the original manslaughter charge dropped. He was the only soldier to be indicted for manslaughter as a result of Operation Cast Lead, in which around 1,400 Palestinians and 13 Israelis were killed. According to reports and testimonies at the time, Majda Abu Hajaj, 35, and her mother, Rayah, 64, were among 30 people, including children, trying to leave a house where they had taken shelter. The group was fired on and the two women were killed. In a statement issued at the time of indictment two years ago, the Israeli military said the charge was based on evidence that the former soldier, a marksman, "deliberately targeted an individual walking with a group of people waving a white flag without being ordered or authorized to do so."

— *Guardian*, August 12, 2012[1]

Still Killing—After All These Years

More than three years have passed since Operation Pillar of Defense hit Gaza, four years since Operation Cast Lead, and more than twenty-two painful years since the Oslo Accords were officially signed on September 13, 1993. The negotiators proclaimed that the accords would serve as interim agreements that would lead to a final peace agreement and an independent Palestinian state within five years. Recently, Palestinian National Initiative leader Mustafa Barghouti stated that the accords turned out to be "a transition to nothing" and had been used as a cover by Israel "to consolidate a system of apartheid."[2]

More than two decades later, thousands of Palestinians are still being killed, wounded, maimed, and oppressed by Israeli governmental forces with little or no international pressure to limit, stop, or prosecute systematic attacks on Palestinian civilians. With its immense, deliberate destructiveness, the Israel Defense Forces (IDF), in Gaza mostly known as the Israeli Occupation Forces (IOF), have systematically attacked and eliminated people as well as predefined physical targets, all based on an Israeli military-political paradigm known as the Dahiya Doctrine.[3]

The aim of these Israeli attacks has been to "send Gaza decades into the past" while at the same time attaining "the maximum number of enemy casualties and keeping IDF casualties at a minimum."[4] During Operation Cast Lead, more than 1,400 Palestinians were killed and 5,400 wounded in a three-week onslaught, while during Operation Pillar of Defense, 190 Palestinians were killed and 1,400 were injured in just one week (PCHR 2009). Palestinian leaders have called on the Palestinian Authority (PA) to abolish the Oslo Accords since Israel has refused to commit to its obligations and instead has continued land grabs and settlement expansion in the West Bank and brutal attacks on civilian society in Gaza.

Negotiations toward a final peace agreement have failed simply because Israel does not want peace.

Jumana

January 2009: The nine-month-old girl was shivering with cold and almost unconscious following anesthesia. I had been asked to attend to her following emergency surgery in one of al-Shifa Hospital's overcrowded operating rooms. I carefully lifted her chin forward to open her airways and secure her breathing. Most of her tiny left hand had to be amputated after a crush injury she sustained in her family's house when the Israeli ground forces attacked it. The hospital room was icy cold for lack of electricity and heating. Not only had the Israeli army assault caused a constant and overwhelming flow of injured, badly wounded, dying, and dead Palestinians to al-Shifa and the other hospitals in Gaza, but the Israeli government had also cut power to the whole Gaza Strip and its civilian population of 1.7 million. The hospitals must rely on old generators that barely work because of a lack of spare parts. The power cut had left corridors and patients' rooms exposed to Mediterranean winter winds. Cold trauma patients bleed more and face higher mortality rates than warm trauma patients. It was an endless, vicious spiral of destruction and death.

Jumana al-Samuni was alone. We did not know her mother's whereabouts. Her father and grandfather were said to have been killed in the attack. Her thumb and second and third fingers had been amputated. The bandage was soaked with blood, but the bleeding had stopped. The little girl had pretty, sharp, almost adult features and strong eyebrows. Her sallow skin color was suggestive of anemia following blood loss, or of the undernourishment from which so many children in Gaza suffer. She seemed to be sleeping peacefully; her closed eyes gave an almost absurdly relaxed appearance. Her skin felt cool and bumpy, as if she was chilled. While I tried to cover her with the thin hospital sheet, one of the nurses told me that the little girl came from the poor quarters of Zaytun in the southern outskirts of Gaza City. She said the Israelis had bombed the family's house and killed eleven that morning. Another nurse said ground forces from an Israeli tank position had forced many of the Samuni family together into one of the family houses overnight, and that the house would have been full of people. The extended Samuni family is a big clan. About a hundred family members, including women, children, and the elderly, had been herded together before the Israeli government forces attacked the building.

Sadly, it turned out to be true. It was no mistake, but a systematic Israeli military operation. Soldiers from the Israeli armed forces had carried out the massacre. My patient, little Jumana, was just one of many victims from the Samuni family that day, as many more were to follow. The appalling details of the massacre of the Samuni family came to light bit by bit. I saw Jumana again about midnight that evening. She looked like a little doll, lying in a bed far too big for her. She was no longer alone; there was an elderly woman dressed in black standing beside the bed, introduced as Jumana's grandmother on the killed father's side. I examined Jumana again. She was alert, with normal vital signs of consciousness. She looked around with a surprised, inquisitive glance. The lady in black was furious. Just like other relatives I met at al-Shifa Hospital, she wanted to express her deep fury over the systematic Israeli killings. We were among the very first outsiders to learn what had happened. We reported. We sent pictures. We gave interviews. The F-16 bombs kept falling. The drones kept shooting rockets. The rivers of Palestinian blood kept running. The Merkava tanks kept shelling. The Dahiya Doctrine played out in all its cruelty.

The Story Was True

We learned that members of the extended Samuni family had been herded together in a big house during the day of January 4, 2009, nearly a hundred men, women, and children of all ages, and were forced to stay in a kind of concrete warehouse of about 200 square meters. They were kept there overnight without food or drink, hostages of the Israeli troops who had taken up position nearby.

Early the next morning, on January 5, the house was bombed by the Israelis. In the attacks, the house was completely demolished and many were killed and more wounded. Jumana's father, grandfather, and grandmother were killed. Jumana's mother and uncle managed to escape. When a few members of the family tried to leave the house, the IDF fired a missile or shell at them, killing one person and wounding two others. A few seconds later, the military fired two more shells or missiles that hit the house directly. The house collapsed on its occupants. Nearly thirty Samuni family members were killed in the warehouse, including nine children and many women. Dozens were injured. People were then trapped in the destroyed house with the dead bodies for three days until Israeli forces allowed rescue services to search for survivors and evacuate those killed.

Amal

One of those trapped for three days was Amal Attila Samuni, a nine-year-old schoolgirl and Jumana's cousin. She had been forced into the building with her father, mother, and siblings. Her father Attila Samuni, aged forty, gathered his family in what he thought to be the safest room. He and his smallest child, Amal's little brother, were shot at point blank when Attila Samuni opened the door to the Israeli soldiers to tell them, in Hebrew, that the building was filled only with civilians, women and children.[5] Amal was hit in the head by a fragment of a shell or a bullet during the bombardment. Her older brother managed to rescue her from the rubble, from the smell of dead and decaying bodies, on January 7, when Israeli soldiers finally allowed him through.

I met them in the ward when Amal was rushed to al-Shifa Hospital at midnight on January 7. Her brother Faraj, aged twenty-two, was tired, almost apathetic. He looked at me with dark, angry eyes.

"We just rescued her. They killed my father and my little brother," he said in a low, intense voice. "Twenty-nine members of my family were killed, including our father. We don't know how many more are lying in the ruins. We could not help the wounded because the Israeli soldiers refused us, the Red Crescent, and Red Cross through."

"But we have already treated little Jumana Samuni. Is she also from your family?" I asked.

"Yes. And there are more still. Have you seen anyone else from my family?"

I told him briefly about Jumana and her grandmother. He knew about them. He was injured himself but kept searching for the rest of the family. He dug out his sister Amal with his own hands and got her to the hospital, then recovered the dead to bury them.

"Amal is completely worn out by thirst, hunger, and the cold. Is she going to survive?" he asked me.

I lifted the blanket and quickly examined the girl. She did not seem to have any serious external physical trauma, but she was cold and extremely exhausted.

"Any other injuries?" I asked Dr. Hamid, a skilled Palestinian physician.

"No, nothing else so far, but very exhausted, as you can see," he replied.

Amal looked like an old lady, not a young schoolgirl, with lips cracked and dried out, the body severely dehydrated. She survived, but, I wondered, how can she go on living? What she survived was not an earthquake or another natural disaster. She was the victim of a truly man-made disaster, executed without mercy or respect for international law and state obligations. She had been attacked and almost killed by soldiers with seemingly profound racist motivations, should one interpret the graffiti drawn by the same soldiers on the walls of her family's houses.

According to a report in the Israeli newspaper *Haaretz*, after the Israeli soldiers took part in the operations in the Zaytun district, brigade commander Colonel Ilan Malka insisted that not a single ambulance should enter the sector under his responsibility, fearing Hamas attempts to capture Israeli soldiers. A soldier said that Malka insisted the wounded should be taken on foot for medical care, to meet ambulances at a distance of over three kilometers away. The ambulances had to halt at a distance, according to the Red Cross, and were blocked from the bombed house by an earth mound put on the road by the Israeli military.

A number of reports from the field confirmed the story that Faraj told me. Civilians who tried to walk to the ambulances were turned back, with soldiers firing at them.[6] When the wounded had finally been evacuated, the IDF demolished the house with the dead bodies inside. It was only possible to remove them from under the debris about two weeks later, after the Israeli army withdrew.

"1948–2009"

Later in 2009, on several walls in one of the remaining Samuni houses, my colleague Dr. Erik Fosse found graffiti scribbled by Israeli soldiers, which he photographed. One was a tombstone with the inscription "1948–2009," another "Die you all" signed with a Star of David. In other destroyed buildings in Zaytun, IDF soldiers marked their mission with more graffiti, some in Hebrew and much written in naive English: "Arabs need 2 die," "Make war not peace," "1 is down, 999,999 to go." On a large peace symbol, three slogans were written in Hebrew: "Death to Arabs," "War on Arabs — Sounds good to me," and "The only good Arab is a dead Arab."[7]

According to a *Haaretz* report, Israeli soldiers testifying to the Breaking the Silence organization were upset by the destructive actions of the IDF, the trigger-happy atmosphere while on patrol, and the virtual reality, as they described it, created by IDF spokespeople inside Israel, to the effect that there was serious fighting in the Gaza Strip. The soldiers said they soon understood that they were not actually confronting the dangerous Hamas resistance for which they had been prepared on the eve of Operation Cast Lead.

Forty-eight members of the Samuni family were killed during the Israeli attacks on Zaytun in one day.[8,9] Twenty-eight homes, a mosque, and a number of farms were destroyed. The Israeli army closed its "investigation" of this massacre in 2012. Major Dorit Tuval, deputy military advocate for operational matters, said that the case was closed after the investigation found that the attack on the civilians, "who did not take part in the fighting," and their killings were not done knowingly and directly or out of haste and negligence "in a manner that would indicate criminal responsibility."[10]

In a letter sent to Israeli human rights organization B'Tselem and the Palestinian Center for Human Rights in Gaza, which filed a complaint on the matter, Major Tuval wrote that the investigation "completely disproved" any claim about deliberate harm to civilians, as well as haste and recklessness regarding possible harm to civilians, or criminal negligence. The military's response does not detail the findings of the investigation, nor does it provide the reasons behind the decision to close the file or any new information about the circumstances.[11]

According to B'Tselem, there has never been a serious investigation into the suspicions raised by them or by other Israeli, Palestinian, and international organizations regarding breaches of international law by the military during the assault on Gaza. No investigation has addressed the responsibility of high-ranking commanders or governmental leaders, instead focusing on the conduct of individual soldiers of lower rank.

Accordingly, only three indictments have been filed against soldiers who took part in Operation Cast Lead: for theft of a credit card from a Palestinian civilian, for use of a nine-year-old Palestinian child as a human shield, and for "manslaughter of an anonymous person." In three other cases, disciplinary action alone was taken. Two officers were disciplined for firing explosive shells that struck a facility of the United Nations Relief and Works Agency for Palestine Refugees in the Near East (UNRWA), and three officers were disciplined for shelling al-Maqadma Mosque, which caused the deaths of at least fifteen Palestinians, nine of them civilians. One officer was disciplined for the use of a Palestinian civilian as a human shield.[12] The investigations were all opened at a very late stage, the first, to B'Tselem's knowledge, in October 2009, ten months after Operation Cast Lead ended. At present, four years after the operation, there is hardly a chance that investigations will lead to further indictments.

No proper independent, international trial has been conducted to hold Israeli military and political leaders responsible and to get all evidence and facts on the table. Several cases have been filed, however, against Israeli army central command officers and the Israeli government for breaches of international law, among them one in Norway. This was the first time in Norwegian legal history that political and military leaders were to be reported for "war crimes and gross violation of international humanitarian law." Since Norway has endorsed the Geneva Conventions and other international law treaties as well as ratified the Rome Statute, it has acknowledged its obligation as a state to be proactive in the prosecution of international crimes and crimes against humanity. Five respected Norwegian solicitors sought to trigger this duty and right and thus filed a legal complaint against Israeli political and military leaders. The Norwegian Bar Association's human rights committee supported the complaint. This complaint was similar to a number of legal campaigns by human rights organizations and by other countries. In Israel, too, calls were made for a legal investigation into what happened in Gaza.[13] Unfortunately, the Norwegian public prosecutor shelved the complaint in November 2009, probably for political reasons. Of course, no mention was made of the obligations the State of Israel carries under the Oslo Accords.

Sanctions, Not Impunity

Not long after Operation Cast Lead, Norway actively participated in the bombing of Libya in order "to protect the civilians."[14] This bombing was enthusiastically supported by the Israeli government, which wanted the same "tough sanctions" to be applied to Iran for "violating civil rights."[15] "If the international community is applying special pressure on Libya and warning its leader and soldiers against violating civil rights, the same warning must be aimed at Iran's leaders and their henchmen," Prime Minister Benjamin Netanyahu said, noting, "At the same time as Gadhafi is massacring his opponents in Libya, the regime of the ayatollahs in Iran is systematically executing its opponents." His comments came on a day when Iranian security forces reportedly fired tear gas during clashes with antigovernment protesters in Tehran demanding the release of two opposition leaders. "I believe that a firm reaction will send a very clear message of encouragement and hope to the Iranian people, that no one has forgotten their struggle for freedom and liberty," the Israeli leader said.[16]

Tear gas does not compare with Israel's systematic bombing of Palestinian civilians in Gaza from F-16 fighter jets, drones, tank artillery, and naval boats, let alone the fact that Gaza's civilian population under Israeli military attack has absolutely no escape routes, nowhere to shelter, and no international protection. The most cowardly way of waging a war must be to bomb a population denied any escape, let alone the protection of their vulnerable members in bomb shelters. Such are the double standards of the Israeli government: provocative, inconsequent, and deeply inhuman. Such are also the double standards of the international community in securing the continuation of Israeli impunity: provocative, partial, profoundly pro-Israeli, and colonial.

The United States, the European Union, the North Atlantic Treaty Organization, as well as Norway repeatedly impose strict economic sanctions, weapons embargos, and military actions including bombing and invasions to "maintain international law" and safeguard the security and rights of "the civilian population," as in the case of Libya, Iran, Iraq, Myanmar, Cuba, and India, to mention a few.[17,18] Yet, the State of Israel enjoys limitless exemptions from the same international laws and fair justice. If anything, the Zaytun massacre, as well as all the other reported collective and individual attacks on Palestinian civilians in Gaza during the Israeli onslaught, once more proves the provocative double standards of the United States and its allies.[19]

Israel's impunity and continuous lack of accountability must be of grave concern for anyone who seeks to uphold some level of peaceful coexistence based on fundamental principles of fairness, equality, justice, and international lawfulness. Israel's regular and systematic military attacks on civilians, its siege and collective punishment of the population, and the tens of thousands killed, maimed, and crippled Palestinians form the stained backstage curtain when the totally failed obligations of the Oslo Accords are to be "celebrated." During the most recent Israeli onslaught on Gaza in November 2012, named Pillar of Defense, the same brutality was demonstrated against the civilian Palestinian population. Working with the doctors, nurses and volunteers at al-Shifa Hospital, I witnessed again how civilian children, women, and elders were injured, maimed, and killed during the Israeli military force's week-long attack. More than 190 were killed in the Gaza Strip, and over 1,490 injured. Of the killed, 48 were children eighteen-years-old or less, while 16 of these were below five years of age; of the injured, 504 were less than eighteen-years-old, 195 of whom were below five years of age, according to the Palestinian Health Information Center, Palestinian National Authority Ministry of Health, Gaza. According to the UN, six Israelis were killed and 224 injured. In the Gaza Strip, 298 houses were destroyed or seriously damaged and more than 1,700 houses sustained minor damage; 10,473 civilians were displaced to emergency shelters in Gaza.

The global boycott, divestment, and sanction movement against the State of Israel is a peaceful, productive, and nonviolent way of forcing Israel to comply at least with fundamental international law: the prohibition against an occupier establishing colonies on occupied land (called 'settlements'); the responsibility to safeguard the security of the civilian population in occupied territories; the prohibition against imposing collective punishment on a population; and the obligation to apply proportional military force in armed conflicts, to mention just a few.

And let us not forget, the Palestinian struggle for freedom, the end of Israeli apartheid and occupation of Palestine, the end of the siege of Gaza, and the right of return of Palestinian refugees is a just struggle well anchored in international conventions and fundamental moral laws. It is just like the struggle of other oppressed people. Health is a fundamental human right, and human security is a key determinant of health (Batniji et al. 2009). The living conditions and security situation for the Palestinian population get steadily worse, not due to natural disasters followed by famine, but due to a chronic, low-intensity, and manmade disaster imposed on it by the government of Israel. As such, it is easily reversible and amendable by lifting the siege and ending the occupation. This should be the concern of all international medical associations and communities, including the World Medical Association and Israel's Medical Association (Yudkin 2009). For those interested and willing to see alternative sources of knowledge, the Lancet's series on health in the Occupied Palestinian Territories offers valuable insight with brilliant research on the connections between the Israeli occupation and population health in Palestine (Horton 2009). As stated in one of the papers, "For too long, the health and welfare of Palestinians within the occupied territory have been secondary to powerful outside interests. . . . The solution lies in justice, sovereignty, and self-determination for the people of the West Bank and Gaza Strip" (Becker et al. 2009).

We cannot rest until the situation is resolved. Or, as Rita Giacaman and colleagues argue, "Hope for improving the health and quality of life of Palestinians will exist only once people recognize that the structural and political conditions that they endure in the occupied Palestinian territory are the key determinants of population health" (Giacaman et al. 2009).

The Human Cost

When the Israeli army launched military attacks on Gaza on July 7, 2014, referred to as Operation Protective Edge, what followed was a scale of destruction, devastation, and displacement over the next fifty days that were unprecedented in Gaza since at least the Israeli occupation in 1967. Gaza is so densely populated and urbanized that nearly the whole population was exposed to these attacks and the resulting clashes after the Israeli ground invasion. From a medical point of view, the human costs of Israel's imposed disaster were seriously aggravated by the entire health sector being already deprived due to the continual siege of Gaza as well as the lack of security for ambulance staff and the Israeli military's extensive destruction and damage to hospitals and primary health-care facilities.[20] The last ten years of the Gaza siege had had terribly negative effects on the health of the residents there, and the most vulnerable are suffering even more. For the first time in five decades, mortality rates have increased among new-born Palestinian refugees in Gaza (van de Berg 2015).

"Outrageous, Unacceptable, and Unjustifiable"

These are the concluding words of UN Secretary General Ban Ki-Moon to the UN General Assembly as he described the Israeli attack on Gaza in July–August of 2014. "The massive death and destruction in Gaza have shocked and shamed the world," he said, placing particular emphasis on the repeated shelling of UN facilities that were "harbouring civilians who had been explicitly told to seek a safe haven there."[21] The secretary general said that "in the most recent case of shelling on a UN facility, the Israelis were informed of the coordinates 33 times," and he called for a swift investigation into "attacks against UN premises, along with other suspected breaches of international law."

Again, Israeli impunity prevails, and these crimes, along with others perpetrated during the most recent assault on Gaza, remain unsanctioned and with no ongoing formal prosecution at the International Criminal Court (ICC).[22] On July 25, 2014, Palestinian officials filed a complaint with the ICC in the Hague, to which an Israeli spokesman responded: "The Israeli military is working 100 percent within the dictates of international humanitarian law."[23]

During this most recent—and most brutal—of the four Israeli military onslaughts on Gaza since 2006, the number of Palestinians who were killed and wounded due to the Israeli bombardment and ground invasion reached disastrous proportions, posing an overwhelming task for the Palestinian health-care system, particularly for ambulances and hospitals. Israel's use of force was disproportionate, non-discriminatory, and constituted yet another significant and collective punishment of the Palestinian people (Omer 2015; Blumenthal 2015). To put this particular assault into perspective, in 2008–2009 during Operation Cast Lead, 3,000 high-explosive artillery shells were fired by the Israeli army on Gaza. In 2014 during Operation Protective Edge, 19,000 shells were fired, a 533 percent increase, which occurred alongside more than 6,000 airstrikes.[24]

Throughout the 2014 war on Gaza, there was genuine fear among the population that no person or place was safe, as evidenced by Israeli attacks on ambulances, hospitals, residential buildings, and schools that had been designated as shelters. Psychosocial distress levels were already high among the population of Gaza from the three previous Israeli military attacks (2006, 2008–2009, and 2012), but they have worsened significantly as a result of the most recent onslaught.

Five Hundred Children, Fifty Days

In the 2014 assault, which lasted just fifty days, more than 12,000 Palestinians were injured, among them more than 3,100 children, with up to 1,000 receiving permanent disabilities. Almost 1,500 children were orphaned. Among the 2,251 killed Palestinians in Gaza, at least 70 percent were civilians, among them at least 502 children and 299 women, according to the UNRWA Protection Cluster. At least 164 children were killed by high-precision drone attacks.[25] On the Israeli side, four civilians, including one child, were killed.

Medical units including hospitals and medical personnel are meant to have special protection under international humanitarian law. Still, the health sector in Gaza suffered severe damage, destruction, and deaths as a result of the widespread Israeli attacks. Eighty-three health personnel were injured, while 21 died; at least 47 uniformed ambulances were damaged. As for hospitals, 17 out of 32 were damaged, and 6 were forced to shut down as a result. Out of 97 primary health centers monitored for damage and closures, 45 reported damage, 17 had to be closed, and 4 were completely destroyed. The primary health care as well as the hospital sector in Gaza was already severely weakened from the preceding eight years of Israeli siege, with limited supplies, renewals, and upgrading of facilities and equipment. The health sector's problems before the Israeli assault had been further worsened by very limited supplies of water, energy (electricity and fuel), and financial resources for staff salaries. The ensuing influx of more than 12,000 casualties, combined with a further reduction of health-care capacity caused by Israel's targeting or destruction of health facilities as well as escalations in the siege and continuous attacks, resulted in unnecessary suffering and an increased number of avoidable deaths among the civilian population. In terms of housing units, 18,000 were destroyed or severely damaged and 44,300 were damaged. At least 26 schools were destroyed and 122 were damaged.

The attacks on Gaza in July–August 2014 caused an estimated $2.8 billion in damages. Even prior to this, growth had slowed from 6 percent in 2012 to about 2 percent in 2013 as a result of political uncertainty, a reduction in aid, the ongoing Israeli siege and blockade, and the collapse of tunnel activity between Gaza and Egypt.[26] As a result of the attacks in the summer of 2014, Gaza's economy contracted by nearly 15 percent. Such negative growth has severely affected unemployment, which has risen to 43 percent in Gaza, with a staggering 60 percent of youths and at least 80 percent of women unemployed.

"Then They Kill Us"

Amal Samuni survived the 2014 Israeli attacks, the fourth so far on her home and her life, even at such a young age. She still suffers intense head pains from shrapnel that became lodged in her brain following the 2009 attacks on her family in Zeytun. I have seen her each time I have visited Gaza since I first met her in 2009, but during the 2014 attacks it was impossible for me to leave al-Shifa Hospital, where I worked during the first part of the onslaught. Still, I was able to interview her (Gilbert 2015).

"It was really, really hard for me this time," she said quietly. "My head hurt badly during the latest war. The pain wakes me up at night and I can't get back to sleep. I wanted Dr. Mads to come and get us. I told my mom to ring him at al-Shifa and ask him to come, even though I knew he couldn't do anything.

"This is the worst attack we've experienced," she continued. "They say they want to get Hamas, but then they kill us. We were terrified."

More than twenty-two years of the Oslo Accords and ten years of the Israeli siege of Gaza has made her and the youth of Gaza's future bleaker than ever. Where are the rights of Gaza's children and youth?[27]

We are all responsible.

Facts on the Siege of Gaza[28, 29]

- Palestinian refugees in Gaza are exposed to the lasting consequences of an Israeli occupation now approaching fifty years, and a ten-year-long blockade, which define every aspect of their lives.
- In the year 2000, roughly 80,000 people in Gaza were reliant on humanitarian assistance, a figure that has risen to over 900,000 today.
- Gaza's high population density and overcrowding may cause it to become unlivable by 2020.[30]
- Since the blockade initiated in 2007, exports from Gaza have been almost completely banned, imports and transfers of cash have been severely restricted, and the flow of all but the most basic humanitarian goods has been suspended. The most recent military operation, in 2014, impacted an already paralyzed economy at a time when socioeconomic conditions were at their lowest since 1967. This operation therefore had a more severe impact on socioeconomic conditions compared to the previous two military operations in 2008 and 2012.[31]
- Over half-a-million Palestinians were displaced during the 2014 attacks, with some one-hundred thousand continuing to be displaced by mid-2015 due to the siege.[32,33]
- Of Gaza's workforce, 43 percent, including over 60 percent of its youth, is unemployed.
- Of the total population, 44 percent do not have food security and about 80 percent are aid recipients.
- Today, 35 percent of Gaza's farmland and 85 percent of its fishing waters are totally or partially inaccessible due to Israeli imposed restrictions.

- A severe fuel and electricity shortage results in power outages for up to twelve to eighteen hours a day.
- Nearly one-hundred million liters of untreated and partially treated sewage are dumped into the sea each day.
- Over 90 percent of the water from the Gaza aquifer is unsafe for human consumption without treatment.
- Of schools in Gaza, 85 percent run on double shifts.

Notes

1. Harriet Sherwood, "Ex-Israeli Soldier Jailed over Deaths of Palestinian Women," *The Guardian*, August 12, 2012, http://www.guardian.co.uk/world/2012/aug/12/former-israeli-soldier-jailed.
2. "Palestinian Leaders Call for Liberation from Oslo Accords," *Ma'an News Agency*, September 15, 2012, http://www.maannews.com/Content.aspx?id=519812.
3. Jonathan Cook, "Israel's 'Dahiya Doctrine' Comes to Gaza,' *Electronic Intifada*, January 20, 2009, http://electronicintifada.net/v2/article10224.shtml.
4. Uri Blau, "GOC Southern Command: IDF Will Send Gaza back Decades,' *Haaretz*, December 28, 2008, http://www.haaretz.com/hasen/spages/1050434.html.
5. Rod Nordland, "One Gaza Family Lost 29 Members in Attacks," *Newsweek*, January 19, 2009, http://europe.newsweek.com/one-gaza-family-lost-29-members-attacks-77919?rm=eu.
6. Amira Hass. "What Led to IDF Bombing House Full of Civilians during Gaza War?" *Haaretz*, October 24, 2010, http://www.haaretz.com/news/diplomacy-defense/what-led-to-idf-bombing-house-full-of-civilians-during-gaza-war-1.320816.
7. Rod Nordland, "One Gaza Family Lost 29 Members in Attacks," *Newsweek*, January 19, 2009, http://europe.newsweek.com/one-gaza-family-lost-29-members-attacks-77919?rm=eu.
8. Israeli and Palestinian human rights organizations have comprehensive documentation of the Samouni massacre. See, NGO Monitor, "The NGO Front in the Gaza War: Compilation of NGO Statements," February 5, 2009, http://www.ngomonitor.org/article.php?operation=print&id=2247; B'Tselem, Testimony: Soldiers Killed and Injured Dozens of Persons from a-Samuni Family in a-Zeitun Neighborhood, Gaza, Jan. '09," January 2009, http://www.btselem.org/testimonies/20090104_soldiers_kill_and_wound_members_of_a_samuni_family; the Goldstone Report before the UN Human Rights Council (2009), para. 713–16.
9. Rory McCarthy, "Amid Dust and Death, A Family's Story Speaks for the Terror of War," *The Guardian*, January 19, 2009, http://www.guardian.co.uk/world/2009/jan/20/gaza-israel-samouni-family.

10. Amira Hass, "IDF Closes Probe into Israeli Air Strike that Killed 21 Members of Gaza Family," *Haaretz*, May 1, 2012, http://www.haaretz.com/news/diplomacy-defense/idf-closes-probe-into-israeli-air-strike-that-killed-21-members-of-gaza-family-1.427583.

11. B'Tselem, "Army Closes Investigation into the Killing of 21 Members of the a-Samuni Family in Gaza," press release, May 2, 2012, http://www.btselem.org/press_releases/20120501_samuni_investigation_closed.

12. Ibid.

13. Eyal Benvenisti, "An Obligation to Investigate," *Haaretz*, January 28, 2009, http://www.haaretz.com/hasen/spages/1059435.html.

14. Nina Berglund, "Norway Backs Extended Libyan Operation," *News and Views from Norway*, June 3, 2011, http://www.newsinenglish.no/2011/06/03/norway-backs-longer-libyan-operation/.

15. "Israel says West Must Treat Iran like Libya," *Ma'an News Agency*, March 1, 2011, http://www.maannews.net/eng/ViewDetails.aspx?ID=364657.

16. Ibid.

17. James Killick, Fabienne Vermeeren, and Sara Nordin, "The EU's New Sanctions against Libya — A Summary of the Sanctions Measures to Date," White & Case, July 2011, http://www.whitecase.com/alerts-07052011/-.UYpRvEqIz3E.

18. "International sanctions," Wikipedia, http://en.wikipedia.org/wiki/International_sanctions.

19. "Report of the Independent Fact Finding Committee on Gaza: No Safe Place," Presented to the League of Arab States, April 30, 2009, http://www.arableagueonline.org/las/picture_gallery/reportfullFINAL.pdf.

20. Mads Gilbert, "Brief Report to UNRWA: The Gaza Health Sector as of June 2014," http://www.unrwa.org/sites/default/files/final_report_-_gaza_health_sector_june-july_2014_-_mads_gilbert_2.pdf.

21. "Recent Israeli, Palestinian Crisis Must Be 'The Last Time,' Secretary-General Tells General Assembly," UN Secretary General, August 6, 2014, http://www.un.org/press/en/2014/sgsm16071.doc.htm.

22. Alice Lynd, "International Human Rights Law: Violations by Israel and the Problem of Enforcement," Historians Against the War, August 2014. http://historiansagainstwar.org/resources/InternationalHumanRights.pdf.

23. Toby Cadman, "Palestine, Israel and the International Criminal Court," *MWC News*, July 31, 2014, http://mwcnews.net/focus/analysis/44032-palestine-israel.html.

24. "The United Nations Independent Commission of Inquiry on the 2014 Gaza Conflict," United Nations Human Rights, Office of the High Commissioner, June 24, 2015, http://www.ohchr.org/EN/HRBodies/HRC/CoIGazaConflict/Pages/ReportCoIGaza.aspx#report.

25. "Operation Protective Edge: A War Waged on Gaza's Children," Defense for Children International: Palestine, April 15, 2015, http://www.dci-palestine.org/sites/default/files/operationprotecteedge.awarwagedonchildren.160415.pdf.

26. "The World Bank: Gaza and West Bank Overview," The World Bank, September 16, 2015, http://www.worldbank.org/en/country/westbankandgaza/overview.

27. Zeina Assam, "Where is Accountability for Gaza's Children?" *Al Jazeera*, September 13, 2014, http://www.aljazeera.com/indepth/features/2014/09/where-accountability-gaza-children-20149973438619725.html.

28. "Gaza Situation Report 127," United Nations Relief and Works Agency for Palestine Refugees in the Near East (UNRWA), January 21, 2016, http://reliefweb.int/sites/reliefweb.int/files/resources/Gaza%20situation%20report%20127%20_%20%20UNRWA.pdf.

29. Ramzy Baroud, "Gaza Speaks: This is What the Decade-Long Siege has Done to Us," *Ma'an News Agency*, January 26, 2016, http://www.maannews.com/Content.aspx?id=769983.

30. "Occupied Palestinian Territory Slides into Recession, Gaza Becoming Uninhabitable," United Nations Conference on Trade and Development (UNCTAD), September 1, 2015, http://unctad.org/en/pages/newsdetails.aspx?OriginalVersionID=1068.

31. Ibid.

32. "Five Years of Blockade: The Humanitarian Situation in the Gaza Strip," United Nations Office for the Coordination of Humanitarian Affairs (OCHA), Occupied Palestine Territory, June 2012, http://www.ochaopt.org/documents/ocha_opt_gaza_blockade_factsheet_june_2012_english.pdf.

33. "5 Years: Gaza Blockade," United Nations Office for the Coordination of Humanitarian Affairs (OCHA), Occupied Palestine Territory, http://www.ochaopt.org/gazablockade/#

References

Batniji, R., Y. Rabaia, V. Nguyen-Gillham, R. Giacaman, E. Sarraj, R.-L. Punamaki, H. Saab, and W. Boyce. 2009. "Health as Human Security in the Occupied Palestinian Territory," Lancet 373 (9669): 1133–43.

Becker, A., K. Al Ju'beh, and G. Watt. 2009. "Keys to Health: Justice, Sovereignty, and Self-Determination." Lancet 373 (9668): 985–87.

Blumenthal, M. 2015. *The 51 Day War: Ruin and Resistance in Gaza*. London: Verso.

Giacaman, R., R. Khatib, L. Shabaneh, A. Ramlawi, B. Sabri, G. Sabatinelli, M. Khawaja, and T. Laurance. 2009. "Health Status and Health Services in the Occupied Palestinian Territory." Lancet 373 (9666): 837–49.

Gilbert, M. 2015. *Night in Gaza*. UK: Skyscraper Publications

Horton, R. 2009. "The Occupied Palestinian Territory: Peace, Justice, and Health." Lancet 373 (9666): 784–48.

Omer, Mohammed. 2015. *Shell-Shocked: On the Ground Under Israel's Gaza Assault.'* New York: OR Books.

Palestinian Center for Human Rights. 2009. "The Dead in the Course of the Israeli Recent Military Offensive on the Gaza Strip between 27 December 2008 and 18 January 2009." Gaza City.

United Nations Human Rights Council. 2009. Human Rights in Palestine and Other Occupied Arab Territories: Report of the United Nations Fact-Finding Mission on the Gaza Conflict. New York. September 25.

United Nations Office for the Coordination of Humanitarian Affairs Occupied Palestinian Territory (UNOCHAOPT). 2012. "Five Years of Blockade: The Humanitarian Situation in the Gaza Strip." Factsheet.

van den Berg, M. M., et al. "Increasing Neonatal Mortality among Palestine Refugees in the Gaza Strip." PloS one 10 (2015): e0135092.

Yudkin, J.S. 2009. "The Responsibilities of the World Medical Association President." Lancet 373 (9670): 1155–77.

17

Public and Primary Healthcare before and after the Oslo Accords: A Personal Reflection

Haakon Aars

Background to the Norwegian Red Cross

The International Committee of the Red Cross (ICRC) is a humanitarian institution based in Geneva, Switzerland. States parties (signatories) to the four Geneva Conventions of 1949 and their Additional Protocols of 1977 and 2005 have given the ICRC a mandate to protect victims of international and internal armed conflicts. Such victims include war wounded, prisoners, refugees, civilians, and other noncombatants.

The International Federation of Red Cross and Red Crescent Societies (IFRC) is part of the International Red Cross and Red Crescent Movement, along with the ICRC and 187 distinct 'national societies.' IFRC, founded in 1919 and also based in Geneva, coordinates activities between the national societies in order "to improve the lives of vulnerable people by mobilizing the power of humanity. On an international level, the federation leads and organizes, in close cooperation with the national societies, relief assistance missions responding to large-scale emergencies.

The Norwegian Red Cross (NorCross) was founded in September 1865. The Norwegian Ministry of Defense authorized the organization for voluntary medical aid in war. NorCross was one of the first national organizations in the International Red Cross. It focuses on the closely interlinked organization development (OD), health, disaster risk reduction (DRR), and humanitarian diplomacy activities. NorCross seeks to address these thematic priorities by working on three structural levels: at the regional level, through the ICRC and the federation zone office; at the national level, through selected Red Cross and Red Crescent national societies; and at the community level, through specific activities of the national societies.

I worked as Health Delegate for the International Federation of Red Cross/ Red Crescent Societies in Palestine from 1998 to 2001. I am a medical doctor, specialized in psychiatry. I also hold a master's degree in public health. This chapter is based on my personal experience and work in Palestine.

The Middle East and Palestine/Israel

The Middle East is home to some of the most complicated and long-standing conflicts in the world. The security situation in the Occupied Territories continues to be fragile, resulting from disparities of an economic, ideological, and political nature. Civil society is weak, with limited political freedom, economic differences, and vulnerabilities. Government structures are dependent on international assistance for basic functions, as the issue of the Palestinian territories becoming a sovereign state remains unresolved.

The State of Israel was established in 1948, after a United Nations resolution, with clearly defined borders — borders that Israel has never respected. The occupation of parts of Palestine is a fact. First in 1948, then in 1967, and still today, Israel has occupied new land in East Jerusalem and in the West Bank. New Jewish settlements are established. These settlements are located on top of water sources and on hilltops, hence on land that is important in terms of political strategy. The settlements are also built on the destruction of Palestinian houses and olive trees.

Palestine has an extreme geographical structure, divided as it is into two main parts: Gaza and the West Bank. The West Bank itself is divided into enclaves of autonomous areas that are located inside civil and military Israeli-controlled areas. For the population of the Palestinian autonomous and occupied territories to cross areas controlled by the Israel Defense Forces (IDF) has been, and still is, difficult, and to a great extent not possible at all. This exacerbates the Palestinian population's trauma and problems of everyday life, such as lack of work, lack of access to proper medical care, lack of proper food, and, not least, psychological distress.

The Gaza Strip is 12 kilometers wide and 45 kilometers long, about the size of a small Norwegian county. Since the withdrawal of the Israeli settlers in 2005, Gaza is no longer 'occupied' by Israel. However, on three sides Gaza is surrounded by enclosures in the form of electric fences and walls, while on the fourth side the sea is guarded by Israeli cannon boats that shoot on anything moving more than a half-mile from the coast. In the air fly Israeli Apache helicopters, which often attack targets on the ground. The targets are mainly civilians, children and women included. With a population of 1.7 million, Gaza is the most densely inhabited area in the world after Hong Kong, with 47 percent of the population under fifteen years of age. While the majority of the population today was born in the Gaza Strip, a large percentage identify as Palestinian refugees, who fled to Gaza as part of the 1948 Palestinian exodus during the 1948 Arab–Israeli War. With a yearly growth rate of about 3.2 percent, the Gaza Strip has the seventh-highest population growth rate in the world. Pursuant to the 1993 Oslo Accords, the Palestinian Authority became the administrative body that governs Palestinian population centers. As mentioned above, Israel maintained control of the airspace, territorial waters, and border crossings, apart from the land border with Egypt. The Gaza Strip forms part of the Palestinian territories. Since July 2007, following the 2006 Palestinian legislative elections and the 'Battle of Gaza,' Hamas has functioned as the de facto leadership in the Gaza Strip, forming an alternative 'Hamas government' in Gaza.

The Palestine Red Crescent Society, Focusing on Public and Primary Healthcare

The Palestine Red Crescent Society (PRCS) was founded in December 1968 in direct response to health and sociocultural needs of the Palestinian people in the Occupied Palestinian Territories and the diaspora. It has 4,200 employees in the West Bank and Gaza, Lebanon, Syria, Egypt, and Iraq, in addition to its volunteer network of more than 20,000 people.

Before the Palestinian Authority was established, the PRCS was the de facto Ministry of Health for the Palestinian people. Following the Oslo Accords and the formal establishment of a Ministry of Health by the Palestinian Authority, the PRCS in 1996 and 1999 was mandated to provide national ambulance, blood transfusion, and pre-hospital emergency services in the Palestinian territories and health service in the diaspora. It assumed the role of a complementary body to the public authorities, targeting the needs of the most vulnerable and disadvantaged groups within the Palestinian population.

IFRC started its assistance to the PRCS with the employment of a regional development delegate in November 1995. The main objective was to help the PRCS in the establishment of a national headquarters in the autonomous territories, thereby ensuring the development of the PRCS into a unified national society. As mandated by the Palestinian National Council from 1969, the PRCS was the main health provider to the Palestinian population, focusing on hospitals (secondary health) and emergency medical services, with mainly curative services. After the Oslo Accords, the health system was taken over by the Palestinian Authority and the PRCS was given an auxiliary role, acting as a national Red Crescent society.

In 1996, on the seventh Congress of the PRCS, a special emphasis was placed on the improvement of health services and public health, and the PRCS' role of improving this for the Palestinian people. As the fifty-year conflict with the Israelis had left the Palestinian population in a war-like situation, primary healthcare needs had over a long period not been met, particularly for the most vulnerable, like women and children.

The Congress defined and ratified the principles and priorities for health services, giving high priority to primary healthcare. Built upon the principles of the Alma-Ata Declaration of 1978 stressing the importance of primary healthcare, as well as on the National Health Plan of 1994, a three-year Development Plan for Primary Healthcare was completed in 1996. This plan stresses the importance of a holistic approach to health, as well as the necessity for more emphasis to be placed on preventive healthcare, in addition to curative care. The plan adopted a proactive community approach, seeking to raise awareness within the population of taking responsibility for its own health, both on an individual basis and on a community one.

Today, the PRCS is a full member of the International Red Cross and Red Crescent Movement.

The eighth Congress for the PRCS in Gaza, in January 2000 stressed the importance of PRCS services starting in the community and ending in the community, as well as the importance of community-based activities.

The Department of Mental Health was established in 1992 as one of the major departments within the PRCS. Its main focus was providing psycho-social support to the PRCS' emergency medical staff. After the beginning of the second

Intifada, the PRCS expanded its psychosocial interventions in the West Bank and Gaza.

To accommodate the PRCS in this major work and reorientation, IFRC proposed to support it with a health delegate with special experience in public health and primary healthcare.

Health Delegate Supporting the PRCS

The first health delegate was employed from June 1997 to September 1998. The mission was based on the three-year comprehensive development plan. I was appointed as health delegate to Palestine from October 1998 to February 2001. I was based in the PRCS' headquarters in al-Bireh in the West Bank.

The PRCS also has a regional headquarters in Gaza City due to the division of Palestine into the two entirely separate entities. The PRCS has branches and the headquarters has departments of administration, primary healthcare, youth and volunteers, emergency medical services (EMS), finance, social welfare, disaster management, dissemination, mental health, and rehabilitation, as well as an EMS school. In addition to me as the health delegate, IFRC had a head of delegation. At the same time, delegates from other Red Cross organizations were implementing bilateral programs in Palestine.

My main task was to assist the PRCS' Primary Healthcare Department with providing adequate medical supplies as well as technical material to the Primary Healthcare Centers. It was also to implement and support the centers' health programs, particularly to help support the people most in need in the different communities. An important program in particular was Primary Health Care and Community-Based Health and First Aid (CBHFA), which trains and mobilizes volunteers to carry out activities in their communities, thereby involving the community, where both the target and the resources reside. The beneficiaries are the community, and volunteers are the backbone of the program. To meet the needs of the most vulnerable is the first issue. The focus is on prevention, preparedness, and the public health aspect, as well as traditional first aid. This includes health education within the community on all important public health issues, such as hygiene, a clean water supply, sanitation, and the prevention of diseases and disasters.

In addition, I worked to obtain financial support for the Primary Healthcare Department and its activities from different national societies.

Before the Intifada started, the PRCS was well into the concept of CBHFA at all levels in the national society. Through this program, a team of one nurse and one social worker was employed in each Primary Health Center run by the PRCS. Another program was the Mother and Child Program, also run via IFRC. Community health groups were established and trained, thus promoting the participation of local communities in dealing with priority health needs. The program focused on health promotion and prevention through community-based activities and the establishment of micro projects in conjunction with a community health committee in each community, consisting of local elected members. The PRCS also established a medical hotline so that communities could ask for help when it was urgently needed, including so-called Focal Points in Gaza with a hotline.

During my tenure as the health delegate, the Department of Mental Health was a newly established department within the PRCS. It had seventy-five social workers and psychologists in the field. The target group was individuals and families in the communities, and the aim was to raise awareness about mental illness, stress management, and support.

The Primary Healthcare Department had twenty-six Primary Health Centers in Gaza and the West Bank. Some PRCS branches also had Primary Health Centers. There were also three mobile clinics, each with a doctor, a nurse, and a driver, which traveled to remote areas, particularly serve the nomads living in these areas. They were in a different community every day of the week and reported back to a Primary Health Center in their area.

My mandate as the IFRC health delegate was to help coordinate public health and primary health services at all levels in the PRCS. My work thus much devoted to traveling and visiting Primary Health Centers in the West Bank, as well as in Gaza.

The Palestinian territories being divided into two entirely different geographical parts, together with the ongoing conflict in the region, particularly after the outbreak of the second Intifada, made my work as a health delegate very difficult.

The Political Situation and Its Consequences for Public and Primary Health in 1998–2000

The political situation in the autonomous and occupied territories at the beginning of my period as health delegate was pressured by the Israeli government's chronic postponement of the implementation of the Wye Agreement of October 23, 1998. The situation seemed even more hopeless by the end of 1998, a year marked by heavy clashes between Palestinians and the IDF and settlers. On three occasions I was personally involved in such clashes, including through direct attacks on my Red Cross/Red Crescent-marked car.

However, there was also much turbulence inside the State of Israel. Deep divisions in Israeli society concerning religious, political, and sociological issues led to mass demonstrations as well as clashes between ultraorthodox groups and more secular groups.

The Israeli elections of May 17, 1999, resulted in a new Labour Party coalition government. Ehud Barak and his 'One Israel' Party gave policy guidelines on Jewish settlements in East Jerusalem and the West Bank, promising no new settlements would be established.

In the meantime the situation was that new settlements were being developed in East Jerusalem and all around the West Bank and the Gaza Strip, with the building of so-called 'bypass roads' on the rise. These are motorways built for the use of Israelis only, not Palestinians. Red Cross/Red Crescent cars were allowed on them during my tenure, but numerous 'checkpoints' make travel difficult and slow. Often, these checkpoints were closed without warning, making access to Palestinian villages to provide medical aid impossible. Although Palestinians' expectations were raised upon the signing of the Sharm al-Sheikh agreement, new settlements were being developed all the time. This was accompanied by serious clashes and demonstrations. As a matter of fact, more settlements were started in this short period under a new prime minister than during the whole Netanyahu period, much to the concern of Palestinians and the expatriate community working in the area. The peace talks were halted and delayed, and an increasing impatience could be felt in the Palestinian population concerning the Palestinian Authority. There was a definite rise in the impatience and level of stress inside the society toward the end of the millennium.

The political situation in the West Bank and Gaza was in this period heavily focused on the peace talks between the Palestinian Authority and the Israelis. There was, however, little development toward a final agreement on the core questions of borders, Jewish settlements, the water supply, refugees, and the status of East Jerusalem. The negotiations between Israel and the Palestinian Authority came to a halt with Camp David.

On May 15, 2000, I was directly involved in a shooting incident. This was in the troubled days around Israeli Independence Day, or al-Naqba Day (the Day of the Catastrophe, as Palestinians call it, referring to the establishment of the State of Israel in 1948). There had been a significant shortage of drinking water and electricity, particularly in Gaza. In the West Bank, more than two hundred villages were experiencing periods without running water. These incidents together with the ongoing conflict and restrictions on travel made the situation for Palestinians worse and worse, both regarding public health and the physical and psychological health of all the people.

The Second Intifada, September 2000 onward

The situation in Palestine on all levels, as well as between Israel and Palestine, changed from difficult to much worse on September 29, 2000, with the outbreak of the al-Aqsa Intifada, also called the second Intifada. The clashes that followed lasted the rest of the time I was in the region. The conflict led to the deaths of many hundreds and the wounding of many thousands, mostly Palestinians. This clearly had a most serious impact both on my work in Palestine and on the Palestinian people as a whole. The situation affected the implementation of all PRCS activities, not least the Primary Healthcare Department, and the public health situation in Palestine in general.

This war-like conflict made visits to Primary Health Centers in the villages by me and even more so for by the staff from headquarters most difficult, and for periods absolutely impossible. The IFRC (myself and the head of delegation) together with the PRCS on different occasions tried to go to Primary Health Centers with aid and medical supplies, but had to return after only being able to give 'back-to-back services' across complete roadblocks to the villages. On many occasions, the work was dangerous, as Israeli settlers were armed. I and my local staff were stopped and even shot at. On many occasions, no respect was paid to the symbol of the Red Cross/Red Crescent on the cars. Many Israeli settlers could not speak English, as many came from Russia or other places where English was not used. Hence, the delivery of medical supplies as well as the implementation of CBHFA and other programs in the Primary Health Centers was often impossible. Many villages were, for periods of time, totally closed off from contact with the outside world due to roadblocks making health services inaccessible. Israeli settlers destroyed roads leading to many villages completely, and also destroyed the supply of clean water by blasting village wells. Hence, many villages faced extreme shortages of food and drinking water. People became sick because they lacked clean water, and their sanitation system had been destroyed, particularly children and the elderly.

At the same time, the Israelis established so-called 'security zones' and motorways to bind Jewish settlements together.

In Gaza, the situation was getting worse all the time. In this last period of my work there, the Gaza Strip was more or less inaccessible, except for to ICRC cars and diplomats. No Palestinians were able to enter or leave, including all PRCS staff.

Recent Years

After I left in 2001, a Danish health delegate took over the position until 2004. After 2005, the support from the Red Cross was provided on a bilateral basis, in accordance with the PRCS' own decision. The Norwegian funding comes via NORAD to NorCross, supporting the PRCS' long-term projects. These include CBHFA, projects on disaster reduction, rehabilitation of the disabled, psychosocial support, organizing support, and support to the ambulance services. There are today about thirty Primary Health Centers that focus on the Mother and Child Program operated by the PRCS, in collaboration with the Ministry of Health together with the United Nations Relief and Works Agency for Palestine Refugees in the Near East. NorCross also supports voluntary work in so-called community committees, which consist mainly of women.

Israel withdrew from Gaza in 2005, closing its settlements. Hamas won the elections in 2006 and has de facto run Gaza since 2007. President Mahmoud Abbas of Fatah is the president of Palestine, although he is resident in Ramallah in the West Bank. Due to Hamas being in power, there were international economic sanctions against the Palestinian Authority from 2007 focused on Hamas-controlled Gaza. These sanctions were stopped in 2008. In this period, it was very difficult to convey money to Gaza especially, and support for civil servants' salaries was partly stopped. This included wages to PRCS staff. About $10 million was withheld. ICRC also had to reduce its financial support to the ambulance services, and Israel stopped the transport of medical supplies to Gaza.

All in all, the Palestinians' extremely difficult situation is placing an enormous burden on primary health services and on the public health situation in the Palestinian territories. In the transitional period of 2008–2009, with the war in Gaza, Israel did serious damage to Gaza's infrastructure, including civilian houses, schools, hospitals, and public buildings. Many hundreds of civilians were killed, including women and children.

The PRCS hospital in Gaza was hit by Israeli bombs, as was the Gaza PRCS headquarters. The water supply was stopped and wells and electricity stations were destroyed. Clean water and electricity has since been in short supply. Most of the sanitation system was destroyed by Israeli shelling and has not functioned since, with all the negative public health consequences this implies.

Today, there are nine 'checkpoints' for travel from Israel to Gaza, in addition to the border crossing from Egypt in Rafah, which is now controlled by Egypt. After the Arab Spring, crossing into Gaza here became easier. However, illegal tunnels from Gaza to Egypt are still believed to be the main conduit for important building materials and probably also medical supplies. Erez is today the main 'checkpoint' for diplomats going to Gaza, as well as for patients going to Israel for treatment.

It is still very difficult to move around in the West Bank. In the 'roadmap' agreement that US President Bill Clinton oversaw, it was decided that the number of 'checkpoints' should be reduced. Instead, lots of so-called 'flying checkpoints' were established, making it even more complicated to move around, and even more unpredictable. People living in villages close to Israeli settlements particularly have difficulties in passing in and out. This also creates extreme difficulties for personnel and patients trying to reach health centers and hospitals. In addition, Israel has constructed a 'security fence,' or wall, all along its border with the West Bank, in many places on Palestinian land. It is especially difficult to move around in the vicinity of this 'fence.' In many places the wall prevents farmers from accessing their olive groves and children from reaching their schools. Some health centers are totally barred off from the outside world.

The West Bank is more and more split up into isolated enclaves. Settler violence is increasing as more and more illegal settlements are built on West Bank territory. The building of these illegal settlements is stealing Palestinian land. The clashes in the West Bank and the shelling of Gaza by Israel kill people. The destruction of houses, wells, the electricity supply, the sanitation system, and olive trees and the blocking of the delivery of medical supplies and food to villages and the stopping of ambulances at checkpoints are all destroying living conditions for Palestinians and having a negative influence on public and primary health. A Palestinian not-for-profit organization, the Health, Development, Information, and Policy Institute, has reported eighty-three deaths when emergency care has been denied. Fifty-two women have given birth at checkpoints after being refused access to hospitals. There are today more than seven hundred checkpoints, blockages, and closures throughout the West Bank, with most Palestinians forbidden to move outside the minor towns.

The latest decision by the Israeli government is to extend the settlement of Ma'ale Adumim to cut off access from the West Bank to East Jerusalem and to carve up the West Bank into two parts.

What Have the Oslo Accords Meant for Public Healthcare?

Oslo I, officially called the Declaration of Principles on Interim Self-Government Arrangements, was an attempt in 1993 to set up a framework that would lead to the resolution of the ongoing Israeli–Palestinian conflict. It was followed by Oslo II in 1995. Neither of these agreements promised statehood, and Palestine has still not obtained this status. On November 20, 2012, however, the United Nations General Assembly overwhelmingly voted to recognize Palestine as a non-member observer state—a move strongly opposed by Israel and the United States.

Since the start of the second Intifada, the Oslo Accords have been viewed with increasing disfavor by both the Palestinian and the Israeli public. Certainly, the Palestinian public health situation and primary health services did not improve in the aftermath of the accords. On the contrary, as described above, they have worsened.

More than twenty-two years after the Oslo Accords, the hope and plan for a future State of Palestine seems increasingly impossible. The health situation for the Palestinian people, too, seems worse in all ways, including primary health, public health, and access to hospital services.

References

Aars, H. 2004. "Review and Assessment of the IFRC Community Based First Aid Program in MENA Region." Unpublished manuscript. International Federation of Red Cross and Red Crescent Societies, Geneva.

_____. 2000. "Final Report, End of Mission, Dr. Haakon Aars, Health Delegate for the International Federation of the Red Cross and Red Crescent Societies, Representation Office for Palestinian O-A/T, al-Bireh, West Bank." Unpublished manuscript. International Federation of Red Cross and Red Crescent Societies, Geneva.

International Committee of the Red Cross. 2011. "Israel and the Occupied Territories." In *ICRC Annual Report 2011*. Geneva: ICRC.

_____. "The ICRC in Israel and the Occupied Territories, http://www.icrc.org/eng/where-we-work/middle-east/israel-occupied-territories/index.jsp.

International Committee of the Red Cross. "Occupation," http://www.icrc.org/eng/war-and-law/contemporary-challenges-for-ihl/occupation/index.jsp.

Stenbäck, P. 2011. *Interim Report on the Implementation of the Memorandum of Understanding and the Agreement on Operational Arrangements Dated 28 November 2005 Between Magen David Adom in Israel and Palestine Red Crescent Society*. Geneva:

International Committee of the Red Cross and the International Federation of Red Cross and Red Crescent Societies.

Norwegian Red Cross. 2012. "Mobilize Volunteers and Communities." Norwegian Red Cross Framework for Middle East and North Africa, 2012–2014.

Palestine Facts, http://www.palestinefacts.org.

18

Facts in the Air: Palestinian Media Expression since Oslo

Matt Sienkiewicz

Writing just before the signing of the Oslo Accords, Edward Said remarked with a certain sense of incredulity on the inability of the Palestine Liberation Organization (PLO) to control its own public profile. He argued that a "semiotic warfare" was waged against the organization as it attempted to stake its claim as the legitimate representative of the Palestinian people (Said 1992: xix). This 'war,' though symbolic in its form, manifested itself concretely in the terms on which negotiations between Israelis and Palestinians took place. According to Said, the media campaign against various Palestinian leaders resulted in an unprecedented situation in which one party to the negotiations, Israel, was effectively able to select both its own representatives and those of its antagonist. This marked yet another example of a decades-long "blocking operation" in which Palestinians were always "spoken for" by others and never themselves.

A few years later, looking back upon the Oslo Accords that resulted from this negotiating dynamic, Said argued that the agreement was a mere "fashion-show" that deprioritized the actual needs of the Palestinian people in favor of a script that matched American and Israeli interests in shaping world perception (1996: 7). Although the ultimate impact of the conflict between Israel and Palestine is felt in the forms of actual violence and dispossession, Said was deeply committed to the notion that the realm of discourse played a key role in creating a global environment in which the situation appeared justified or even necessary. His work, as much as anything, represented a call to action for Palestinians to seize opportunities to tell their own stories in every public forum possible.

Despite the well-publicized failings of the accords themselves, Palestinians have, in fact, made considerable progress over the past two decades in bringing their own narratives into the public sphere. Perhaps nowhere has this success been more apparent than in the realm of international cinema, where Palestinian productions have become a mainstay. The films of Michel Khleifi, Elia Suleiman, Hany Abu-Assad, Rashid Masharawi, and others have brought representations of Palestinians, by Palestinians, to festival screens across the world. Abu-Assad's *Paradise Now* and Emad Burnat's *5 Broken Cameras* (produced with Israeli film-maker Guy David), films that dig deeply into the Palestinian perspective on Israeli occupation, have found truly global audiences with the help of Academy Award nominations. In one of his final statements on the subject, Said noted the progress that had been made, arguing that finally the world had access to "a visible incarnation of Palestinian existence" that stood in opposition to the dominant western-Zionist narrative (2006: 3). Were he alive today, Said would perhaps include international news outlets such as Al Jazeera in this effort, as the democratization of broadcast technologies has most certainly made public a more diverse array of perspectives on the Middle East.

Lost within this discourse, however, is the struggle that has taken place over domestic Palestinian media, a battle, I argue, that has been permanently hampered by the ways in which the international community reacted to the Oslo process and its extremely limited acceptance of Palestinian sovereignty. While individual Palestinian artists have thrived in the years since the accords, more systematic media efforts, such as Palestinian broadcasting, have been weighed down by the intense international scrutiny that Oslo invited upon Palestinian culture. Although I wish to stop short of claiming that any western involvement in Palestinian broadcasting is inherently damaging, this chapter aims to sketch some of the ways in which the Oslo Accords invited new structural limitations upon a struggling media sector already beset by the impositions of Israeli occupation.

The Early Years

As scholars Daoud Kuttab (1998), Amal Jamal (2004), Naomi Sakr (2007), and Helga Tawil-Souri (2007) have noted, Palestinian broadcasting has faced tremendous obstacles from the moment of its inception. The Oslo Accords ended the decades-old moratorium on electronic media produced by Palestinians in the West Bank and Gaza Strip that reached back to the period before Israel's occupation in 1967. Although the accords offered Palestinians only a tiny sliver of spectrum space, even this represented an unprecedented opportunity to express Palestinian perspectives without "Arab governmental pressures [or] . . . fear of Israeli airstrikes" (Kuttab 1998). Yasser Arafat, in fact, placed such an emphasis on the establishment of the Palestinian Broadcasting Corporation (PBC) that he incorporated the institution and dedicated its Gaza City headquarters prior to his own return from exile in Tunis in 1994 (Jamal 2000: 499). After years of being forced to broadcast indirectly via a variety of outside mediators in surrounding Arab states, Arafat and the Palestinian Authority saw indigenous broadcasting as a crucial step in creating a sense of national unity within the borders of what was now officially the proto-state of Palestine.

However, while the accords provided a broadcasting opportunity in terms of spectrum space for Palestinians, it did little to promote the effective use of these newly allocated resources. As Israel began to reduce its presence in the Area A spaces that were handed over to the Palestinian Authority's limited sovereignty as a result of Oslo, it took with it the core elements of the region's broadcasting infrastructure. As a result, the Palestinian Authority, though eager to begin broadcasting, was left not only with a deficit in regards to technical know-how but also without the high-power antennas necessary to reach its citizens.

Thus, a moment that could have worked to further the goals of the Oslo process by establishing a strong sense of a unified imagined community within the newly declared Palestinian territories through broadcasting was not just delayed but fractured. As the Palestinian Authority worked to establish its central broadcasting presence, entrepreneurial micro-broadcasters began popping up throughout the West Bank and Gaza, seizing upon an opportunity to garner small amounts of local notoriety and advertising revenue by broadcasting pirated programming. The Palestinian Authority, wishing to lay permanent claim to the Oslo-granted spectrum space, allowed these extralegal stations to operate, establishing what Kuttab describes as "facts in the air" that would prevent future seizure of the spectrum by Israel.[1] These small stations catered to highly localized audiences, contributing to what Tawil-Souri (2006) criticizes for playing a role in preventing the establishment of a widely shared, democratically conceived sense of unity among citizens living in the Palestinian territories. This virtual cantonization of the media sphere thus paralleled the physical compartmentalization the Oslo process laid out as the first step to the establishment of Palestinian political sovereignty in atomized, noncontiguous territories (Tawil-Souri 2006: 11).

Although there are many reasons to argue for the existence of the alternative media sphere that small, private stations can provide, the lack of detailed foresight in the Oslo Accords approach to national broadcasting is indicative of the agreement's general deficit of vision. As advocates for public television across the world have long held, it is not nearly enough simply to offer spectrum space to a new broadcasting entity. The process of producing high-quality television requires a tremendous level of financial investment and infrastructural foresight. Had the framers of the Oslo Accords been fully appreciative of the importance of allowing for a coherent internal Palestinian voice to be broadcast, this could have been accounted for early in the process through a negotiated exchange of broadcast technology. Instead, a slow, fractured rollout of Palestinian media came to parallel the slow, fractured process of turning over physical space to Palestinian sovereignty. Whereas media might have played a role of bridging physical and political gaps, it was instead allowed to exacerbate them.

Hypersurveillance

Another ramification of the Oslo Accords for the realm of Palestinian media expression resulted from the intense scrutiny that came with the process' massive influx of international money. The utter dependence of Palestinian institutions, including the PBC, on foreign aid left them vulnerable to both passive and aggressive measures aimed at severely limiting local decision making. In the realm of broadcasting, this came in the form of a cottage industry devoted to monitoring every aspect of Palestinian media expression in order to report the results back to donor states and, in the majority of cases, advocate for ceasing of support.

The Oslo Accords were made possible in large measure by an increase in foreign aid funding from western nations. Unable to find a consensus with regards to the fundamental questions of final borders, refugees, and the status of Jerusalem, western powers engaged in a strategy that Lasensky (2004) and others have described as "paying for peace," whereby Israelis and Palestinians were encouraged to accept partial and unsatisfactory terms in exchange for vastly inflated aid packages. In the years following the accords, American aid to the Palestinian

Authority increased exponentially, tripling to $3 billion in the first half of the 1990s alone (Brynen 2000: 7).

In addition to papering over fundamental problems and placing into question the ultimate economic independence of a Palestinian state, this strategy brought the world of Palestinian broadcasting into the sphere of international debate. Although relatively small in terms of proportion of total investment, the content of Palestinian media produced by the Palestinian Authority and thus ultimately funded by the Palestinian Authority's western supporters became a political lightning road. A wide range of organizations, including NGO Monitor, Palestinian Media Watch (PMW), the Taxpayers' Alliance, and the Middle East Media Research Institute emerged in the wake of the accords. Although each of these watchdog institutions has interests that go beyond the content of the Oslo Accords, their work is bolstered by, and is in some cases dependent on, the relationship between western funding sources and the accords.

PMW, for example, provides near-daily video and text reports translating and exposing the content of Palestinian print and broadcast media in a highly compressed, decontextualized format. These reports are generally produced in the form of brief media samples alongside summaries that detail the way in which PMW's editors believe the clips or quotes reflect Palestinian society's relationship to the peacemaking process. Overwhelmingly, these reports are aimed at exposing aspects of the Palestinian media that might disturb a western viewer. They are also often accompanied by an explanation of the ways in which western nations are implicated in the production of the offending media, whether through direct financial support or through political alliances that date back to Oslo. In many cases, PMW's focus, though subject to a severe case of tunnel vision, details moments of Palestinian media that are all but certain to disturb viewers from across the political spectrum. In particular, its reports that illustrate the acceptance of child suicide violence in the Palestinian media are deeply troubling, as the phenomenon's causes are more complex than PMW's analysis suggests.[2]

These reports are intermingled with others documenting Palestinian infractions that are primarily problematic in the context of western funding and the Oslo Accords. Alongside categories such as "Suicide terror" and "Children as combatants," the PMW Research Center features reports that chronicle far less morally obvious concerns. These include reports that reprimand Palestinian broadcasters for describing cities such as Haifa as "Palestinian," despite their being part of the established Israeli borders outlined by Oslo. While this is certainly a political statement, describing Haifa or Tel Aviv as Palestinian is by no means an obvious failing or provocation, given the history and sizable Arab population of the cities. PMW, however, denounces such articulations as fundamentally wrong due to their implication that Palestinians, despite signing the accords, have not stripped these cities out of their national identity.

Along similar lines, PMW chronicles and denounces acts of Palestinian resistance that, while neither violent nor obviously immoral, betray what PMW understands to be the essence of the Oslo agreement. For example, in 2011, PMW issued a report detailing the Spanish government's support for a television advertisement advocating a boycott of Israeli products. One day later the Spanish government disowned and condemned the advertisement.[3] The expressions being exposed by PMW in these reports can be questioned in terms of their wisdom, but they are by no means the sort of media that would be scrutinized under normal circumstances.

The Oslo Accords have brought a sense that the hypersurveillance of Palestinian media is not only justified but also an effective form of anti-Palestinian resistance. Reports by groups such as PMW have had documented, tangible effects on Palestinian broadcasting. The most obvious of these is seen in United States Congressional debates that took place in the early days of the PBC, during which it was argued that "the PBC consistently broadcasts programming that attempts to undermine all the United States seeks to achieve in the Middle East" (Congressional Record 1999: 19323). Based on information provided by watchdog groups, this line of argument led to Section 584 of the 1999 Foreign Operations Appropriations Bill, which prohibits the disbursement of American funds to the PBC (Rennack, Mages, and Chesser 2009: 12). The result is a strange situation in which the United States supports the Palestinian Authority with large sums of money for operating expenses, yet at the same time treats its broadcasting wing as a hostile organization parallel to outlets such as Hezbollah's Al-Manar.

The reason for this fractured worldview would seem to be a divergent understanding of what broadcasting's role was to be in the process of Palestinian nation building. From the perspective of America and western watchdogs, the PBC ought to have placed the Oslo Accords first, shaping its portrayal of Palestinian identity to the new political order that 1993 brought to the region. The Palestinian Authority, however, understood the PBC as a means of fostering a unified sense of nationalism without regard to the particularities of Oslo. If the majority of Gaza and West Bank residents understand Haifa as Palestinian, for example, the PBC was not about to contradict this and threaten its own legitimacy in order to avoid crossing the Oslo-induced red lines that watchdogs such as PMW were created to enforce.

Media Assistance

The Oslo Accords brought more than surveillance to the world of Palestinian media. As donor money flooded into the Palestinian territories in the 1990s and early 2000s, a variety of western-funded initiatives targeted at media production emerged. Organizations such as Internews created training programs for journalists, most of which were geared toward a process of professionalization and capacity building. Although these initiatives have served as training grounds for numerous members of the current Palestinian mediasphere, critics have identified them as yet another patronizing "gift, from the developed West to the 'transitional' or developing Rest" (Miller 2009: 10).

But media assistance in the Palestinian territories has gone far beyond training activities and educational programs. Beginning in the late 1990s, a number of western nations invested in the development of alternative media institutions aimed at supplementing or supplanting the PBC as the premier voice of Palestinian broadcasting. The most prominent of these has been the Bethlehem-based Ma'an Network. Billing itself as the only independent broadcaster in the Palestinian territories, Ma'an has grown substantially over the past decade, now representing the only consistent indigenous alternative to official Hamas and Fatah television.

Originally known as the Shams Network, Ma'an began as a loose alliance of the West Bank independent micro-broadcasters described above. Its original investment came from the Danish government, whose interests lay not only in establishing a European-style public broadcasting service in the West Bank but also in achieving a level of international respect. According to Christian Jessen, a Danish Foreign Service officer who spearheaded the original project, Denmark's enthusiasm for supporting Palestinian media was bolstered by a desire to escape the shadow cast by Norway's breakthrough in facilitating the Oslo Accords. As in all areas of Palestinian culture and politics, broadcasting represents not only a local reality but also a symbolic plain upon which global actors display influence and gain prestige.[4]

The Danish broadcasting experiment in Palestine was relatively short-lived, however, as the second Intifada finally ended the enthusiasm and accessibility that the Oslo agreement had brought to the region. Left for dead, the Ma'an Network was eventually resuscitated by the American government, which infused the institution with money and provided it with broadcasting resources that would eventually make it a significant force in the region's media environment. After eight years of broadcasting via ultra-high frequency (UHF), Ma'an now operates a satellite channel known as Ma'an/Mix TV that features some of the most popular domestic Palestinian programming in history. Most notably, the singing competition *Palestine New Star* has attracted an audience that dwarfs that of entertainment programming on the PBC.

Ma'an is a complicated institution and one that is very much indicative of the complex dynamic that has marked the west's relationship with Palestinian entities since Oslo. On the one hand, Ma'an is an independent broadcaster, free to produce any programming it desires and staffed entirely by locals and international personnel hired by local decision makers. The institution has created a variety of interesting shows, ranging from public affairs programs such as *Hebrew Press Tour*, which features a live Arabic translation of Israel's Hebrew Channel 2 news broadcast, to culturally rich entertainments such as *New Star*. Using production and satellite uplink technology provided by the west, Ma'an has added a layer of diversity to Palestinian television that even the most stringent of its critics must acknowledge.

However, although Ma'an is technically an independent organization, the economic and political realities of Palestinian existence undermine any sense of true autonomy. Yes, Ma'an is able to make programs of its own initiative, but media production, like nation building, is extremely expensive and requires a level of financial security that only large, established external institutions can provide. Ma'an thus chooses to produce the majority of its programming either in partnership with western nongovernmental organizations (NGOs) or as work-for-hire, with the clients being western states. Thus, for every program such as *New Star* that Ma'an produces, it creates many documentaries paid for specifically by the European Union, intended to increase the EU's prestige in the minds of Arabic speakers across the world.

Many of Ma'an's programs have come through NGOs such as Search for Common Ground that receive their funding primarily from the US Department of State. As such, these programs tend to avoid issues that would stir up controversy for American politicians on the domestic front. For example, Ma'an has produced a series of fictional programs focusing on the theme of conflict. However, as opposed to engaging with the reality of the Israeli–Palestinian dilemma, these productions have, without exception, focused on internal Palestinian unrest. Most notably, the film *Enough* and the television drama series *The Team* have devoted dozens of hours to domestic Palestinian political division while never directly addressing the impact of Israeli occupation on these complex, often violent internal conflicts. Although these series certainly confront important elements of contemporary Palestinian life, they are also remarkable in their silence not only on the conflict with Israel but also on the role the west has played in perpetuating in the conflict.

Repercussions

Ma'an's inability to address these crucial concerns represents a disturbing microcosm of the Palestinian political situation since Oslo. Having little choice but to accept external help, Ma'an has taken on an extensive relationship with the west. This has brought with it new opportunities. Ma'an programming boasts impressive production values, employs a relative diversity of on- and off-air personnel, and tells stories about the daily sorts of internal Palestinian matters that would never grace the screen at the Cannes Film Festival. Yet, this freedom brings with it an inability to address the structural limitations that might prevent Ma'an from developing into a truly independent institution. Constantly monitored by organizations such as PMW and held to standards beyond that of most broadcasting outlets across the world, Ma'an's source of economic freedom is also its prison. As an independent station, the outlet should be able to debate all aspects of Palestinian life, including the role the western architects of the Oslo Accords play in the prospects for an equitable and permanent peace with Israel. However, as much as western donors might proclaim the freedom of Ma'an, the ability of monitoring organizations to take bits of media and turn them into powerful indictments forestalls any true freedom of expression. Funded through the mechanisms of Oslo, Ma'an and other Palestinian broadcasters are unable to question the orthodoxies codified by the agreement, the most prominent of which is the central place of America and Europe in the ultimate resolution of the Israeli–Palestinian conflict.

There is no question that Palestinian cultural expression has expanded since the signing of the Oslo Accords. On the international level Palestinian storytelling is perhaps reaching a golden age. In the domestic sphere there is a far greater diversity of voices outlining the Palestinian narrative. There are even ways in which the structural elements of the Oslo Accords have contributed to this progress. Ma'an and the PBC have pushed one another over the past decade, with the latter notably liberalizing and diversifying its offerings. There is good reason to believe that, alongside the influence of international outlets, the PBC has been adapting in order to keep up with Ma'an as a local competitor.

This progress would seem to be inherently limited, however. Such incomplete forms of independence as those offered under the strictures of Oslo can only go so far. In the case of Ma'an, the institution has been struggling to break out from the golden chains of western funding in order to address Palestinian culture in ways beyond the purview of those approved by America and Europe. It has done this to some extent with *New Star*, a program that not only is financially viable but also freely mixes Palestinians from both sides of the Green Line, perhaps implicitly throwing into question the reality of Oslo. However, for every example of this sort of freedom, many more can be found that display the partial, often illusory independence that has been given to Palestinians since Oslo. The west can perhaps play a role in encouraging both a free Palestinian media and a free state. But, just as offering limited contained spheres of autonomy has failed politically, limited contained spheres of discursive freedom will ultimately lead nowhere.

Notes

1. D. Kuttab, "Independent Media in the Face of Change," *This Week in Palestine*, May 2006, http://www.thisweekinpalestine.com/details.php?id=1702&ed=114&edid=114.
2. I. Marcus and N. Zilberdik, "Mother Places Suicide Belt on Her Child:

   'I Will Put It on You and You Will Go to Your Death on Fatah-Lebanon
   Facebook Page,'" http://palwatch.org electronic mailing list message, October 29, 2012.
3. I. Marcus and N. Zilberdik, "Spanish Government Denies Knowledge of Its Funding of PA TV Ad Advocating Boycott of Israeli Products," http://palwatch.org electronic mailing list message, January 12, 2011.
4. Interview with Christian Jessen, Danish Foreign Ministry, January 10, 2010.

References

Brynen, R. 2000. *A Very Political Economy: Peacebuilding and Foreign Aid in the West Bank and Gaza*. Washington, D.C.: United States Institute of Peace Press.

Jamal, A. 2003. *State Formation and Media Regime in Palestine*. Tel Aviv: Tami Steinmet Center for Peace Studies, Tel Aviv University.

_____. 2000. "State-Formation, the Media, and the Prospects of Democracy in Palestine." *Media, Culture and Society* 22 (4): 497–505.

Kuttab, D. 1998. "The Palestinian Media and the Peace Process: The Palestinian Media from the Dark Period of the Intifada to the Emergence of the PNA." *Palestine-Israel Journal* 5 (3/4), http://www.pij.org/details.php?id=372.

Lasensky, S. 2004. "Paying for Peace: The Oslo Process and the Limits of American Foreign Aid." *Middle East Journal* 58 (2): 210–34.

Rennack, D., L. Mages, and S.G. Chesser. 2009. *Foreign Operations Appropriations: General Provisions*. Washington, D.C.: Congressional Research Service.

Said, E.W. 2006. "Preface." In *Dreams of a Nation*, edited by H. Dabashi. London: Verso.

_____. 1996. *Peace and Its Discontents: Essays on Palestine in the Middle East Peace Process*. New York: Vintage.

_____. 1992. *Orientalism*. New York: Vintage.

Sakr, N. 2007. *Arab Television Today*. London: I.B. Tauris.

Tawil-Souri, H. 2007. "Global and Local Forces for a Nation-State Yet To Be Born: The Paradoxes of Palestinian Television Policies." *Westminster Papers in Communication and Culture* 4 (3): 4–25.

United States Congress. 1998. *Congressional Record*. Washington, D.C.: Government Printing Office.

19

Networking Palestine: The Development and Limitations of Television and Telecommunications since 1993

Helga Tawil-Souri

Constricted Self-Determination

While the Oslo Accords enabled Palestinian state building, they also set the stage for Palestinians in the Occupied Territories to have their own technology and media infrastructures. Between 1948 and 1967, television and radio broadcasts occurred extraterritorially, under Jordanian and Egyptian control in the West Bank and the Gaza Strip, respectively, or through political parties in exile beaming signals from Amman, Beirut, or Cyprus. Under Israeli occupation from 1967 to 1993, Palestinians could watch and listen to Israeli broadcasts (some of which were in Arabic) or obtain signals from neighboring countries. During that time telephone lines were extremely difficult to obtain, and after the first Intifada everything from fax machines to modems became illegal, so that what little connection was available to the Internet or other telecommunications networks was done surreptitiously by dialing up through an Israeli telephone company to providers in other countries. The media production that existed was tightly controlled and surveilled by Israeli officials, highly self-censored, or underground (see Bahabh 1985; Shinar 1987; Hillel and Rinnawi 2003).

Media and technology restrictions eased after the Oslo Accords, specifically after Oslo II, signed in 1995, when the Palestinian Authority (PA) was given permission to build some of its own infrastructure. The outcomes have been contradictory: Palestinians were given some freedom over their own (mediated) lives, but such self-determination would remain constricted. In the twenty-two years since Oslo, television and telecommunications — the most widely diffused technologies — have paradoxically emerged and flourished under conditions of illegality or inhibiting dependency.

For the first time in their modern history, the Palestinians were afforded, by the accords, the freedom for collective self-expression through mediated forms, such as radio and television. Palestinians were also permitted to build their own telecommunications infrastructure for land and mobile telephony, establish digital services, and engender an industry that would eventually make up a significant amount of the Palestinian Gross Domestic Product (GDP) and play an important role in Palestinian society.

And yet, the accords also inhibited the formation of these very industries. None of these media fields would be representatively or geographically national, many have operated quasi-illegally, and all of them continue to be hindered by Israeli policies and by the conditions of PA–international funding agreements that Oslo made possible.

The development of media and technology infrastructure has to be understood in the context of a conjuncture of events, some related to the Oslo Accords and some not. The early 1990s witnessed the global growth of the hi-tech sector, state building and international development efforts that would place primacy on privatization and liberalization (often called the Washington Consensus), and the fervor over what came simply to be called globalization. That Israel became a successful hub in this new global economy would itself impact on Palestinians, as development of a Palestinian hi-tech sector would be naively framed as a means to compete with Israel's or, at the least, to piggy-back off of it. Within this matrix, much of state-building efforts focused on new technologies as means for (neoliberal) economic growth. It also problematically was assumed to be able to bring about all kinds of societal changes, such as peace, democratization, and women's empowerment, to name only some (Tawil-Souri 2007b). This kind of hi-tech globalization was posited as the route through which to overcome confinement and localization, and, in a sense, networked Palestinians into channels of international capital flows, neoliberal state-building efforts, and hi-tech firms.

Equally important, the Oslo Accords gave birth to the PA and the influx of international development and private investment into the Territories that would make infrastructural development possible. As such, telecommunications, television, and an information technology sector more widely are very much products of Oslo and the kinds of economic policies the PA would adopt, most of which would not challenge continuing, albeit changing, Israeli control. The accords, meant to create and demarcate Palestinian self-administered territory and hand the PA responsibilities over civilian life and its related infrastructure, also resulted in the reorganization of Israeli power over Palestinians, rather than Israeli withdrawal. The supremacy of 'Israeli security' combined with Palestinian territorial fragmentation (such as the creation of Areas A, B, and C, let alone the expansion of settlements and establishment of checkpoints, bypass roads, and eventually the 'security barrier') would delineate the realm of possibility under which media and telecommunications would develop.

Oslo II stated that "Israel recognizes that the Palestinian side has the right to build and operate separate and independent communication systems and infrastructures, including telecommunication networks, a television network, and a radio network" (Annex III, Art. 36, Sec. B1), but the devil would be in the detail, which would in actuality hinder independent and viable systems, as detailed in the following sections.

Television

The establishment of the PA's official mass media outlets occurred soon after the establishment of the PA itself. The Palestinian Broadcasting Corporation (PBC) began radio broadcasts from Jericho in July 1994 and intermittent television broadcasts from Gaza City in December 1995. The birth of the PBC was important, as it was the first official voice of Palestinians' new government. Given the precarious ways in which the newly returned exiles of the PA attempted to embed themselves in and control Palestinian society, the PBC would be micromanaged by Yasser Arafat and his loyalists. Entertainment and news reflected Fatah's interests and political moods, to the exclusion of other voices (Jamal 2001; Jamal 2005; Jayyusi 1998; Jayyusi 2002).

It is critical to recognize, however, that PBC, and all broadcasting, would be limited by the agreements. The Oslo Accords specified the precise locations of broadcasting towers, tower heights, and signal strengths, so that no Israeli signals would be interfered with, whether radio signals for military needs or commercial cellular use in settlements. PBC could only broadcast in six cities. Since its birth, then, the PBC could not be considered a truly national channel: it neither politically represented the entirety of Palestinians nor geographically reached everyone in the Territories.

The accords determined an even narrower frame for other potential broadcasters by simply making any other television channels beyond the six permitted for PBC illegal. This did not prevent Palestinian entrepreneurs from establishing private (and illegal) television channels, as early as April 1994. In fact, Palestinian mass media proliferated at a startling rate, resulting in, at a maximum, forty-two private television stations and forty-six private local radio stations, along with a dozen production companies. Television would become the most widely diffused medium, with more than 90 percent of Palestinian households owning a set by the decade's end.

The growth of television viewership and a Palestinian television industry occurred at the same time as the pan-Arab satellite boom. Local political upheavals — namely the second Intifada and the Hamas–Fatah conflict — would simultaneously change the media landscape and be reflected in media's changes. Private television evolved in three overlapping phases: the illegal period (from 1994 onward), the networking period (from 2000 onward), and the factional period (from 2005 onward).

In the first phase, everything about television was highly politicized and tenuous. First, with the exception of PBC, all channels would remain illegal according to the Oslo Accords. What this translated into was an "enforced localization" (Tawil-Souri 2007a), in that all channels' broadcasting range did not go much beyond a few miles, if that, so as to attempt to remain 'under the radar.' A national televisual experience across the West Bank, Gaza, and East Jerusalem would remain unattainable. This in turn would limit stations' growth and professionalization, as stations found it hard to justify financial and technical investments and had difficulty obtaining outside funding. Consequently, most stations would remain small, relatively unprofessional, and run by a handful of employees who were often family members. For the first few years, much programming was illegal itself, relying on pirated videocassettes and DVDs or rebroadcasting pan-Arab and foreign satellite channels for local viewers. The dependence on satellite channels to fill programming time would also hinder the stations' development in that they would never be able to compete with them, whether in terms of professionalization, content, or access within the Territories. This would exacerbate their fiscal difficulties and keep their viewership relatively low.

Second, the PA dealt with the illegality of these channels in ambiguous ways. The PA permitted the channels to erect transmission towers and signals as a strategy to build its own 'facts in the air' as Palestinians' negotiation cards (Sakr 2007). The various legal attempts to assimilate broadcasting under the control of PA ministries was mired in larger political strategies, many of which originated in the PA's need to appease the population's growing disagreement with negotiations with Israel. The growth of channels was a factor of the PA allowing room for a carefully balanced plurality that would not fundamentally politically or ideologically oppose the PA and yet gave a semblance of democratic tolerance.

The majority of channels were established as for-profit businesses and seldom challenged the PA and Fatah. Still, whenever a channel broadcast content that the PA found oppositional, it would have no qualms about shutting it down — under the premise of being illegal under the accords (see Batrawi 2001; Jamal 2005). What existed was a market plurality that was extremely localized, since throughout the 1990s signals in a city would rarely be available in other locations, sometimes even impossible within the city itself.

The PA also approached media policy in contradictory ways. For example, in its 1996 media regulations, the PA was careful to use language as if Israeli limitations were nonexistent, rather than admitting its protostatus over which Israel would maintain much control. More important, however, broadcasting regulations would continue to be disagreed upon until well after the industry burgeoned, and 'regulated' as if in a permanent 'state of emergency.' Thus, the PA would offer broadcasting licenses, in opposition to the accords, on annual terms. This temporariness — based on frequency control by Israel, annual licenses, the various ministries vying for control over media regulations, and fear of Israeli reprisals against stations as well as a measure of self-censorship present in all media in the Territories — would come to define private broadcasting from 1994 until around 2000.

Paradoxically, local private channels were part of a changing global media landscape and, in a different way, helped network Palestinians into international media flows. It would not be uncommon, for example, for viewers to rely on pan-Arab satellite newscasts, rebroadcast illegally through a local channel, to obtain news on what was going on down the street, in another Palestinian city, or farther afield, just as it would not be uncommon for local programming to be influenced by foreign content.

The second Intifada would mark an important shift. Local stations, which had shied away from overtly political programming, began broadcasting patriotic and nationalistic programs. Some aired content advocating resistance to both Israel and the PA. The PA's radio and television channels in the meantime had been bombed and taken off the air by Israeli forces, fundamentally changing the relationship between PBC and the private illegal channels, which PBC had to rely on to broadcast its content until it could rebuild its system. Thereafter, the PA would be more supportive of private channels and changed its policies toward them.

The Intifada marked the televisual landscape in other ways. Given the territorial constraints broadcasters faced, exacerbated by an increase in checkpoints, closures, and the inability of people to move around, private station owners began planning a more national approach, both geographically and televisually. The Ma'an Network was thus born to ease the sharing of content, and eventually became the largest private station in the West Bank.

Lastly, the precarious political landscape meant that foreign funding would become increasingly channeled into media by European and American nongovernmental organizations (NGOs). Much of the foreign funding that went into programming content, program creation, professional training, and, to a lesser extent, equipment would be ideologically or politically driven, whether by an orientalizing discourse, by the hope of peacebuilding and democratization, or, as the political landscape changed again, the intention of weakening support for Hamas. Previous to the Intifada, only Al Quds Educational TV was bolstered by international funds. Thereafter, increasing aspects of media would become networked in international funding structures (see Sienkiewicz 2010). The influx of foreign funding, ongoing reliance on foreign programming (legal and illegal), the creation of a network of affiliated private stations, and the move toward conglomeration defined this networking period, which continued into the present.

The next change in the Palestinian televisual landscape—the factional phase—would be related to Hamas' ascent. Hamas' Al-Aqsa TV had attempted to broadcast (illegally, as all others) in 2005 from secret locations in the Gaza Strip, but would be continuously shut down by the PA (Salama 2006). (The PA gave Hamas a radio license in 2003 for its *The Voice of Al Aqsa*, which quickly became Gaza's most listened to station.) The TV station reemerged again in Gaza a few days before the national elections in January 2006, and thereafter would remain relatively uninterrupted, now the target of Israeli rather than PA shutdowns. After 2006, Hamas would itself shut down other media outlets throughout Gaza, confiscate equipment, and censor journalists and media professionals (Abuzanouna 2012). Hamas' rule over the Gaza Strip would eventually result in its own media empire, albeit localized and contained within Gaza and under constant threat of being taken off the air—as it often was—by Israeli forces, whether through direct bombings, drone interceptions, or limited spectrum allocation (which would be reflected in the telecommunications realm, described below).

The presence of Al-Aqsa TV in Gaza and the PBC in the West Bank (it had moved to Ramallah in the late 1990s) would mirror the political Hamas/Gaza and Fatah/West Bank division. Each party approached media as its official voice, and each would attempt to suppress dissent in its area. Despite Prime Minister Salam Fayyad's neoliberal visions and policies, and his promises in the late 2000s to turn PBC into a 'public institution' with administrative and financial independence rather than a strictly governmental one, the PA's official media outlets are still run by Fatah loyalists. In the meantime, private channels in the West Bank would manage to carve out a slightly wider political spectrum. As commercially driven, for-profit businesses, however, their owners would generally be more interested in promoting their own political and economic interests than fostering a democratic public sphere.

Twenty-two years after Oslo, Palestinians have managed to create a media industry and boast a number of media tycoons. Their private stations have gained more permanency, and regulations are targeted toward increased professionalization. But the landscape has resulted in a partisan and factional media that does not foster a culture of tolerance or democratic pluralism, instead serving as an ideological battle ground for power and privilege in the political sphere. While television viewership has reached near total penetration, most of what is watched continues to come from abroad in Arabic and other languages available on hundreds of free-to-air satellite channels, an arena on which Palestinian channels have yet to make a significant mark.

Telecommunications

In the early 1990s, a little more than 2 percent of Palestinian households had telephone lines. Cellular phones and fax machines were prohibited. Telephonically, Palestinians were enclavized, living under a regime that restricted access to the outside world and to each other. Not until the accords were Palestinians permitted to own and build their own voice and data telecommunications infrastructure, whether for land, cellular, or Internet uses.

Unlike television, however, where the entirety of the industry and its infrastructure had to be built from scratch, the PA was handed the largely debilitated telecommunications infrastructure existent in the Territories. After Israel handed over responsibility in 1995, the PA established a simulacrum of an independent telecommunications system. Its underlying workings, as well as many aspects related to its future development, would be dependent on Israel and/or constrained by Israeli controls.

Reflecting its neoliberal agenda and that of its foreign donors, the PA passed responsibility for telecommunications to the private sector. PALTEL, whose largest investors already wielded substantial economic power that would increase exponentially with the growth of telecommunications, was awarded a license to build and operate landlines, a global system mobile (GSM) cellular network, data communications, paging services, and public phones. Dismissing both the benefits of universal access and telecommunications as a public good and opting instead for a privatized for-profit structure, the PA rendered telecommunications only symbolically national as they became available only to those who could afford the services.

More important, however, would be the territorial and other forms of limitations that telecommunications would face, which PA policies would never challenge but simply find ways around, while the PA and PALTEL financially benefited. Fifteen years after its start, PALTEL's market capitalization in 2010 represented more than half the value traded on the Palestinian Stock Exchange. The corporation contributed over one-third of the PA's tax income and its revenues accounted for more than 10 percent of Palestinian GDP. But PALTEL would also become one of Israel's largest — dependent — clients.

As with television, and as detailed in the Oslo Accords, Israel would control all allocation of frequencies and determine where the building of new infrastructure would be allowed. Since part of the landline infrastructure already existed, its geographic condition would not fundamentally change: most exchanges were located in Israeli cities. This meant that all international traffic — initially for land, and later for cellular communications and Internet as well — would have to be routed through Israeli providers to which PALTEL and its subsidiaries would pay connection and termination fees. Israel would also forbid PALTEL its own international gateway, thus cementing dependency on Israeli providers until today.

Connection between the West Bank and Gaza would befall the same fate. For example, Article 36 of Oslo II stipulated that "Israel recognizes the right of the Palestinian side to establish telecommunications links (microwave and physical) to connect the West Bank and the Gaza Strip through Israel." A microwave link was installed in 1995 to connect the two areas, but it was quickly saturated because of the Israeli communication ministry's refusal to provide more bandwidth, so that traffic had to be rerouted back through Israeli networks. PAL-TEL was later forbidden to import equipment (such as telephone exchanges and broadcasting towers) that could have allowed it to build a network that could connect across all Palestinian territories. Even the majority of inter-West Bank and inter-Gaza connections would have to depend on Israeli networks. Calls between Gaza and Khan Younis, for example, are routed through Ashkelon and calls between Ramallah and Nablus are routed through Afula.

The territorial fragmentation that Oslo fomented would also constrict tele-communications, as most infrastructure was — and still is — only permitted within Area A, seldom in Area B, and never in Area C. Along the eventual 'secur-ity barrier' and in Israeli-defined 'buffer zones' and other locations inside the Ter-ritories, Palestinians would be forbidden to install infrastructure, resulting in a network that is fragmented, pocketed, and necessarily dependent on Israeli net-works, both in places where Palestinian infrastructure does not exist and in places where it does but it is not permitted directly to connect.

This fragmented infrastructure is the system on which both landline and Internet traffic rely. Hadara, PALTEL's Internet service provider, which became a monopoly in 2005, is not permitted an Internet trunk switch to allow Internet traffic to circumvent Israel. Hadara is mandated by Israeli authorities to provide limited bandwidth for Palestinian Internet use, making it invariably slower to surf the Internet in the Territories than in Israel. Israeli providers sell bandwidth to Hadara at substantially higher rates than to providers in Israel, making access rela-tively more expensive for Palestinian users. Moreover, the Israeli government has enforced strict limitations on the kinds of equipment permitted. The combina-tion of higher costs, slower speeds, and limited technologies results in a bondage of bandwidth, meaning that Internet flows are limited, as is Palestinians' integra-tion into the larger global network. Especially in its dependence on Israeli infra-structure, telecommunications demonstrates Oslo's core paradox: self-determination under continued occupation.

It is the realm of cellular communications, however, that is most precarious. This is the most widely used, the most profitable, and the most politicized sector, and around it occur the most political, economic, and legal contentions. PAL-TEL's cellular subsidiary, Jawwal, began service in Gaza in July 1999, and a few months later in the West Bank. Jawwal's entire infrastructure was built from scratch, although no cellular system can wholly function without landlines, whether for international connections or something as obvious as calling a fixed-line number. A working cellular system requires not only thousands of towers (cells) but also the allocation of frequency (among other technicalities that I will not detail here). As per Oslo, the Israeli communications ministry approves frequency allocation for Palestinian use. Although the accords stated that Israel would release more bandwidth "as soon as any need arises," Jawwal continues to operate on the same narrow frequency allocation it was first awarded. In layman's terms, this means that the network can only support a certain number of callers (in this case a hundred and twenty thousand) before calls are dropped, unless more and/or stronger towers are built.

As with the limitations that exist for landlines, Palestinian-owned cellular infrastructure is only allowed in Area A and limitations are imposed on the kinds of equipment and new technologies Jawwal is permitted. The result is a cellular network that is overburdened (because the number of subscribers has reached two million and continues to grow but frequency allocation has remained the same), territorially fragmented, and, as with landlines, often dependent on the Israeli backbone. In late 2009, after much political difficulty with Israeli authorities and pressure from institutions such as the World Bank toward competition, a second cellular provider, Wataniya, began operating in the West Bank. Wataniya was allocated less spectrum by Israel's communications ministry than initially promised, has not yet been given approval to operate in Gaza, and faces many of the same limitations as Jawwal. Both Jawwal and Wataniya are forced to be segregated from yet dependent on Israeli networks.

Neither Jawwal nor Wataniya emerged in an empty cellular landscape. Israeli cellular providers already serviced many parts of the West Bank and Gaza in the 1990s. In fact, Israeli cellular service continues to be generally available throughout the Occupied Territories because Israeli providers build and install technologically superior infrastructure throughout Israel *and* the West Bank, usually on and along bypass roads, on hilltops, in settlements, in outposts, and in military installations. While there is no Israeli-owned infrastructure inside post-2005 disengagement Gaza, cellular signals from Israeli towers along the perimeter reach well within the narrow sliver of the Strip. Moreover, the four Israeli cellular providers collectively boast signals more than two thousand times stronger than those of Jawwal or Wataniya. Since Israeli providers do not pay extra charges for connection and termination and function in a more competitive landscape, their services are substantially cheaper. Since 1999, Jawwal has garnered a larger market share, but an estimated 20 to 40 percent of Palestinian cellular users today still use Israeli cellular service for reasons ranging from cheaper service to a stronger signal, and sometimes because there is no other choice.

According to Oslo, such practices are illegal. Any provider operating in PA territory ought to obtain permission from the PA (which itself must obtain permission from Israel) and have economic, social, or political accountability to the PA, such as payment of taxes on revenues. The Israeli cellular companies contend that they cannot control such activity, although it is technologically easy to monitor and mostly prevent. By the late 2000s the PA had introduced regulations that render it illegal for Palestinians to use Israeli services, even if the PA cannot actually stop Israeli signals from beaming into its territory. Although the ratio of Palestinian cellular users on Palestinian networks to Israeli ones has grown, this illegal 'competition' remains quite rampant (Tawil-Souri 2012).

Palestinian telecommunications are constrained by various kinds of practices, many of which originated with the Oslo Accords. Telecommunications face territorial limitations, combined with 'legal' and military measures that include confiscating and forbidding the importation of equipment, illegal competition by Israeli providers, limited bandwidth, limitations on what equipment can be installed and where, delay or denial of approvals, and destruction of machinery and infrastructure. Moments of heightened violence often impact on Palestinian telecommunications in debilitating ways. For example, much infrastructure was bombed in the West Bank during the 2002 Israeli military incursions, as it was throughout Gaza, most notably in 2008–2009 and again in 2012. Throughout the past twenty years, telephone and broadcast signals have been jammed and hacked into by the Israel Defense Forces. Infrastructure has been destroyed in far less violent moments. Examples include purposefully severing the only landline connection between southern and northern Gaza, digging up fiber-optic cables throughout parts of the West Bank, uprooting transmission towers, as well as confiscating equipment and holding up purchased multimillion-dollar equipment and charging Palestinian firms 'storage' fees.

Israeli-imposed controls exist through(out) the disruption of everyday life. Palestinian telecommunications networks are continually shut down for various reasons, including PALTEL's failure or delay in paying its Israeli providers and for Israeli-defined 'security' issues. On any 'normal' day, a Palestinian's phone call is routed through Israel, his phone service may be shut down or tapped, his Internet connection surveilled and rendered relatively slower, and he must pay substantially more for all of these than his Israeli counterpart. Should he live in an area where Palestinian cellular service is either substandard or nonexistent, he can, illegally, use and pay for Israeli service. Despite these various limitations, telecommunications has experienced phenomenal growth. This, too, however, would be a result of Oslo: PALTEL, like the PA, while dependent agents of Israeli control, have nonetheless handsomely profited from the situation.

Conclusion

The Oslo process shaped the state-building process, and by extension the media and telecommunications industries, in critical and contradictory ways. Neither television nor mobile telephony would have existed without the 'peace process.' Phenomenal growth has occurred in the development and eventual professionalization of television, for example. The success of telecommunications has been even more formidable. Palestinians now have two cellular providers, they can connect to the Internet, and the still largely monopolistic PALTEL has contributed to significant economic growth, whether in terms of GDP, employment, charitable contributions across sectors of Palestinian society, or fabulous gains made by its investors and shareholders.

Yet, the limited status of these industries, as described above, is directly related to how the Oslo Accords failed to address important factors in long-term state-building needs (such as territorial control), as well as how the accords themselves set limits on the industries that have played a restrictive role. Moreover, governmental patterns within the PA and its various institutions, driven in large part by processes of globalization and state building to which Oslo opened the floodgates, have influenced the shape of these industries. Technology infrastructure highlights how Palestinians are at once incorporated into a global network (of technology, international development, capital, media flows, and so forth) and contained through a combination of Israeli policies.

The never-quite-sovereign state of media and telecommunications also demonstrates what is true of the larger political contradictions that Oslo has enabled over the past twenty-two years: dynamic restrictions over territoriality, politics, economics, and communications, and, ultimately, the impossibility of an independent state.

References

Abuzanouna, B. 2012. "Enhancing Democratic Communication? Television and Partisan Politics in Palestine." PhD diss., University of Westminster.

Bahabh, B.A. 1985. "Perspectives in Conflict: The Role of the Palestinian Media in the West Bank, the Gaza Strip, and East Jerusalem — A Palestinian View." *Journal of Communication* 35:17–21.

Batrawi, W. 2001. "Private Television in Palestine." MA diss., Leicester University.

Jamal, A. 2005. *Media Politics and Democracy in Palestine: Political Culture, Pluralism, and the Palestinian Authority*. Portland, OR: Sussex Academic Press.

_____. 2001. "State-Building and Media Regime: Censoring the Emerging Public Sphere in Palestine." *Gazette: The International Journal for Communication Research* 63 (2/3): 263–82.

Jayyusi, L. 2002. "'Voicing the Nation': The Struggle over Palestinian Broadcasting." *Intersections* 2 (3/4): 39–49.

_____. 1998. "The 'Voice of Palestine' and the Peace Process: Paradoxes in Media Discourse after Oslo." In *After Oslo: New Realities, Old Problems*, edited by G. Giacaman and D.J. Lonning, 189–211. Chicago: Pluto Press.

Nossek, H. and K. Rinnawi. 2003. "Censorship and Freedom of the Press under Changing Political Regimes: Palestinian Media from Israeli Occupation to the Palestinian Authority." *International Communication Gazette* 65(2): 183–202.

Sakr, N. 2007. *Arab Television Today*. London: IB Tauris.

Salama, V. 2006. "Hamas TV: Palestinian Media in Transition." *Transnational Broadcasting Studies* 16, http://www.tbsjournal.com/Salama.html

Sienkiewicz, M. 2010. "Hard Questions: Public Goods and the Political Economy of the New Palestinian Televisual Public Sphere." *The Velvet Light Trap* 66:3–14.

Shinar, D. 1987. *Palestinian Voices: Communication and Nation Building in the West Bank*. Boulder, CO: Lynne Rienner.

Tawil-Souri, H. 2012. "Digital Occupation: The High-Tech Enclosure of Gaza." *Journal of Palestine Studies* 41 (2): 27–43.

_____. 2007a. "Global and Local Forces for a Nation-State Yet to Be Born: The Paradoxes of Palestinian Television Policies." *Westminster Papers in Communication and Culture* 4:4–25.

_____. 2007b. "Move over Bangalore. Here Comes . . . Palestine? Western Funding and 'Internet Development' in the Shrinking Palestinian State." In *Global Communications: Toward a Transcultural Political Economy*, edited by P. Chakravartty and Y. Zhao, 263–84. Boulder, CO: Rowman and Littlefield.

20

The European Union and Israel since Oslo

Harry van Bommel

Never before had the hope for a Palestinian state and thus an end to the Israeli occupation been so great as it was twenty-two years ago when the Oslo Accords were signed.[1] Since the outbreak of the second Intifada in September 2000, however, there has no longer been any room for doubt about the failure of 'Oslo.' Subsequent peace initiatives have produced even less noteworthy results and died a comparatively early death.

On both the Palestinian and the Israeli side, one can pinpoint reasons for the failure of Oslo and of later peace initiatives. On the Palestinian side, for example, there were the suicide attacks in the mid-1990s, which were a major obstacle. It is, however, crystal clear that absolutely no possibility of peace exists as long as Israel continues to expand its settlements and the occupation of the Palestinian territories remains in place or becomes even more entrenched. The fact that Israel expanded the settlements during Oslo, from some 280,000 inhabitants in 1993 to around 390,000 in 2000,[2] demonstrates this failure better than anything. The further enlargement of the settlements to more than 500,000 inhabitants explains in large part the failure of later peace initiatives.[3]

With the rapid extension of the settlements and by maintaining the high-pressure occupation of the Palestinian Territories, Israel has not met its peace obligations. The fact that during Oslo the settlements grew at a faster pace than they had done in the period preceding the talks says a great deal, moreover. For the European Union (EU) none of this was apparently a problem. Relations with Israel during the breakdown of Oslo as well as during other fruitless peace initiatives did, after all, grow stronger. A 2009 statement from Javier Solana, the then EU high representative for foreign affairs, made clear the results of this deepening of relations:

> There is no country outside the European Union that has this type of relationship that Israel has with the European Union . . . . Israel, allow me to say, is a member of the European Union without being a member of the institution. It's a member of all the programmes, it participates in all the programmes. And I'd like to emphasize and underline, with a very big, thick line [that Israel participates] in [helping us deal] with all the problems of research and technology, which are very important.[4]

Deep Diplomatic Relations

Shortly after the Oslo process began, the EU and Israel initiated negotiations on broadening their cooperation. This led to the signing of the EU–Israel Association Agreement in 1995. As well as economic cooperation, which was established as early as 1975 in a cooperation agreement, this new treaty included other areas, such as scientific and technical research. The treaty also offered a framework for political dialogue. Due to a lengthy ratification process, the agreement did not come formally into force until 2000, the year that stands out as a symbol of Oslo's failure. One of the reasons for this delay was a debate on whether products from the settlements should come under the favorable terms the agreement extended to Israeli exports. After much deliberation, the answer was in the end negative.

In 2004 the EU adopted the European Neighborhood Policy (ENP). The following year, Israel became one of the first countries with which an action plan was agreed on the basis of this new policy instrument. The ENP includes far-reaching cooperation in a range of areas and has deepened relations between Israel and the EU.

In more recent years the relationship between the EU and Israel has been deepened further. The European parliament, for example, voted in 2012 in favor of a trade accord governing medical products.[5] A few months previously the EU–Israel Association Council had given its approval for closer cooperation on dozens of policy areas.[6] In 2014 the EU and Israel signed the Horizon 2020 scientific cooperation agreement, which gives Israel equal access with EU member states to the largest-ever EU research and innovation program. The program has a total budget of nearly €80 billion over seven years.[7] Apart from the EU, some EU member states intensify their cooperation with Israel on a bilateral basis. Dutch Prime Minister Mark Rutte, for instance, signed a Netherlands-Israel Cooperation Agreement in late 2013.[8] Apart from the above, the EU and Israel work closely with each other via a range of other, smaller partnerships.[9] The fact that some of these developments do not literally involve a deepening of relations should not distract us from seeing that this is precisely what they represent. Given the intensive cooperation between the EU and Israel, the statement from Solana quoted above should not surprise us.

Support for the Occupation

In itself, there is nothing wrong with the deepening of economic, scientific, cultural, and political relations between countries. The deepening of relations between the EU and Israel, however, means indirect support for the Israeli occupation and the policy of expanding the settlements. Such deep relations as the EU has maintained with Israel since Oslo are impossible without the EU becoming involved in the numerous violations of international law perpetrated by Israel, which go hand in hand with the ongoing occupation. In fact, the deep relations legitimize the many violations.

The export of products from the Israeli settlements to the European market is a case in point. An enlightening 2012 report on the issue entitled *Trading Away Peace: How Europe Helps Sustain Illegal Israeli Settlements* starkly reveals that the economic relations the EU has constructed with the Palestinian Territories do not compare to those it has with the Israeli settlements:

> The most recent estimate of the value of EU imports from settlements provided by the Israeli government to the World Bank is $300m (€230m) a year; this is approximately fifteen times the annual value of EU imports from Palestinians. With more than four million Palestinians and over 500,000 Israeli settlers living in the Occupied Territory this means the EU imports over 100 times more per settler than per Palestinian. (APRODEV et al. 2012)

Many of these settlement products find their way, labeled 'Made in Israel,' into European supermarkets. In this way the Israeli exporter qualifies for tax benefits on the basis of the EU–Israel Association Agreement and the consumer is squarely misled. After years of deliberation, this practice might finally end. In late

2015 the EU published new guidelines for labelling products made in Israeli settlements.[10] The guidelines mean Israeli producers must explicitly label farm goods and other products that come from settlements built on land occupied by Israel if they are sold in the EU, though it is too early to tell whether this will indeed put an end to consumer misleading. Much depends on applying the new rules. In practice this might be quite difficult, especially when Israel does not cooperate.

The fact that cooperation with Israel in relation to science is not pure and innocent can be seen clearly from David Cronin's book, *Europe's Alliance with Israel: Aiding the Occupation*. Once again the title leaves no room for doubt on the EU's role when it comes to illegal Israeli policies, while the book itself is full of examples of dubious cooperation between the two trading partners. One example concerns unmanned aircraft, better known as drones. The EU invested financial resources in a project for their development under the leadership of Israel Aerospace Industries. Officially, this was a civil project that explored the possibility of using drones in civilian air transport (Cronin 2010: 96–97). Everyone knows, however, that the same drone technology could be used for Israeli combat operations in the Palestinian Territories. It is not rare for Israel to do just that. In November 2012 Hamas member Ahmed Jabari was extrajudicially executed by means of an Israeli drone, an act that led to a week of unnecessary bloodshed in Gaza and dozens of innocent Palestinian deaths.[11] Since January 2013, a further research project on drones has been financed with EU money. Any pretence that this is a civilian project has completely disappeared, with the goal advertised as being to stop "non-cooperative vehicles in both land and sea scenarios by means of Unmanned Aerial Vehicles."[12]

Intensive economic relations between the EU and Israel are leading on a regular basis to European corporations contributing to Israel's illegal building practices in the Palestinian Territories. Consider, for example, the bulldozers supplied by Swedish corporation Volvo that were used a few years ago to level Palestinians' houses to the ground (Cronin 2010: 127–31). Dutch firm Riwal has delivered cranes for the building of the 'separation wall' on Palestinian land. The fact that a few years previously the International Court of Justice had declared the wall to be illegal was evidently no problem for the company.[13]

The trade in arms between the EU and Israel is the clearest demonstration of the link between the two sides' close relationship and the occupation. Weapons supplied to Israel have a direct and major impact on the Israeli–Palestinian conflict. They also affect the broader conflict in the region. Of course, the vast majority of weapons imported by Israel — some 90 percent — come from the United States, but the EU is far from being an unimportant player in the game. More than ten EU countries have for a number of years stood in the list of the world's top twenty arms exporters to Israel (Cronin 2010: 112). Germany, for example, has already supplied four submarines to Israel and will in the next few years add a further two, despite the Germans having known for decades of the existence of an Israeli nuclear weapons program. The delivery of the submarines constitutes active support for this program, given that Israel has armed them with nuclear missiles. These submarines could be deployed to enforce the illegal blockade of Gaza. In addition to German submarines, Israel receives Apache helicopter parts from companies in the Netherlands. The helicopters regularly used to sow death and destruction in Gaza are often in part 'Made in Holland.'[14]

As well as the export of arms by the EU, their import from Israel should also be mentioned here. One does not have to be clairvoyant to know that the hundreds of millions of euros that Israeli state-owned enterprise Rafael receives from various EU member states for its Spike rockets could easily be contributing to further military disasters in the Palestinian Territories (Cronin 2010: 122–23). With these millions, new weapons can be developed for the oppression of the Palestinians.

A Change in Course Is Both Necessary and Possible

Weighing up developments in the twenty-two years since Oslo, one can only conclude that the deepening of relations between the EU and Israel has in no way served the interests of the hopes for a Palestinian state or an end to the Israeli occupation raised by the accords. The ongoing enlargement of the settlements, the building of the wall on Palestinian soil, the collective punishment of Palestinians in Gaza, and the continuing economic catastrophe in the Palestinian Territories are just a few examples of how these hopes have been dashed. The fact that Israel in this context can count on persistent support from the EU in the form of the deepening of relations is inexplicable. It is therefore high time that the EU took a drastic change of course.

Existing agreements with Israel offer the EU useful instruments to effect such a change of direction. For example, Article 2 of the Association agreement states, "Relations between the Parties, as well as all the provisions of the Agreement itself, shall be based on respect for human rights and democratic principles, which guides their internal and international policy and constitutes an essential element of this Agreement."[15] Because Israel fails to respect human rights in all sorts of areas, this article can now be cited in order to have the agreement suspended until Israel begins to exhibit such respect. It is, of course, remarkable that this article has not to the present day led to the treaty's suspension.

The ENP also offers possibilities for putting more pressure on Israel to meet its obligations under international law. Since the upheavals in the Arab world, the phrase "more for more, less for less," used in the ENP, has been in vogue. Respect for human rights is one of the criteria for this policy instrument. The more a country respects human rights, the deeper goes cooperation with the EU. When reforms are postponed and human rights abridged, cooperation becomes less intense. Remarkably enough, this instrument has been used regularly against Arab countries in transition, such as Egypt, but not against Israel.[16]

Finally, the legally binding European criteria for the export of weapons give every opportunity to stop their export to Israel. In particular, the criteria include stipulations that "Member States will not allow exports which would provoke or prolong armed conflicts or aggravate existing tensions or conflicts in the country of final destination" and that "Member States will not issue an export license if there is a clear risk that the intended recipient would use the proposed export aggressively against another country or to assert by force a territorial claim."[17] David Cronin correctly concludes that "if both the spirit and the letter of this code were properly applied, EU countries would not sell a single weapon — or even a component of a weapon — to Israel" (2010: 111).

Sanctions Can Work

For a long time now European ministers have been asserting that sanctions against Israel do not work and that it is precisely from within the context of a friendly relationship that more influence can be exerted on Israel. A good friend is, after all, listened to more attentively than an enemy. Former Minister of Foreign Affairs for the Netherlands Maxime Verhagen expressed this standpoint in 2009:

> We have a friendly relationship with Israel. In a friendly relationship you can usually simply say if you don't agree with the other's policy . . . . You only threaten sanctions if you are confident that in so doing you can change undesirable behavior to behavior more advisable. My estimate is that this will absolutely not work in this way in the case of Israel—on the contrary—that it would be counter-productive . . . . Sanctions imposed by the European Union would have most Israelis saying, "So now we know the European Union, namely as a friend of the Palestinians and critics of Israel." Threatening them with sanctions would simply reinforce Israel's isolation, would not make Israel any more flexible or

compliant, and would lead to a further radicalization within Israel. Of that I am totally convinced.[18]

If the twenty-two years since Oslo have made anything clear, it is that this theory is completely untenable. Occasionally letting it be known that one is not in agreement with one or another aspect of the illegal Israeli policy while at the same time expanding relations with the country has not changed the way Israel thinks. More seriously still, in Israel this European attitude is simply interpreted as support for its policy.

It could be different. In 1990, before Oslo and during the first Intifada, the EU did indeed for once show its teeth. In that year Israel closed a range of educational establishments on the West Bank. Following urging from the European parliament, the European Commission reacted to this collective punishment by freezing scientific cooperation projects. Immediately afterward, Israel reversed the closures (Van Agt 2009: 221).

Since 1990 the EU's influence on Israel has only increased, as the relationship described above indicates. In the economic sphere in particular, Israel's dependence on the EU is significant. Bilateral trade between the EU and Israel has grown enormously in recent years and the EU is Israel's most important trading partner. Almost two-thirds of Israeli exports go to the European market, while 40 percent of Israel's imports originate in the EU (Van Agt 2009: 221). Even more than in 1990, the EU has available the means to call on Israel to keep within the bounds of international law.

The failure of Oslo and every peace initiative since should be reason enough for the EU to step back from its bankrupt policy toward Israel and in unmistakable terms make it clear that without significant improvements in relation to international law and progress toward peace there can be absolutely no question of intensification of relations with the EU.

The enormous enlargement of settlements by thousands of dwellings under the Netanyahu government makes the urgency of such a change of direction more than clear. One commentator drew the correct conclusion when she wrote that "by every objective measure, the Netanyahu government has demonstrated that it is determined to use settlements to destroy the very possibility of the two-state solution."[19] Former Dutch Minister for Foreign Affairs Frans Timmermans stated at the end of 2012 that "the enlargement of the settlements represents the biggest threat to a two-state solution."[20]

The sense of urgency that policies need to change seems to be increasingly shared within the EU.

Notes

1. This chapter was translated from the Dutch by Steve P. McGiffen.
2. Foundation for Middle East Peace, "Israeli Settler Population 1972–2006," http://www.fmep.org/settlement_info/settlement-info-and-tables/stats-data/israeli-settler-population-1972-2006
3. B'Tselem, "Land Expropriation and Settlements Statistics," April 22, 2013, http://www.btselem.org/settlements/statistics
4. Raphael Ahren, "Solana: EU Has Closer Ties to Israel than Potential Member Croatia,"*Haaretz*, October 21, 2009.
5. Andrew Rettman, "EU–Israel Drugs Pact Contains Legal Pitfall," *EU Observer*, October 24, 2012, http://euobserver.com/foreign/117982.
6. Benjamin Fox, "EU to Boost Israel Trade Relations despite Settlements Row," *EU Observer*, July 24, 2012, http://euobserver.com/economic/117045.
7. European Commission, Press Release Database, "EU, Israel Sign Horizon 2020 Association Agreement," June 8, 2014, http://europa.eu/rapid/press-release_IP-14-633_en.htm.
8. Netherlands Embassy in Tel Aviv, Israel, Press Release, December 8, 2013, http://israel.nlembassy.org/binaries/content/assets/postenweb/i/israel/netherlands-embassy-in-tel-aviv/joint-statement-nicf-2013.pdf
9. For an extended overview of relations between the EU and Israel, see, Delegation of the European Union to Israel, "Political and Economic Relations," http://eeas.europa.eu/delegations/israel/eu_israel/political_relations/index_en.htm
10. Peter Beaumont, "EU Issues Guidelines on Labelling Products from Israeli Settlements," the *Guardian*, November 11, 2015, http://www.theguardian.com/world/2015/nov/11/eu-sets-guidelines-on-labelling-products-from-israeli-settlements.
11. Nick Meo, "How Israel Killed Ahmed Jabari, Its Toughest Enemy in Gaza," *Daily Telegraph*, November 17, 2012.
12. Nikolai Nielsen, "EU and Israel Research Crime-Stopping Drones," *EU Observer*, February 7, 2013, http://euobserver.com/justice/118951.
13. Cnaan Liphshiz, "Dutch Gov't Warns Company to Stop Work on W. Bank Fence," *Haaretz*, July 9, 2007.
14. Soemoed, "Europese militaire relaties met Israel," Campagne tegen Wapenhandel, November 2010, http://www.stopwapenhandel.org/node/779 (author's translation).
15. EU–Israel Association Agreement, June 21, 2000, http://eeas.europa.eu/delegations/israel/documents/eu_israel/asso_agree_en.pdf
16. European Commission and the High Representative of the European Union for Foreign Affairs and Security Policy, "Delivering on a New European Neighbourhood Policy," May 15, 2012, http://eur-lex.europa.eu/LexUriServ/LexUriServ.do?uri=OJ:L:2008:335:0099:0099:EN:PDF

17. European Union Code of Conduct on Arms Exports, June 5, 1998, http://www.consilium.europa.eu/uedocs/cmsUpload/08675r2en8.pdf

18. "Oud-minister van Buitenlandse Zaken Maxime Verhagen, Verslag van een Algemeen Overleg," April 8, 2009, https://zoek.officielebekendmakingen.nl/kst-23432-299.html (author's translation).

19. Lara Friedman, "Laying Bare the Facts about Netanyahu and the Settlements," *The Daily Beast*, January 18, 2013, http://www.thedailybeast.com/articles/2013/01/18/laying-bare-the-facts-about-netanyahu-and-the-settlements.html?utm_medium=email&utm_source=newsletter&utm_campaign=zionsquare&cid=newsletter%3Bemail%3Bzionsquare&utm_term=Open%20Zion.

20. Answer to parliamentary question from Harry van Bommel, member of parliament for the Socialist Party, on the enlargement of settlements by Israel, December 3, 2012, https://zoek.officielebekendmakingen.nl/ah-tk-20122013-730.html (author's translation). This was said in reference to the former government. The fact that it is a similarly accurate description of the current Netanyahu government points to the continuity of Israeli settlement policy.

References

APRODEV et al. 2012. *Trading Away Peace: How Europe Helps Sustain Illegal Israeli Settlements.*

Cronin, D. 2010. *Europe's Alliance with Israel: Aiding the Occupation.* London: Pluto Press.

Van Agt, D. 2009. *Een schreeuw om recht: De tragedie van het Palestijnse volk.* Amsterdam: Bezige Bij.

21

A War of Ideas: The American Media on Israel and Palestine post Oslo

Laura Dawn Lewis

Your opinion is your opinion, your perception is your perception — do not confuse them with 'facts' or 'truth.'
—John Moore, *Quotations for Martial Artists*

I am neither an academic nor a public figure. I am one of the millions of ordinary people throughout the world on every continent, of every faith, ethnicity, and political persuasion, who work behind the scenes toward peace and justice. Many of us, myself included, originally approached the issue of Israel and its occupation as strong supporters of Zionism. We failed to notice the inequities, unasked questions, and lack of historical context in the reporting until, one day, something caused each of us to question. For me it was the news coverage following September 11, 2001, an article about the Jenin massacre of 2002,[1] and the survivors of USS *Liberty*.[2] For others it was something else.

We each have our change agents. Ultimately we discover this is an issue where the perceived wisdom, accepted narrative, and historical facts often are at odds. We become driven through a combination of moral outrage and compassion, fortified through self-education, questions, and months of introspection. We do not realize it at first, but we all find ourselves conscripts in a massive war of ideas. The weapons are information and perception laced with cognitive dissonance. The prizes sought are justice, land, water, money, weapons, political and economic clout, self-determination, respect, and even eternal life, depending upon the battlement occupied. The battlefield is the media.

This chapter will look at several of the entities and tactics shepherding the opinions that Americans follow regarding Israel and Palestine, the experience journalists and others have in attempting to report on or expose this issue, and the oft-overlooked impact of Christian media on the perception, politics, and continuation of the status quo.

Media and Perception since Oslo

Perception is reality.
—Lee Atwater

The American media hailed Oslo as a momentous breakthrough in the Middle East peace process. Today it is often cited by pro-Israel advocates to shore up a narrative that Palestinians are incapable of upholding an agreement and that Israel tries again and again to appease them to no avail. The Israeli narrative is how most Americans perceive Oslo.

Critically, within the international academic and political circles, Oslo is considered a one-sided disaster for the Palestinians. They gave up much with scant reciprocity. Additional stakeholders in the region, including Lebanon, Jordan, and Syria, each with large communities of Palestinian refugees from either the 1948 or the 1967 expulsions, were not consulted. This side of Oslo is rarely discussed in the United States media. Nor does the US media provide sufficient background to the actual issues causing the sixty-six-year conflict between the Israelis and the Palestinians.

Oslo accomplished putting the 'Middle East peace process' into the vocabulary of the average American. It also escalated the information war between the Palestinian experience and the Israeli narrative, a war played out in the media.

American Media

In 2013, people from outside the United States often look at the media reporting within the United States with confusion. How does a country that values its First Amendment cultivate a media that seems more interested in polarization, celebrities, and sensationalism than in reporting the news? It is a criticism heard in the newsrooms and answered in popular culture by hit scripted shows like *The Newsroom*. The answer as to how we got here is a little more academic.

It began with the repeal of the Fairness Doctrine in 1987, which eliminated the requirement that broadcasters devote a portion of airtime to matters of public interest with contrasting views. The repeal opened the door to opinion-based news that reinforces opinions rather than discusses them. It also meant that television networks no longer had to give both sides of contentious issues. The year 1989 saw the fall of Communism and the growth of conservative versus liberal programming, led by the success of talk radio host Rush Limbaugh. In 1991, CNN cashed in on the invasion of Kuwait and the twenty-four-hour news cycle came into its own. Soon competitors appeared and the need for a constant stream of news followed.

By 1993, Oslo was in the news and the Internet loomed on the horizon. The commercialization of the Internet and the movement of media onto it in 1995 made global news accessible to anyone with a modem. This was succeeded by the 1997 Telecommunications Act, which removed many of the barriers to media ownership. What followed was mass consolidation of media, culminating in five major corporations owning most of the United States' news sources.

The rise of Fox News in the late 1990s established a market for opinion-fortification infotainment, that is, news that matches your opinions and entertains, factual or not. MSNBC followed suit, leaning to the opposite persuasion, with the remainder catering less obviously to one side or another. By the turn of the century, it became increasingly popular for Americans to identify their political persuasion by the news channel on which they relied. It was during this time that Christian media truly went mainstream as well.

Oslo may have brought the Israeli occupation of Palestine back into the media but it was the reporting on Iraq and Afghanistan that exposed a media that could be played. This prompted many who had not paid attention to the coverage to ask questions not only about Iraq but also Israel.

With the war drums, apathy toward the media increased within intellectual and activist circles, leading to a questioning and the growth of alternative news sources covering niche markets. In relation to the Middle East and American politics, alternative media found its market in the disillusioned. The media that benefited included the Washington Report on Middle Eastern Affairs, Institute for Middle East Understanding, LinkTV, Free Speech Television, and Democracy Now. On the Internet, trusted sources that emerged included Counter Punch, Common Dreams, AlterNet, Huffington Post, Electronic Intifada, as well as several Israeli, Palestinian, and international joint efforts, including the International Middle East Media Center and the Palestine Chronicle.

With the success of the Internet, the war of ideas went global, covering mainstream media and thousands of outlets ranging from multinational media conglomerates to independent bloggers. With so many new sources for information dissemination, managing the narrative of Israel and Palestine, regardless of the position, required new tactics and new ideas. Enter the players.

A Sampling of the Players

In a war of ideas it is people who get killed.
— Stanislaw Lec

Where do the ideas come from and why is one narrative superseded by another?

American Monitors

An analysis of the US mainstream media's reporting on Israel shows that the media invariably follows the basic talking points originating from the Israeli government press office and its disseminators. There is nothing wrong with that. Where it gets interesting is when the reporting or actions of a publication, organization, group, or individual do not support the promoted Israeli narrative.

For example, the editor of *The Oak Leaf*, the student newspaper of Santa Rosa Junior College in California, received death threats and was forced temporarily to close the paper's doors in April 2003 after publishing an opinion piece entitled "Is Anti-Semitism Ever the Result of Jewish Behavior?"[3]

Publications hold no exclusivity on the sting associated with deviating from the accepted narrative on Israel. In September 2011, the Museum of Children's Art in Oakland, California, planned an art exhibit by Palestinian children entitled "A Child's View from Gaza." The event was canceled due to "a concerted effort by pro-Israel organizations in the San Francisco Bay Area."[4]

These are two examples of the challenges facing journalists, activists, and others in bringing a balanced view of the occupation to the American people.

There are thousands of examples from the past sixty-six years. Allison Weir, founder of the non-profit If Americans Knew who now heads the Council for the National Interest, has documented over fifteen years of media bias relating to this issue.[5] Fairness and Accuracy in Reporting (FAIR), a nonpartisan organization, documents media bias in the United States on many issues, not only Israel and Palestine. On February 12, 2013, it released a post entitled "PBS [Public Broadcasting System] Goes to Israel and Palestine–Mostly Israel."[6] On its website, over ten pages of results appear when "media bias Israel" is searched. Media Matters is another source that regularly analyzes news stories for accuracy, although it tends to focus on what has come to be called the 'conservative press.' Search its site for 'Israel' and you get 1,287 results, recently ending with a post entitled "In the Wake of Boston Marathon Attack, Fox Turned to Anti-Islam Commentators."[7] Finally, Project Censored, also a nonpartisan source from Cotati, California, publishes a list of the top twenty-five most censored or underreported stories of the past year every September. For more than a decade, the Israeli occupation of Palestine has made almost every issue.

Each of these organizations seeks to educate and hold accountable the media within the United States. However, with journalist staff being cut due to falling revenues and media consolidation, coupled with an increased demand for news to fill a twenty-four-hour news cycle, there has been a rise in the reliance on think tanks and resources that provide near-boilerplate releases, talking heads, and pundits, especially in the more expensive stories to cover, involving international news and the military. For every Media Matters and FAIR, there is a counter-resource for any contentious topic.

Israeli Monitors

In relation to Israel and Palestine, three of the more popular promoters of the accepted Israeli narrative are the Middle East Media Research Institute (MEMRI), Honest Reporting, and the Israel Project.

MEMRI, which states that it "emphasizes the continuing relevance of Zionism to the Jewish people and to the State of Israel," was founded in 1998 by former Israeli intelligence officers Meyrav Wurmser (wife of Principal Deputy Assistant to Vice President Dick Cheney for National Security Affairs, David Wurmser) and Colonel Yigal Carmon. Both founding members have come out publicly as critical of the Oslo Accords.

Source Watch, an online entity delving into who is behind various think tanks, resources, and publications, urges caution when dealing with information distributed by MEMRI, stating, "MEMRI is operated by a group closely associated with the Israeli intelligence organizations."[8] It cites the following as an example: "Psychological warfare officers were in touch with Israeli journalists covering the Arab world, gave them translated articles from Arab papers (which were planted by the IDF [Israel Defense Forces]) and pressed the Israeli reporters to publish the same news here."[9]

Honest Reporting is the pro-Israel counter to FAIR and Media Matters on issues relating to Israel. The nonprofit monitors news coverage of Israel and related issues, most notably in the US and Canada. Whenever a story comes out that fails to portray the situation to its satisfaction, the organization and its supporters contact the offending publication, noting the offending passages they consider biased and requesting changes to the reporting. A cursory survey of its site and the stories considered biased suggests that Honest Reporting's criteria include anything that does not fit the preferred image of Israel as a democratic state under constant threat or that in some way humanizes non-Jewish residents of the state or under occupation.

The Israel Project's objectives are aptly summarized by founder and president Jennifer Laszlo Mizrahi in her foreword to the 2009 Global Language Dictionary: "We offer this guide to visionary leaders who are on the front lines of fighting the media war for Israel. We want you to succeed in winning the hearts and minds of the public." The Global Language Dictionary teaches people how to talk to the press and other opinion leaders and to insure that their language is used when framing the occupation and its issues. The Israel Project specifically targets media and student organizations for advocacy on the premise that it is not what Israel does that is important but how it is perceived. It argues that perception is formed through the media as a war of words and ideas through a consistent message disseminated in a variety of ways.

Euphemisms, Obfuscations, and Omissions

It's not what you say that counts. It's what people hear.
—Dr. Frank Luntz, foreword to 2009 Global Language Dictionary

Part of controlling a narrative is controlling what people hear and the words used to describe the situation. This happens through repetition. Euphemisms and obfuscations rather than accurate terms are deployed. Facts are softened and details omitted.

For example, 'settlements' is used to describe the illegal housing developments that one must be Jewish to live in, built on land already settled by Palestinians. A 'settlement' according to Webster's dictionary is "a place or region newly settled." The Israeli developments referred to as settlements are not settlements, they are colonies. A colony displaces the population currently living in the area with another and excludes the original tenants.

'Security fence' is the term used to describe the hundreds-of-miles-long conglomeration of cement, razor wire, no man's land, guard towers, and roads that reach as high as twenty-five feet in some areas built by Israel largely on stolen Palestinian land. 'Fence' is defined by Webster's as "a barrier intended to prevent escape or intrusion or to mark a boundary; such as a barrier made of posts and wire or boards." 'Wall' is defined as "a high thick masonry structure forming a long rampart or an enclosure chiefly for defense — often used in plural." The Israeli 'security fence' is in fact a wall. The term 'security' is also debatable as the wall is built on land not within the state's boundaries. It was first proposed by Ariel Sharon in 1973 and first drawn out in 1978, eleven years before the first Intifada, which suggests that its purpose is not security but rather conquest.[10]

Other insertions and deletions include continued references to Israel as 'a democracy,' despite it having no constitution guaranteeing equal rights and multiple laws on its books withholding citizenship, housing, resources, equal education, equal participation, freedom of movement, just compensation, and more. Tying Israel to democracy is strategic, according to a 2003 Luntz Research memo on communications strategies stating, "So far, one of Israel's most effective messages has been that Israel is the only democracy in the Middle East."[11]

A democracy is void of hereditary or arbitrary class distinctions or privileges. Israel is *built* on hereditary and arbitrary class distinctions defined by faith and race. Israel is a republic guided by democratic principles. It is theocratic. It is militaristic. It espouses all fourteen points of fascism[12] in relation to its non-Jewish residents and the occupation, including its two-tiered legal system. It is not nor has it ever been a democracy.

Additional fallacies repeated in the American media without question include the seamless transition from "recognize Israel," which occurred at Oslo, to "recognize Israel as a Jewish state," something that would disenfranchise all non-Jewish persons living within the yet-to-be-defined borders, as well as referencing the Occupied Territories as disputed territories when according to international law they are occupied and the application of civil criminal language such as 'kidnap' to the capture of an Israeli soldier on active duty during a military operation by opposing forces.

War of Ideas: Why?

Somebody said once, "Follow the money," and that is what it is all about.
— Murray Walker

Why is there such a strong emphasis on the Israeli position by its supporters and a concentrated effort to make that position the perceived wisdom? Based on statements in Israel Project publications, notations by the Luntz Group, and numerous Congressional appeals and other documents of public record, the real motivation, though often covered with religious or historical analogies, is money—a lot of money in the form of foreign aid, grants, military equipment, and political clout:

> All the arguments about Israel being a democracy, letting Arabs vote and serve in government, protecting religious freedom, etc., won't deliver the public support to secure the loan guarantees and the military aid Israel needs—not when it comes to U.S. tax dollars. There must be a national security angle—one that clearly links the interests of both Israel and America.[13]

Israel receives 40 percent of US foreign aid.[14] This money allows it to rank within the top ten military powers in the world despite having one of the world's smallest populations.[15] It has nuclear capability. It has the sixteenth-highest standard of living[16] and is the twenty-eighth-richest country in the world.[17] In addition, it receives diplomatic shields, interest-free loans that never get paid back, military equipment, favored status, and access to strategic reserves.

Should US public opinion turn against Israel, these benefits would come under scrutiny. American public opinion is predicated upon a specific perception. For the money to continue to flow, the message must remain sympathetic and the perception favorable. The media is key, but message management extends to academia and politics.

John Mearsheimer and Stephen Walt, in *The Israel Lobby and U.S. Foreign Policy*, state, "One of the lobby's central concerns is to ensure that public discourse about Israel echoes the strategic and moral rationales" (2008: 168). Politicians who question policy in relation to Israel may be targeted and often find themselves voted out. Former Congressman Paul Findley details this experience in his book, *They Dared to Speak Out*. Congresswoman Cynthia McKinney, Congressman Ron Paul, and Congressman Darryl Issa, a Palestinian-American, have also been targeted. In Issa's case, extremists from the Jewish Defense League attempted to bomb his offices.[18]

Although a press conference was held and a sitting US Congressman was targeted, within three months of September 11, 2001, the mainstream US media was largely silent. CNN carried a single story on the attempted bombing on December 13, 2001.[19] Had the religion of the terrorists been different, would the coverage have been different? Subsequent US media coverage of thwarted bomb plots in which the suspects are Muslim suggest that this is the case. However, it is unclear whether the reporting would have been similarly scant had the faith of the terrorists been Christian.

Reporting on the Middle East

I think it's important for the public to know, great reporting starts with a publisher who has guts and an editor who has guts
— Dan Rather

In a war of ideas, reporting can be complicated. Editors and publishers often do not want the grief that comes with telling the whole story.[20] Calls from watchdog groups, visits from the Anti-Defamation League, threats of advertising dollars being withheld, charges of anti-Semitism, boycotts of the publication, death threats, demotions, and reassignments all play into whether reporting the full story is worth it.

Mel Frykberg from Inter Press Service and Dahr Jamal from Al Jazeera have been covering the Middle East, including Israel, for well over a decade. When asked what their biggest challenge is in reporting on the Middle East in the US media, Frykberg responded, "Getting my editor [of the third biggest media outlet in the US] to think covering the facts I raised in reply to the previous question are newsworthy. American apathy as well." Jamal responded, "Censorship. First, I'm not invited on any of the mainstream programs to talk about Iraq, or any of the other conflicts in the Middle East I've covered over the last decade. Anyone (like myself) whose reportage regularly challenges the mainstream's dominant rhetoric on the region or whatever conflict is being addressed, is simply not going to be given air time. And that kind of censorship is the most powerful tool there is when it comes to controlling the message." Asked whether they feel their coverage of events in the region is accurately portrayed in the US media or edited down to soften the impact, Frykberg states,

I think the American media lacks introducing the contextual background for the events occurring in Israel-Palestine today and I think this is imperative in understanding the conflict in general. There is still a double standard, however, in the reporting of atrocities against Palestinian civilians, which happen on a regular basis and are hardly covered, whereas atrocities against Israeli civilians make big news always. My reports for American media often just want the bare facts of an incident in a bubble without giving readers enough understanding.

Jamaal notes,

Most certainly mainstream coverage of events in the region, whether it be on CNN or even on Al Jazeera English, is edited down to soften the impact. It continues to be a rare instance indeed when we would see Ali Abunimah or even Norman Finklestein talking on CNN about international law and the ongoing Israeli violations and abuses of said. In addition, we still will not be shown Palestinian babies blown to pieces by Israeli air strikes. By and large, most media coverage on the issue continues to be propagandistic.

Asked whether US media coverage of Israel has improved since Olso, Frykberg responds, "It has gone from very bad to poor, which I suppose is some improvement." When asked whether the Oslo Accords were a catalyst to better coverage of the issues relating to the occupation, Israel, Palestine, and the greater Middle East, or if something else has perpetuated improved coverage, Frykberg says,

Not so much the Oslo Accords, which did make the Israeli-Palestinian conflict front page news again. I think the Goldstone report following the war on Gaza from December 2008 to January 2009 was influential in highlighting Israel's excessive behaviour as well as the attack on the Mavi Marmara humanitarian ship to Gaza. I think the invasion of Iraq and the lies surrounding this has also made many Americans more aware of the propaganda of American military action in the Mideast.

Jamal, meanwhile, states,

At least in the US, I don't think the Oslo Accords had much to do with the fact that it is now easier to question Israeli policies. Again, I think it's been the barbarism of the Israeli policies—taking more land despite UN objections, their blatant land grabs and settlement announcements just as major US political figures come to Israel, or just after they leave, the savage attack on Gaza in 2008 was also a real turning point. Granted, I still feel there is a very long way to go as far as truly educating the general public in the US about the situation, international law being squarely in favor of the Palestinians, etc . . . . but, the tide is certainly now beginning to flow against the Israelis.[21]

When it comes to covering the occupation of Palestine, little has changed since Oslo. Some headway has been made through groups such as Media Matters, Project Censored, and FAIR, but these are non-profits up against major funding on the Israeli side. The mainstream media continues to repeat ad nauseam Israeli demands that the Palestinians cease violence against Israelis, recognize Israel's right to exist as a Jewish state, and uphold past agreements. The same criterion is rarely applied to Israel in relation to the Palestinians.

Christian Media

The media's the most powerful entity on earth. They have the power to make the innocent guilty and to make the guilty innocent, and that's power. Because they control the minds of the masses.
—Malcolm X

What is often overlooked or dismissed by studies of US media coverage relating to Israel is the impact of the Christian media on public perception of the issues. In part this is due to the fact that the majority of journalists are not devoted followers of any particular faith.[22] In part it is due to religious doctrine rather than fact being used to frame stories. Ignoring this is unfortunate. Over 70 million people in the United States identify with Christian Zionism, and it is estimated that 50 percent (121 million) of all US Christians (77 percent of the US population, or 243 million)[23] are influenced by the Dispensationalist narrative of the Bible, whether they know it or not.[24] Without the support of Dispensationalists (Christian Zionists), Israel would not have the political and economic clout necessary to continue unfettered.

The Dispensationalist movement is heavily insular. Its followers often self-identify as 'born again,' 'evangelical,' or 'fundamentalist' and are taught to avoid any media, information, books, people, and institutions that do not support their definition of a Christian worldview. Dispensationalists have their own language and catchphrases and believe they are on God's mission. They have their own media, which includes the Bible Network, Sky Angel, Trinity Broadcasting Network, Cornerstone Television, FamilyNet, LeSEA Broadcasting, Middle East Television, and the Christian Broadcasting Network, as well as programs like the *700 Club, Christian World News*, and *John Hagee Today*.

In addition, there are a series of books, including multiple versions of the Bible embedded with footnotes supporting their beliefs, the *Left Behind* series, films, documentaries, magazines, newspapers, radio, music, festivals, and websites. The influence extends from an entire home-schooling curriculum to tertiary education institutions, including Jerry Falwell's Liberty University, Oral Roberts University, and Patrick Henry College.

Origins of Christian Zionism

At this point in America's history, we are plainly rejecting the Word of God because, according to Joel 3, we are helping to divide the land of Israel. We, through billions in foreign aid, are pressuring Israel to abandon the covenant land that God has given to the Jewish people forever. America is in the valley of decision, and we are making the wrong decision.
—Rev. John Hagee, founder of Christians United for Israel[25]

The history of the rise of Christian Zionism ties directly to the media and how issues are reported. Understanding it is essential to understanding the ties of these Christians to the State of Israel and the influence the media has on their position.

Dispensationalists are the backbone of support for Israel, and they are true believers. They believe that the State of Israel is the fulfillment of a biblical prophecy and that to act in any way that might prevent Israel from becoming 100 percent Jewish would prevent the return of Jesus Christ. They believe that any action against Israel is a sin. They believe the Jewish temple must be rebuilt where al-Aqsa Mosque currently stands, that sacrifices must be resumed in the temple, and that the Muslim nations surrounding Israel are the enemy.[26] They believe this because it has been written into their Bibles, taught in their seminaries, and repeated in their media.

These teachings are not part of the mainstream Protestant and Catholic faiths (Weber 2004; Currie 2004; Halsell 2002), but through media saturation, this version of biblical analysis is penetrating into traditional Christian churches. To ignore the impact of Christian media on the political landscape is to ignore the political, financial, and religious motivations of those who effectively prevent resolution through their support, influence, and votes.

The occupation in Israel is a political issue, not a religious one. Christians, Jews, and Muslims have lived together in relative peace in the Holy Land for centuries, right up until the twentieth century. That narrative changed due to two movements, both originating in the mid-nineteenth century: Dispensationalism and Zionism.

Dispensationalism first appeared in Scotland in 1832 with a young clergyman named Charles Darby, who based upon a vision of 'rapture' by a teenager, Mary McDonald, formulated the foundations of what came to be known as Christian Zionism. Darby traveled to the United States preaching this form of Christianity. The Dispensationalist movement gathered momentum in the 1860s within the Pentecostal and Evangelical Christian movements, most notably becoming a key component of the Protestant revival movement spearheaded by Dwight Lyman Moody, an entrepreneur and clergyman. In 1886, Moody founded the Moody Bible Institute. Central to the teachings of the institute was the doctrine of Dispensationalism.

In 1908, these ideas were written into the Bible by Cyrus Ingerson Scofield and published by Oxford University Press in the Scofield Reference Bible. This Bible used footnotes and annotations to explain predominantly Old Testament passages in accordance with Dispensationalist ideas, the primary being that the world has been on hold for the past two thousand years and that Jesus Christ cannot return until all the Jewish people of the world have returned to the land of Israel and it is once again their home. The book became an instant bestseller and the primary study Bible in Christian Evangelical circles (Canfield 2005).

While Darby and Moody were perfecting the foundations of Dispensationalism, Theodor Herzl, a secular Jewish man in Austria-Hungary, was forming the foundations of modern Zionism. In 1882, Herzl published *The Jewish State*, in which he outlined what would come to be known as Zionism. With increasing racial tensions in Europe, the idea began to spread. By 1897, the first world conference on Zionism was held in Switzerland to decide on a location and direction. Kenya, Uganda, Argentina, and Palestine were all considered. For various reasons, including the end of the Ottoman Empire, the rise in Christian Zionism, and the ability to tie the name to the Bible, Palestine became the logical choice. Proclamations and agreements within the British government during 1915–17 sealed it.

With the choice of Palestine over the other locations, the yet-to-be-named state would inherit well-funded eager allies in the Dispensationalist Christians. It could now be argued that the establishment of such a state was ordained by God. Marrying this belief with the political objectives of Zionism provided a narrative, funding, supporters, and political protection. The Holocaust in Germany would provide the final motivation and justification.

By 1924, when Dr. Lewis Sperry Chafer founded the Evangelical Theological College (later the Dallas Theological Seminary), a portion of Palestine was to go to the Zionists and the Scofield Bible was in its second printing. Its footnotes were duly altered to reflect current events and the rise of Zionism in Europe. This college is notable as it graduates a large percentage of the televangelists and celebrity preachers controlling 90 percent of all Christian broadcasting on the radio and television in the United States.

Christian Zionism in the next decades would explode as political events appeared to match scripture. Its promoters would acquire extreme wealth selling fear of Armageddon with the promise of a rapture and go on to build powerful media conglomerants that include television, radio, films, websites, books, newspapers, and magazines.

By the end of the 1960s, Scofield's Bible would go through four revisions,[27] each updating the footnotes to coincide with historical events occurring in Palestine and the establishment of the State of Israel in 1948 and its conquest of Palestine and the Sinai in 1967. Dispensationalism continued to reside within evangelical circles until 1970, when Dallas Theological Seminary graduate Hal Lindsay's novel *The Late Great Planet Earth* became a bestseller. The book captured the 'end times' narrative of the Dispensationalist movement, to which Israel is central. As a bestseller, it penetrated popular culture. After its success, many prominent evangelical preachers created their own footnoted Bibles tying current events to biblical passages for consumption by their followers.

The melding of Zionist objectives with the Dispensationalist movement created an unlikely dependency. For Israel to achieve its founder's vision of a Jewish-only Greater Israel, it needs the Dispensationalists to continue supporting and defending it, as well as blocking politically and financially any repercussions due to its actions. The continuation of Israel toward a Jewish-only state is equally essential to the Dispensationalists. It is the foundation of their identity and the cornerstone of their version of Christianity. Their Bibles say this is true. Their media confirms it. They are regularly warned against seeking outside knowledge because it does not support their definition of a Christian worldview.

Conclusion

The growth of Christian media has been explosive over the past forty years, but most notably since Oslo. The Oslo Accords threatened Dispensationalism. They threatened a contiguous Greater Israel by creating a two-state solution. A two-state solution destroys the Dispensationalist narrative of a Jewish-only Greater

Israel that leads to Armageddon and ultimately to the return of Jesus Christ. A one-state solution would have the same effect because it would apply equal rights to all, not simply Jewish residents, thus making Israel not purely Jewish. The majority of the Christian media promotes the Dispensationalist narrative. Awareness of Dispensationalism within the mainstream churches and concentrated efforts to educate Christians about its goals, tools, and teachings continue to gain momentum. With a growing awareness of the conflicts between the Dispensationalist narrative and the text of the Bible within the Catholic and Protestant mainline denominations, coupled with the preponderance of Dispensationalism in the Christian media, the Christian community is slowly addressing this within the faith. These efforts have yet to be reported indepth in the mainstream media, despite their affecting nearly 75 percent of the population in the United States. For example, on October 5, 2012, fifteen major American Christian churches came together and wrote a letter to Congress urging the United States to end its unconditional support for Israel.[28] Although unprecedented, it received almost no US mainstream media coverage. However, its importance cannot be understated as it indicates a growing public division within the faith over a foreign policy issue.

The Christian media is one component, but not the only one, of the media that is coming under scrutiny from Americans. Although still predominantly within the intellectual, academic, and advocacy circles, these people are the thought leaders and opinion makers within much of society. The *Goldstone Report*, the attack on the Mavi Marmara, Operation Cast Lead, the 2006 assault on Lebanon by Israeli forces, and what is increasingly seen as heavily racist attitudes within the political right are influencing reassessment, especially among moderate conservatives, those identifying as liberal, and many in the Jewish faith who see the attachment of Israeli actions to their faith as a problem.

Adding to the shift in public opinion and understanding are the invasions of Iraq and Afghanistan, coupled with the increasing brutality of Israel's actions against Palestinian Christians and Muslims as well as Jewish persons of the Arab race. The publication of books such as former President Jimmy Carter's *Peace Not Apartheid* and Mearsheimer and Walt's *The Israel Lobby and US Foreign Policy* has made it more acceptable to discuss Israel in a critical fashion. Books by Jewish authors, including Anna Balzer's *Witness in Palestine* and Susan Nathan's *The Other Side of Israel*, bring the occupation to a younger audience in personalized stories. Films including *The Kite Runner* (2007), *Occupation 101* (2006),

Mural (2011), and *Paradise Now* (2005), and even *Syriana* (2005), have helped to humanize the Palestinian and Iranian perspectives.

Even reporting, though still far from ideal, is slowly penetrating the gauntlet of perceived narrative and fact. The process is slow, but one day it will happen. One day, the war of ideas, on this issue at least, will pass.

Notes

1. "I Made Them a Stadium in the Middle of the Camp," *Electronic Intifada*, May 31, 2002, http://electronicintifada.net/content/i-made-them-stadium-middle-camp/4459.
2. *USS Liberty Dead in the Water*, DVD (BBC, 2002), http://www.youtube.com/watch?v=52U-uXmhJ_M.
3. Joe Eskenazi, "Free Speech Clashes with Anti-Semitism in Santa Rosa," *Jweekly*, April 18, 2003, http://www.jweekly.com/article/full/19711/free-speech-clashes-with-anti-semitism-in-santa-rosa.
4. Middle East Children's Alliance, "Oakland Museum of Children's Art Shuts Down Palestinian Children's Exhibit," September 8, 2011, http://www.mecaforpeace.org/news/media-advisory-oakland-museum-childrens-art-shuts-down-palestinian-children%E2%80%99s-exhibit.
5. If Americans Knew, "Media Reports Cards: Grading Accuracy in News Coverage of Israel and Palestine," http://ifamericansknew.org/media/report_cards.html.
6. Peter Hart, "PBS Goes to Israel and Palestine — Mostly Israel," *Fairness and Accuracy in Reporting*, February 12, 2013, http://www.fair.org/blog/2013/02/12/pbs-goes-to-israel-and-palestine-mostly-israel/
7. Frank Gaffney, "In the Wake of Boston Marathon Attack, Fox Turned to Anti-Islam Commentators," *Media Matters*, April 22, 2013, http://mediamatters.org/research/2013/04/22/in-the-wake-of-boston-marathon-attack-fox-turne/193722.
8. Source Watch, "Middle East Media Research Institute," http://www.sourcewatch.org/index.php/Middle_East_Media_Research_Institute.
9. Amos Harel, "IDF Reviving Psychological Warfare Unit," *Haaretz*, January 25, 2005.
10. Regan Boychuk, "Arial Sharon and the 'Security Fence,'" *Dissident Voice*, December 13, 2003, http://dissidentvoice.org/Articles9/Boychuk_Apartheid-Wall.htm.
11. "Wexner Analysis: Israeli Communication Priorities 2003," The Luntz Research Companies and the Israel Project, April 2003, 10.
12. See fourteen points of fascism in Lawrence Britt, "Fascism Anyone?" *Free Inquiry* (Spring 2003), 20; Naomi Wolf, "Fascist America, in 10 Easy Steps," *Guardian*, April 24, 2007.
13. Israel Project, *2009 Global Language Dictionary* (unpublished), 67.
14. See foreign assistance by country office, http://foreignassistance.gov.

15. Multiple lists by various government agencies and military groups rank Israel's military strength between five and ten, depending on the criteria applied.
16. See the United Nations 2013 Human Development Index.
17. International Monetary Fund, "World Economic Outlook Database," April 2012, http://www.imf.org/external/pubs/ft/weo/2013/01/weodata/index.aspx.
18. "Transcript: Issa on Bomb Plot," *Washington Post*, December 12, 2001.
19. "Two JDL Leaders Charged in Bomb Plot," *CNN*, December 13, 2001.
20. There are a number of books and documentaries covering this, including Findley (2003) and Mearsheimer and Walt (2008). Films include *American Radical*, about Prof. Norman Finkelstein, and *Shadows of Liberty*, which does not cover the Israel–Palestine issue but discloses other instances of special interest intimidation of the media. Media intimidation is not limited to the subject of Israel. It has grown in the past twenty years on a number of topics, including Iraq, Iran, Afghanistan, oil, energy, corporate crime, and a number of other issues with well-funded lobbies.
21. Interviews with Dhar and Mel were conducted by the author via e-mail.
22. Pew Research Center for the People and the Press, "2002 Religion & Public Life Survey," April 9, 2002, http://www.people-press.org/2002/04/09/2002-religion-public-life-survey.
23. Frank Newport, "In US, 77% Identify as Christian," *Gallup Politics*, December 24, 2012, http://www.gallup.com/poll/159548/identify-christian.aspx.
24. Interview, Chuck Carlson of We Hold These Truths, who has been studying and engaging the movement since 1992. Evangelical statistics are those given by Christian Zionist organizations to underline their strength.
25. Kristen Scharold, "Low Expectations Follow Annapolis Summit," *Christianity Today*, November 30, 2007.
26. During the first part of the twentieth century, communists played this role. As communism waned, Islam became the new Gog and Magog. In centuries past, the Roman Empire, the papacy, and other groups have been cast in this role.
27. *Christian Zionism: The Tragedy and the Turning*, part I, film (Straight Gate Ministries, 2006).
28. Jerry L. Van Marter, "Religious Leaders Ask Congress to Condition Israel Military Aid on Human Rights Compliance," *Presbyterian Church (USA)*, October 5, 2012, http://www.pcusa.org/news/2012/10/5/religious-leaders-ask-congress-condition-israel-mi/

References

Canfield, J.M. 2005. *The Incredible Scofield and His Book*, 2nd ed. South Portland, ME: Ross House Books.

Currie, D.B. 2004. *Rapture: The End-Times Error that Leaves the Bible Behind*. Bedford, NH: Sophia Institute Press.

Findley, P. 2003. *They Dare to Speak Out: People and Institutions Confront Israel's Lobby*, 3rd ed. Chicago: Chicago Review Press.

Halsell, G. 2002. *Forcing God's Hand: Why Millions Pray for a Quick Rapture ... and Destruction of Planet Earth*, rev. ed. Beltsville, MD: Amana Publications.

Mearsheimer, J.J. and S.M. Walt. 2008. *The Israel Lobby and US Foreign Policy*. New York: Farrar, Straus and Giroux.

Weber, T.P. 2004. *On the Road to Armageddon: How Evangelicals Became Israel's Best Friend*. Grand Rapids, MI: Baker.

22

Corporate Complicity in Human Rights Abuses under Oslo

Yasmine Gado

Around the time that protesters across Arab nations were calling for the downfall of dictatorial regimes, in small demonstrations in Palestine they called for the downfall of Oslo.

Palestinian opposition to the Oslo 'peace process' is increasing, with many viewing boycotts, civil disobedience, and hunger strikes as more effective mechanisms to assert their rights than a negotiated settlement with Israel. This loss of faith is not surprising given the dramatic worsening in living conditions over the twenty years since the first Oslo agreement was signed. In the forty-eighth year of the occupation, illegal settlement construction is ongoing, with approximately five hundred thousand settlers currently living in the West Bank, including East Jerusalem. Movement restrictions in the West Bank include hundreds of checkpoints and roadblocks, settlements and bypass roads, and the denial of access to Gaza and Jerusalem. Settler violence and arbitrary arrests are regular occurrences. Even the Palestinian Authority (PA) tried (unsuccessfully) to bypass the Oslo negotiations and seek statehood through the United Nations. It has stated that it will not negotiate with Israel without a settlement freeze.

Throughout the post-Oslo period, Israel has continued to commit egregious violations of international human rights law in the Occupied Territories without being held to account in any substantial or meaningful way. Many of these violations would not be possible without the assistance of private corporations. The Palestinian-led boycott, divestment, and sanctions (BDS) movement is a response to this corporate complicity.

Another response came from lawyers and activists in the United States and Canada who made use of domestic tort and corporate liability laws to demand redress for Palestinian victims of corporate complicity in Israel's rights violations. Significant gains had been made in the area of corporate legal accountability for human rights abuses since the early 1990s, and it was thought that such mechanisms could be of use to further that accountability in the context of corporate involvement in Israeli human rights violations. Those cases were not successful in this regard and established only negative precedents. As a result, as discussed below, Israel's corporate partners have enjoyed the same level of legal immunity as the Israeli state with regard to such violations.

Types of Corporate Exploitation of the Occupation

The Oslo 'peace process' began in 1993 with Israel and the Palestine Liberation Organization (PLO) signing the Declaration of Principles on Interim Self-Government Arrangements (Oslo I). The declaration provided for the establishment of a self-governing, Palestinian authority that would be in power for no more than five years, while negotiations between the parties for a permanent settlement would begin no later than the third year of that period.

In 1995, the parties signed the Interim Agreement on the West Bank and the Gaza Strip (Oslo II), which divided the West Bank into three areas. Area A comprises seven major Palestinian towns and was placed under Palestinian control. Area B consists of the remaining Palestinian population centers and was placed under Palestinian civilian control and Israeli security control. Area C consists of the remaining area and was placed under total Israeli control, in terms of security, planning, and construction. It contains most Israeli settlements and is home to three-hundred-thousand settlers.[1] While Areas A and B are designated as under Palestinian control (sole or shared), they are noncontiguous areas separated by and contained within areas under full Israeli security control. Israel also maintains control over the West Bank's external borders with Israel and Jordan.

Beginning in 1993, Israel imposed what it calls "closure," dramatically restricting Palestinians' freedom of movement. Movement and trade between the West Bank and Gaza effectively ceased. Most West Bank Palestinians are denied access to Jerusalem, and exit to Jordan is subject to Israeli permission. Movement within the West Bank is restricted by hundreds of checkpoints, settlements, and bypass roads. This closure policy may not have resulted from the Oslo regime per se, but it has been a "defining feature" of the Oslo period (Roy 2002).

Oslo provided Israel with legal control over a majority of West Bank land and control over the passage of people and goods across borders, giving Israel greater freedom to build and expand the settlements in Area C, exploit its natural resources, and build the 'separation wall' inside the West Bank. These activities have provided lucrative opportunities for corporate exploitation, and in most cases Israel could not conduct them without corporate assistance. The involvement of corporations in providing goods and services relating to Israel's occupation of the West Bank has been categorized by researchers into three areas: (i) the settlement industry, (ii) exploitation of captive consumer and labor markets, and (iii) population control (Wistanley and Barat 2011: 53).

Settlement Industry

The Who Profits from the Occupation organization documents the activities of at least four hundred corporations that support illegal West Bank settlements.[2] Over twenty settlements produce agricultural goods that are sold in Israel and abroad, and Israeli industrial zones contain large factories that also produce goods for export. These activities are encouraged by the Israeli government through tax incentives and subsidies. They also benefit from reduced labor and environmental regulations, among other support (Wistanley and Barat 2011).

Manufacturers in the settlements exploit cheap Palestinian labor at an average daily wage of about half the Israeli minimum wage.[3] Evidence suggests that labor abuses are widespread, with Palestinian laborers working excessive hours, often in unsafe conditions or with toxic substances without safety training, medical aid, or compensation for job-related injuries (Wistanley and Barat 2011: 61–62). Under Oslo II, Area C is excluded from the PA's legislative control and thus from Palestinian labor law.

Apart from manufacturing in the settlements, corporations are involved in the construction of housing units and other infrastructure and in the provision of a range of necessary support and services required for settlements to function, including security, transportation, telecommunications, waste management, and water. Companies provide bus transport to and from Israel, build bypass roads, operate banks and restaurants in the settlements, and sell consumer goods.

Exploitation and Population Control

Within the 'exploitation' category, corporations benefit from Israeli control of land, borders, and movement by exploiting captive consumer markets (and captive labor, as described above), by confiscating natural resources such as water and dead sea minerals, and by using Palestinian land to dump toxic waste from Israel. The 'population control' category covers corporations that assist in the construction of the 'separation wall' and checkpoints and provide surveillance technology (Wistanley and Barat 2011).

Some Well-Known Complicit Corporations

In November 2011, the Russell Tribunal on Palestine (2010) held a two-day session in London on corporate complicity in Israel's occupation. The examples under discussion are taken from its findings.

Caterpillar is a US manufacturer that since 1967 has supplied the Israeli military with specially designed militarized bulldozers used to demolish Palestinian homes illegally and to build illegal settlements and the illegal 'separation wall' in the West Bank. These uses have resulted in civilian deaths and injuries and extensive property damage.

Elbit Systems, an Israeli company, provides surveillance equipment for the 'separation wall' in the occupied West Bank as well as unmanned aerial vehicles used by the Israeli military.

Motorola, through a subsidiary, provides surveillance systems to Israeli settlements, phone services to Israeli soldiers and settlers in the West Bank, and communication systems to the Israeli military.

G4S, a multinational British-Danish corporation, through a subsidiary supplies luggage, scanning equipment, and full-body scanners to checkpoints in the West Bank built as part of the 'separation wall,' whose route was declared illegal by the International Court of Justice in 2004. The company also supplies security services to businesses in West Bank settlements and to Israeli prisons dedicated to holding Palestinian political prisoners illegally transferred from the Occupied Territories.

Ahava manufactures bauty products using mud from the Dead Sea shore in an illegal settlement and exports them overseas labeled as originating from "the Dead Sea, Israel."

The above corporations have been targeted by activists for their activities. In addition, Caterpillar was sued in the United States by victims alleging they were injured by the corporations' alleged complicity in human rights abuse. Another suit was brought in Canada against the Canadian companies Green Park International and Green Mount International by the village of Bil'in over the companies' involvement in building residential units in an adjacent illegal Israeli settlement. Both of these suits were unsuccessful.

Legal Challenges to Corporate Complicity in Israeli Violations of International Law

Over the past two decades, efforts have been made by a variety of actors, including state governments, lawyers, UN agencies, and activists, to advance corporate accountability for human rights abuses.

Alien Tort Statute

An important US legal mechanism, the Alien Tort Statute (ATS), has been used to hold corporations accountable for their involvement in international human rights violations. Enacted in 1789 by the US Congress, the ATS allows aliens (non-US citizens) to bring civil tort suits in US federal courts for violations of the 'law of nations' or a US treaty.[4]

In the early 1990s, foreign plaintiffs began using the statute to sue corporations in US courts for human rights abuses committed overseas. After Texaco Inc. was sued in the US in 1993 through use of the ATS for its oil-production activities in Ecuador, a wave of ATS claims were filed against corporations for alleged human rights abuses, most alleging complicity with a state actor. In 2004, the US Supreme Court upheld the use of the ATS for this purpose, provided that the international legal norms the plaintiff sought to enforce were specific, universal, and obligatory.[5]

However, in 2013, the US Supreme Court ruled in the landmark case of *Kiobel v. Royal Dutch Petroleum Co.*,[6] that the ATS is subject to a presumption against extraterritorial application of US laws, and thus will generally not apply to claims based on allegations of human rights abuses alleged to have taken place overseas.

In that case, Nigerians had sued the company alleging it conspired with the Nigerian government to commit torture, extrajudicial killing, and other atrocities in Nigeria. The Supreme Court affirmed the Second Circuit Court of Appeals' holding that because the defendant's conduct took place outside US territory, there was not a sufficient connection between the US and either the defendant corporation (a foreign corporation) or the alleged violations to justify trying the suit in a US court. The court also held that even in cases in which the defendants do have a significant connection to the US (such as when the defendant corporation is based there), there is a strong presumption against extraterritorial application of US laws, which "serves to protect against unintended clashes between US laws and those of other nations."[7] While the *Kiobel* ruling may be seen as a setback for the corporate accountability movement, some argue that "significant international human rights litigation will still continue in US courts."[8]

United States: Corrie v. Caterpillar, Inc.

Although it may be more difficult after the *Kiobel* ruling to challenge overseas corporate human rights abuse in US courts, Palestinians who had used the law earlier to bring a claim in the US were not successful anyway for a different reason. The only ATS case involving a corporation's activities in the Occupied Palestinian Territories is *Corrie v. Caterpillar, Inc.,*[9] a case against a US corporation. In 2003, an Israel Defense Forces (IDF) officer deliberately crushed to death a twenty-three-year-old American activist, Rachel Corrie, using a bulldozer manufactured by Caterpillar while Corrie attempted to prevent the demolition of a Palestinian home in the Gaza Strip while the family was in the home.

The Center for Constitutional Rights (and cooperating counsel) sued Caterpillar in a US court using the ATS on behalf of the parents of Corrie and several Palestinian families whose relatives were injured or killed when bulldozers demolished their homes on top of them. They sought monetary compensation and an injunction on future sales until the bulldozers ceased to be used for illegal demolitions of Palestinian homes. The plaintiffs alleged that Caterpillar aided and abetted the Israeli government in committing war crimes, extrajudicial killing, and cruel, inhuman, or degrading treatment or punishment by selling bulldozers to Israel and the IDF while knowing they would be used for illegal purposes and specifically tailoring their construction for such purposes.

The US Court of Appeals for the Ninth Circuit dismissed the case on the grounds that it presented a "non-justiciable" political question—that is, a question that is not appropriate for a court to decide because it is textually committed by the US Constitution to the authority of Congress or the executive branch. The court held that because the US paid for the bulldozers, deciding the case would question foreign policy decisions of the executive branch.

Even prior to the *Kiobel* ruling, therefore, the *Caterpillar* precedent provided that a corporation that assisted the Israeli government in committing egregious human rights violations against Palestinians would be immune from suit if the US government financed or otherwise enabled the corporation's involvement in such violations.

Canada: Bil'in v. Green Park

Aside from efforts in the United States under the ATS, Palestinians sought redress for violations of international law via domestic tort law in Canada. In the 2008 case, *Bil'in v. Green Park*,[10] the people of Bil'in village in the West Bank brought a civil suit in Canada against two Canadian corporations, Green Mount and Green Park International, for building illegal settlements in their village. The plaintiffs alleged the corporations violated Canadian law by aiding and abetting Israel's violation of the Geneva Conventions, which prohibit an occupying power from transferring part of its own civilian population into occupied territory. They sought monetary compensation and a halt to the corporations' activities.

While the court adopted the plaintiffs' argument that knowingly participating in a war crime is a civil wrong under Canada law, it dismissed the case on the grounds that Canadian courts were not the appropriate forum since Israeli courts had a stronger connection to the case. The court based its finding on the fact that the parties, witnesses, evidence, alleged violations, and injuries were all located in the West Bank; that relevant documents were likely to be in Hebrew or Arabic; and that the judgment would have to be enforced outside of Canada. The court found that Israeli courts are sufficiently impartial to provide a fair judgment.[11]

The plaintiffs appealed the case, arguing that the lower court erred in declining jurisdiction because an Israeli court would not have jurisdiction, and even if it did, it would not have the legal precedent to apply the Geneva Conventions. (This is because Israel does not consider the conventions applicable to the territories on the grounds that there is no legal sovereign over them.) Bil'in also argued the court erred by sending the case to a court of the same country whose government hired the corporations to assist in the commission of war crimes. In 2010, the Quebec Court of Appeal dismissed the appeal, holding that deciding the case would interfere with the discretion of the lower court and the Supreme Court of Canada did not grant the leave to appeal.

Market-Based Mechanisms: Boycotts and Divestment

While lawyers have not had success with domestic tort litigation on behalf of Palestinians, and the avenue provided by the ATS has been narrowed to foreign victims of overseas human rights abuses, the Palestinian-led boycott, divestment, and sanctions (BDS) movement has made substantial progress since it was announced in 2005. Major global companies doing business with the Israeli government or enabling and profiteering from the occupation have faced boycotts and divestment due to activist campaigns.[12]

The French multinational telecommunications company Orange announced in January 2016 that it had terminated its relationship with its Israeli affiliate.[13] This followed a six-year boycott campaign that began in France and included a group of activists in Egypt calling for a boycott of Mobinil, a subsidiary of Orange.

In 2015, Veolia divested from the Jerusalem light rail project, ending all of its investments in Israel. Prior to that, the Swedish National Pension Fund had divested from Alstom and the Dutch ASN bank had divested from Veolia, both over those companies' involvement in the light rail project. In addition, Veolia's subsidiary Connex had failed to obtain public service contracts in Sweden and Ireland after a campaign by activists publicizing its connection to the project.

As of 2015, Barclays bank is no longer a shareholder in Elbit Systems, an Israeli company that provides surveillance equipment for the 'separation wall' and unmanned aerial vehicles to the Israeli military. This followed a campaign of sit-ins at over twenty of its branches.[14] In a significant earlier divestment in 2009, Norway's government Global Pension Fund divested from Elbit Systems because of its role in supporting Israel's occupation of the West Bank.

Also in 2015, the United Church of Christ voted overwhelmingly to divest from companies profiting from Israel's occupation and to boycott products of Israeli companies based in the West Bank.[15] This followed a 2014 narrowly passed divestment vote by the Presbyterian Church (US).[16]

According to the World Bank, consumer boycotts were also a key factor in a 24 percent drop in Palestinian imports from Israel in the first quarter of 2015.[17]

Trade unions also have explicitly embraced the BDS movement. In 2015, the United Electrical, Radio and Machine Workers of America became the second US union to back the BDS boycott call (after the Connecticut branch of the AFL-CIO, representing 200,000 workers).[18] Quebec's confederation of trade unions, representing 325,000 workers has joined the call as well.[19] They join the British Trades Union Congress (representing six-and-a-half million workers) and unions in Sweden, Norway, Brazil, Belgium, and India.

Following Israel's attack on the Freedom Flotilla in 2010, dockworkers in Stockholm and Oakland, California, refused to unload Israeli ships. In February 2009, dockworkers in Durban, South Africa, blockaded Israeli ships in response to the aggression in Gaza.

Conclusion

The Oslo territorial division of the West Bank and Israel's closure policy combined to give Israel legal and practical control over a majority of the West Bank. It has control over the movement of people and goods between fragmented Palestinian territories inside the West Bank and between the West Bank and East Jerusalem, Gaza, and Jordan. Having formal legal control over Area C, Israel continued colonizing and exploiting the resources in that area with greater ease, offering lucrative opportunities for corporations in the process. From the perspective of corporations, therefore, Oslo provided opportunities to profit from trapped labor, captive markets, land, and resources. Despite the nearly simultaneous development of a movement to advance corporate accountability for human rights abuses through the use of domestic tort laws, the use of these mechanisms on behalf of Palestinians have been unsuccessful. For the time being, the success of boycotts and divestment suggest that market mechanisms may be more useful to effect change in Palestine rather than the slow, incremental progress of law-based mechanisms.

Notes

1. United Nations Office for the Coordination of Humanitarian Affairs, Occupied Palestinian Territory, "Area C of the West Bank: Key Humanitarian Concerns, update August 2014," https://www.ochaopt.org/documents/ocha_opt_area_c_factsheet_august_2014_english.pdf. The agreement did not mention Greater Jerusalem, which has been annexed by Israel.
2. See Who Profits' posts, http://www.whoprofits.org/.
3. The Palestinian average daily wage in the West Bank is 104 NIS for the publicsector and 83 NIS for the private sector. International Labor Organization (ILO), 2015, Report of the Director-General, "Appendix: The Situation of Workers of the Occupied Arab Territories." Based on a five-day work week, the monthly minimum wage would be 2,080 NIS ($525) and 1,660 NIS ($419),respectively (ILO 2015: 14). By comparison, the Israeli monthly minimum wage is 4,300 NIS ($1,184). See "Guide for Migrant Workers," Israel Government, http://www.gov.il/FirstGov/TopNavEng/EngSituations/ESMigrantWorkers-Guide/ESMWGRights/
4. 28 USC. § 1350.

5. Sosa v. Alvarez-Machain, 542 US 692 (2004).

6. Docket No. 10– 1491, Slip. Op., US Supreme Court (April 17, 2013), http://www. supremecourt.gov/opinions/12pdf/10-1491_8n59.pdf.

7. Kiobel v. Royal Dutch Petroleum Co., 569 US ____ (2013), Slip Opinion at 4 (citing EEOC v. Arabian American Oil Co., 499 US 244, 248 (1991)).

8. Hoffman & Stephens, International Human Rights Cases Under State Law and in State Courts, 3 U.C. IRVINE L. REV. 9 (2013). The authors argue that if a US state court (as opposed to a federal court) has personal jurisdiction over a defendant, "that court will generally have jurisdiction to hear claims arising out of human rights violations in a foreign state." Id. at 10. They also argue that such claims will continue in federal courts as well "under the remaining core of the ATS and . . . other federal statutes." Id.

9. DC No. CV-05-05192-FDB, US Court of Appeals for the Ninth Circuit (September 17, 2007), http://ccrjustice.org/files/Ninth%20Circuit%20Opinion%2007.7.06.pdf. For further information and court documents, see http://ccrjustice.org/ourcases/current-cases/corrie-et-al.-v.-caterpillar.

10. Case No. 500-17-044030-081, Canada Superior Court (September 18, 2009), http://www.asser.nl/upload/documents/DomCLIC/Docs/NLP/Canada/Bilin_v_GreenPark_Complaint_9-7-2008.pdf.

11. See http://www.ccij.ca/content/uploads/2015/07/Bilin-QC-Sup-Ct-judgment-2009 qccs4151.pdf.

12. See the website of the BDS Movement, http://www.bdsmovement.net/.

13. "Orange Drops Israel Affiliate Following Inspiring BDS Campaign," BDS Movement, January 7, 2016, http://bdsmovement.net/2016/orange-drops-israel-affiliate-13648-sthash.WLw8lHF4.dpuf.

14. "BDS: Full 2015 Round-Up," BDS Movement, December 29, 2015, http://bdsmovement.net/2015/bds-full-2015-round-up-13628#sthash.Y4Mzh7QR.dpuf.

15. "United Church of Christ Votes to Divest from Israeli Companies in Occupied Territories," Religion News Service, June 20, 2015, http://www.religionnews.com/2015/06/30/united-church-christ-votes-divest-companies-israeli-occupied-territories/.

16. Anugrah Kumar, "Presbyterian Church USA Votes to Divest from Companies Israel Uses in West Bank; Jewish Group Denounces 'Radical, Prejudiced' Decision," The Christian Post, June 23, 2014, http://www.christianpost.com/news/presbyterian-church-usa-votes-to-divest-from-companies-israel-uses-in-west-bank-jewish-group-denounces-radical-prejudiced-decision-121990/#mBzF8rdG46zUUOAg.99.

17. Ali Abunimah, "How the Israel Boycott Movement Struck Major Blows in 2015," Electronic Intifada, December 30, 2015, https://electronicintifada.net/blogs/ali-abunimah/how-israel-boycott-movement-struck-major-blows-2015.

18. Ibid.

19. Ibid.

References

Roy, S. 2002. "Why Peace Failed: An Oslo Autopsy." *Current History* 100 (651): 8–16.

Russell Tribunal on Palestine. 2010. *Findings of the London Session: Corporate Complicity in Israel's Violations of International Humanitarian and International Human Rights Law.*

Wistanley, A., and F. Barat, eds. 2011. *Corporate Complicity in Israel's Occupation.* London: Pluto Press.